Gestalt Therapy

The Gestalt approach is based on the philosophy that the human being is born with the healthy ability to regulate needs and wants in relationship with the environment in which she/he lives. Heightening of personal awareness and exploration of needs is enabled by the therapist who actively engages in supporting and assisting the therapeutic journey of the client.

Gestalt Therapy: Advances in Theory and Practice is a collaboration of some of the best thinkers in the Gestalt therapy approach. It offers a summary of recent advances in theory and practice, and novel ideas for future development. Each chapter focuses on a different element of the Gestalt approach and, with contributors from around the world, each offers a different perspective of its ongoing evolution in relation to politics, religion and philosophy.

Incorporating ideas about community, field theory, family and couple therapy, politics and spirituality, this book will be of interest not only to Gestalt therapists but also to non-Gestalt practitioners, counsellors, psychologists, psychiatrists and other mental health professionals. Counselling, behavioural science and psychotherapy students will also find this a valuable contribution to their learning.

Talia Bar-Yoseph Levine BA, MA (Hons), DPsych is a co-founder of the Jerusalem Gestalt Institute; past head of the MSc programme in Gestalt psychotherapy at Metanoia Institute, London; registered clinical psychologist since 1981. Talia is the managing director of Choice Psychotherapy and Management Consultancy Ltd, UK, and is a business consultant in Israel, Europe, USA and Asia and an international trainer. She has published numerous journal essays and is a member of the IPA (Israeli Psychological Association).

Advancing Theory in Therapy
Series Editor: Keith Tudor

Most books covering individual therapeutic approaches are aimed at the trainee/student market. This series, however, is concerned with *advanced* and *advancing* theory, offering the reader comparative and comparable coverage of a number of therapeutic approaches.

Aimed at professionals and postgraduates, *Advancing Theory in Therapy* will cover an impressive range of theories. With full reference to case studies throughout, each title will

- present cutting-edge research findings
- locate each theory and its application within its cultural context
- develop a critical view of theory and practice.

Titles in the series

Body Psychotherapy
Edited by Tree Staunton

Transactional Analysis: A Relational Perspective
Helena Hargaden and Charlotte Sills

Adlerian Psychotherapy: An Advanced Approach to Individual Psychology
Ursula E. Oberst and Alan E. Stewart

Rational Emotive Behaviour Therapy: Theoretical Developments
Edited by Windy Dryden

Co-Counselling: The Theory and Practice of Re-evaluation Counselling
Katie Kauffman and Caroline New

Analytical Psychology
Edited by Joe Cambray and Linda Carter

Person-Centred Therapy: A Clinical Philosophy
Keith Tudor and Mike Worrall

Psychodrama: Advances in Theory and Practice
Edited by Clark Baim, Jorge Burmeister and Manuela Maciel

Neurolinguistic Psychotherapy: A Postmodern Perspective
Lisa Wake

Constructivist Psychotherapy: A Narrative Hermeneutic Approach
Gabriele Chiari and Maria Laura Nuzzo

Lacanian Psychoanalysis: Revolutions in Subjectivity
Ian Parker

Gestalt Therapy

Advances in Theory and Practice

Edited by Talia Bar-Yoseph Levine

Routledge
Taylor & Francis Group
LONDON AND NEW YORK

First published 2012
by Routledge
27 Church Road, Hove, East Sussex BN3 2FA

Simultaneously published in the USA and Canada
by Routledge
711 Third Avenue, New York NY 10017

Routledge is an imprint of the Taylor & Francis Group, an Informa business

Copyright © 2012 selection and editorial matter *Talia Bar-Yoseph Levine*; individual chapters, the contributors.

All rights reserved. No part of this book may be reprinted or reproduced or utilised in any form or by any electronic, mechanical, or other means, now known or hereafter invented, including photocopying and recording, or in any information storage or retrieval system, without permission in writing from the publishers.

Trademark notice: Product or corporate names may be trademarks or registered trademarks, and are used only for identification and explanation without intent to infringe.

British Library Cataloguing in Publication Data
A catalogue record for this book is available from the British Library

Library of Congress Cataloging-in-Publication Data
Gestalt therapy : advances in theory and practice / edited by Talia Bar-Yoseph Levine.
    p. cm.
  ISBN 978-0-415-48916-4 (hbk.) – ISBN 978-0-415-48917-1 (pbk.)
  1. Gestalt therapy. I. Bar-Yoseph, Talia Levine.
  RC489.G4G4837 2011
  616.89'143–dc22

                                                          2011001404

ISBN: 978-0-415-48916-4 (hbk)
ISBN: 978-0-415-48917-1 (pbk)
ISBN: 978-0-203-15776-3 (ebk)

Typeset in Times by Garfield Morgan, Swansea, West Glamorgan
Paperback cover design by Sandra Heath
Printed and bound in Great Britain by TJ International Ltd, Padstow, Cornwall

Contents

List of contributors		ix
Preface		xiii
Acknowledgements		xv
Introduction		xvii
1	Gestalt in the new age JAY LEVIN AND TALIA BAR-YOSEPH LEVINE	1

PART I
Gestalt therapy and theory 13

2	Flexibility in theory formation: point and counterpoint ERVING POLSTER	15
3	Reconsidering holism in gestalt therapy: a bridge too far? CHARLES BOWMAN	27
4	The interactive field: Gestalt therapy as an embodied relational dialogue MICHAEL CRAIG CLEMMENS	39
5	Personality: co-creating a dynamic symphony CARMEN VÁZQUEZ BANDÍN	49
6	Critiquing projection: supporting dialogue in a post-Cartesian world LYNNE JACOBS	59
7	Sensing animals/knowing persons: a challenge to some basic ideas in gestalt therapy DAN BLOOM	71

8	Mind and matter: the implications of neuroscience research for Gestalt psychotherapy PETER PHILIPPSON	83
9	Spirituality in gestalt therapy PHILIP BROWNELL	93

PART II
Aspects of Gestalt practice 105

10	Creating an embodied, authentic self: integrating mindfulness with psychotherapy when working with trauma LOLITA SAPRIEL	107
11	The four relationships of Gestalt therapy couples work GARY YONTEF	123
12	Gestalt family therapy: a field perspective BRIAN O'NEILL	137
13	A neo-Lewinian perspective on gestalt group facilitation SEÁN GAFFNEY	149

Epilogue 161

14	Awareness instead of rules: Gestalt ethics ERNST KNIJFF	163
15	Culture change: conversations concerning political/religious differences PHILIP LICHTENBERG	175

Index 185

Contributors

Dan Bloom, JD, LCSW, is a psychotherapist in private practice. He studied with Laura Perls, Isadore From, and Richard Kitzler. He is a fellow of the New York Institute for Gestalt Therapy and a full member of the European Association for Gestalt Therapy. Dan is past president of the Association for the Advancement of Gestalt Therapy and the New York Institute for Gestalt Therapy. His writings have appeared widely.

Charles Bowman is past president of the Association for the Advancement of Gestalt Therapy (AAGT) and Co-President of the Indianapolis Gestalt Institute. He has published commentary on a variety of topics, most related to Gestalt therapy, and is the editor of the AAGT newsletter and co-editor of the online journal *Gestalt!* He is a Gestalt trainer, psychotherapist and business consultant in Indianapolis, Indiana, USA.

Philip Brownell, MDiv, PsyD, is a registered clinical psychologist in Bermuda and a licensed clinical psychologist in Oregon and North Carolina, USA. He is editor of the *Handbook for Theory, Research and Practice in Gestalt Therapy*, the author of *Gestalt Therapy: A Guide to Contemporary Practice*, and series editor for *The World of Contemporary Gestalt Therapy*.

Michael C. Clemmens, PhD, is a psychologist in Pittsburgh, PA in the US, working with individuals and couples. He trains therapists throughout the US and Europe emphasizing relational physical process. Michael is a professional staff member of the Gestalt Institute of Cleveland. His publications include *Getting Beyond Sobriety: Clinical Approaches to Long Term Recovery* and other articles on Gestalt therapy.

Seán Gaffney, PhD, was born and raised in Dublin, Ireland, and has been a resident of Sweden since 1975. He is a Gestalt therapist, Gestalt OSD consultant, and university lecturer in Cross-cultural Management. He is a full member of the New York Institute for Gestalt Therapy (NYIGT) and a senior trainer at Gestalt Institutes worldwide.

Lynne Jacobs, PhD, lives in two psychotherapy worlds. She is co-founder of the Pacific Gestalt Institute and training analyst at the Institute of Contemporary Psychoanalysis. She is co-author (with Rich Hycner) of *The Healing Relationship in Gestalt Therapy*, and co-editor of *Relational Approaches in Gestalt Therapy*. She has also written numerous articles for Gestalt therapists and psychoanalytic therapists.

Ernst Knijff is a NVAGT and EAP Registered Gestalt psychotherapist and has been a Teaching and Supervising Member of the Flemish Dutch Gestalt Psychotherapy & Training Institute MultidiMens for 20 years. He is author of *De therapeut als clown, randopmerkingen van een gestalttherapeut* (EPO, Berchem 2000) and one of the editors of the book *Praktijkboek Gestalt* (de Tijdstroom, Utrecht 2009) and the Dutch Flemish Gestalt Journal, *Gestalt, Tijdschrift voor Gestalttherapie*.

Jay Levin, MA (Clin. Psych.) LMHC, has practised and taught psychotherapy internationally for over 20 years. His interest in how values shape personal behavior and therapeutic interventions is mirrored in published articles that reflect his vision of a more hospitable world.

Philip Lichtenberg is Mary Hale Chase Emeritus at Bryn Mawr College and founder and senior faculty member of the Gestalt Therapy Institute of Philadelphia. He is author of many articles and six books, to specify just a few: *Psychoanalysis: Radical and Conservative*; *Community and Confluence: Undoing the Clinch of Oppression*; and *Encountering Bigotry: Befriending Projecting Persons in Everyday Life* (with Janneke van Beusekom and Dorothy Gibbons).

Brian O'Neill, BA (Hons), MAPS, is director of the Illawarra Gestalt Centre, past president of AAGT and on the editorial boards of the *Gestalt Review* and *Studies in Gestalt*. He has published on topics such as field theory, relationship therapy and community, and completed chapters (with his wife Jenny) on Gestalt couples therapy and the use of groups in training.

Peter Philippson, MSc (Gestalt Psychotherapy), is a UKCP registered Gestalt psychotherapist, teaching and supervising member of the Gestalt Psychotherapy & Training Institute UK, founder member of Manchester Gestalt Centre, full member of the New York Institute for Gestalt Therapy, senior trainer for GITA (Slovenia) and guest trainer for many training programmes internationally. He is past president of the AAGT and the author of *Self in Relation* (Gestalt Journal Press) and *The Emergent Self* (Karnac/UKCP).

Erving Polster, with his late wife, Miriam, founded the Gestalt Training Center–San Diego. He has authored *Gestalt Therapy Integrated, Every Person's Life is Worth a Novel, A Population of Selves, From the Radical*

Center and *Uncommon Ground*, as well as many anthology chapters. He is currently teaching and writing about transforming private therapy into a communal format.

Lolita Sapriel is a Licensed Clinical Social Worker in private practice in Santa Monica, CA. She is a member of NASW (National Association of Social Workers).

Carmen Vázquez Bandín, PhD, is a clinical psychologist and a Gestalt therapist. She is the founder and director of CTP Training Institute for Gestalt Therapy, Madrid, Spain, and a Member of the AETG, EAGT, EAP, and AAGT. She is a full member of the New York Institute for Gestalt Therapy (NYIGT), an international trainer and supervisor. She is an expert in communication and in the processes of mourning and grief, and co-director of the Gestalt therapy publishing company *Los Libros del CTP*. Carmen is the author of books, papers and chapters about Gestalt therapy and a translator into Spanish of Gestalt literature and is also the President of the Spanish Association for Gestalt Therapy (AETG).

Gary Yontef, PhD, ABPP, clinical psychologist in Los Angeles, has been on the UCLA Psychology Department faculty, Faculty Chair of GTILA, on the editorial board of the *International Gestalt Journal*, the *Gestalt Review*, and an editorial advisor of the *British Gestalt Journal*. He is a co-founder of the Pacific Gestalt Institute and author of *Awareness, Dialogue and Process: Essays on Gestalt Therapy* and numerous articles and chapters.

Preface

This series focuses on advanced and advancing theory in psychotherapy. Its aims are: to present theory and practice within a specific theoretical orientation or approach at an advanced, postgraduate level; to advance theory by presenting and evaluating new ideas and their relation to the particular approach; to locate the orientation and its psychotherapeutic applications within cultural contexts, both historically in terms of the origins of the approach, and contemporarily in terms of current debates about philosophy, theory, society and therapy; and, finally, to present and develop a critical view of theory and practice, especially in the context of debates about power, organisation and the increasing professionalisation of therapy.

I have a particular association with gestalt therapy as my first two therapists, back in the early 1980s, were gestalt therapists. I then went on to train in gestalt therapy and contribution training with Peter Fleming at the Pellin Centre in London, UK, and in Montecorice in Italy. Although I went on to train in other therapeutic approaches, I remained – and remain – interested in gestalt and its developments. In continuing my professional development in the late 1980s and early 1990s, I attended various gestalt workshops at the Metanoia Institute in London where I met Talia Bar-Yoseph Levine. I was struck then, not only by her knowledge, skill, and elegance as a trainer, but also by how she was able to bring and hold disparate people and groups together. When, more recently, I approached her with the commission to edit a volume on gestalt theory and therapy for this series, I was delighted that she accepted the challenge, and that she has brought her particular skills to bear to collect and complete this particular contribution to the series. True to gestalt principles, she considered and consulted with the field, and entered into dialogue with a number of people to contribute to the volume; and, indeed, the process of editing – of the book itself and of the book as part of the series – has been marked by continued dialogue. It has not always been an easy process, but has been one which, I think, has borne good fruit, with a result: a rich, eclectic volume which shows gestalt therapy looking back, in reconsidering some of its foundations (such as holism); looking outwards (for example, to neuroscience); and looking forwards (in developing, for instance, neo-Lewinian perspectives on groups, as well as the editor's own work proposing a gestalt philosophy of being).

Keith Tudor

Acknowledgements

Thank you Keith for inviting me to take on this important yet humbling project; you gave me a special opportunity to carry the Gestalt word into the wider field. Thank you all writers for hanging in there with me, for your quick responses, acceptance and for sharing your most fresh concepts and thoughts, not to forget the two generous translators. To you Joanne and Sarah I am indebted for walking the thin line between writers and publishing demands with grace and respect. Sean, you helped me, a non English speaker, to maintain the person behind the translated chapters, thus enrich the book and supported a value dear to me. Jay Levin, my dearest friend, you held my hand, supported, edited, challenged and were such a generous writing partner, it would have been much harder without you. Last by no means least, many thanks to my family who were patient, protective and helpful each in their own way – Benni, Neta, Michael and you Adi who also acted as the technical support.

Introduction

Talia Bar-Yoseph Levine

How does one introduce such a book while at the same time remaining succinct, alive and inviting? I wonder. This requirement distils the important from the less important, sharpens my thinking in challenging to lead the reader into the book, takes me down memory lane to when it all started, and more so to why I felt compelled to accept the request from Keith Tudor, the series editor, to take on this project.

"Advanced thinking about Gestalt therapy," Keith said, and lit the first spark. "In a series that Routledge is publishing" – the prospect of an established publisher that would carry our thinking to the wider field fired the second spark; and the challenge to bring together the best possible thinkers and practitioners was the third. It took only a moment to say "Yes," at the price of putting a book that I was editing and writing for exploring organizational interventions following the Gestalt school of thought on the back burner.

My socialist, political and idealistic interests were touched by the opportunity to present our therapeutic approach in particular, and its implicit concepts of existence in general, to a wider readership. I felt compelled to oblige yet strangely free. Knijff, in his chapter in this volume (Chapter 14) gives the words: "Freedom means here the ability to choose; to choose to be involved with the situation and the people involved. This is what we call responsibility. Freedom is the ability to respond in a certain situation" (p. 167). My responsibility was my freedom.

My enthusiasm must have been also true for the authors who submitted proposals for chapters for this book. It took less than two weeks for about 20 of the professionals that were approached to get back with an excited "Yes." The invitation was to submit a proposal for an chapter exploring that which excites them the most about the Gestalt school of thought, theory, and practice leading into the future. It is with regret that I remember those who wanted to contribute and in the end for a variety of reasons were not able to so do. Still, you were blowing a helpful wind on our backs.

My wish was to create a book composed of people's utmost exciting, current, based-on-experience, mind-liberating thoughts. I wanted the writers to come from different professional and personal backgrounds, age groups, and native languages. The latter presented an interesting challenge.

Being one of the latter group, I am acutely aware of how much is lost in translation, be it a thought, individuality, personal style, imagery and, at times, the soul of the writer. On the one hand, publication must be up to specific publishing standards in its respective language; on the other, the writer needs to be met as who she or he is . . . such a difficult bridge to build and maintain.

Indeed, to make certain that pedantic language does not take over the writer's intention and personality is a derivative of a more general principle: how much should the editor intervene? When is the purpose defeated and the meaning – and the writer – lost? This was also a challenge that I confronted when I edited the book *The Bridge – Dialogues Across Cultures* (Bar-Yoseph Levine 2005). As a clown on a wire, high up in the air, I balanced between the wish to make a chapter right by me, respecting the authors as whole human beings, being careful that the chapters read well and last but not least fulfilled the objectives of the book.

One example was when Ernst Knijff agreed to contribute his refreshing thinking about ethics: he warned me that his English was not that good, hence, he felt unable to contribute fully to the chapter once translated – a crystallizing example of the complexity presented to the editor. It left me, on my own with my consent, to be the keeper of that delicate balance spelt out above. Once I read the first translated draft (and thanks to Frans Meulmeester for initiating the contact and for the translation) it was clear to me that this chapter must have a voice in English and be included into the book. I respected his wish to write in a non-academic manner and took a decision to stop working the translation to death, supported by Seán Gaffney's additional editorial input on this chapter as a native English-speaking being.

Another example is Vázquez Bandín who chose to submit a complete chapter translated by Susan L. Fischer and scrutinize it herself. By doing so she relieved me of the delicate task described above.

In Judaism, *knowledge is defined as the ability to put together information and thought*. My intention in sharing the thinking behind my editorial decisions is to allow you, the reader, to approach the chapters from a knowledgeable point of view.

It is clearly impossible to address every aspect of Gestalt therapy theory and its practice in one collection. In accepting this reality I became interested to have excellent thinkers and practitioners share their excitement with others, bearing in mind that the book should be of interest to the wider professional community.

So, you, our reader, are invited to read in this volume a wide diversity of thinkers who take the Gestalt theoretical view one step ahead from "now" to "next." The contributors to this volume, who are leading practitioners and thinkers in a Gestalt philosophy-of-being based therapy, were invited to share their ideas. Each was asked to write about that which is closest to his/her heart and that interests them the most. As a result the reader is presented with a feast for the mind, heart, and soul.

The first "next" or difference I want to introduce is the term "Gestalt philosophy of being," a term used to describe accurately the field commonly called "Gestalt therapy." The term Gestalt philosophy of being encapsulates the breadth of applications of our school of thought: from therapy to friendships, via organizations, educational systems, in fact any form of human relating.

A brief look at the table of contents gives a sense of much of the contemporary thinking in our discipline. Levin and Bar-Yoseph Levine start by inviting the reader to identify the seeds of the contemporary in the original writing, as well as taking the lead to develop Bar-Yoseph Levine's suggestion that Gestalt therapy is one aspect of a "Gestalt philosophy of being." Their chapter provides some infrastructure for the reader, especially if less familiar with the Gestalt school of thought.

In Part I eight chapters explore Gestalt therapy and theory. Polster opens up this part sharing his thinking about community life. Bowman (in Chapter 3) takes the historical concept of "holism" forward. One might say that "holism" paved the ground for "Field theory" to be embraced, explored and expanded, which Clemmens does (in Chapter 4) when he looks at the self, dialogue and field from a body perspective and, while doing so, reminds the reader of the whole – body, mind and spirit of which the human being is composed. He thus provides a fundamental reminder to all that the human whole is to be taken into account at all times. Gaffney (in Chapter 13) also continues the development of the field perspective. In Chapter 5 Vázquez Bandín explores the self, as do Bloom (Chapter 7) and Philippson (Chapter 8), each from differing, enriching perspectives.

A number of chapters challenge a central concept in Gestalt: in Chapter 6 Jacobs, as she often does, offers a challenge, this time about projection, as does Bar-Yoseph Levine to the term "Gestalt therapy," Bowman with his chapter on holism, and Knijff (in the Epilogue) on ethics. Then (in Chapter 8) Philippson views the implications of neuroscience research for Gestalt therapy and (in Chapter 9), Brownell adds "God" to the therapy room, again both enlarging the therapeutic as it used to be more commonly viewed to include a spiritual entity (Brownell) and scientific research (Philippson). Brownell takes a controversial question, shares his strong clear views and takes the risk of evoking strong feelings.

As expected, contemporary thinking by its nature challenges the current conventional wisdom, hence one would expect each chapter to challenge a thought, technique, terminology . . .

In Part II four chapters look at aspects of Gestalt practice. Sapriel, Yontef, O'Neill, and Gaffney stress the value of Gestalt thinking when working with systems as does Polster in Part I. Polster breaks the boundaries of closed systems and looks at the importance of communities; Sapriel (Chapter 10) discusses mindfulness and therapy in trauma work; Yontef (Chapter 11) examines couples work; O'Neill (Chapter 12) explores family therapy; and Gaffney (Chapter 13) looks at larger systems.

The last section of the book is an Epilogue which comprises two chapters. In the first, Knijff shares his inner thoughts, feelings and view of ethics and defines ethical behavior. The fashion in which he writes reminds us of the rebellious nature of the ancestors of Gestalt therapy, the strength of personality and of will. In the second, Lichtenberg adds a cultural perspective to his well-known interest in communities and thus concludes the book in a way which highlights my conviction that attention to culture and larger social system is essential to the well-being of us all. This, precisely, is the reason that Polster's chapter opens the book (after the lead-in chapter), so the community aspect both opens up and closes down the book.

To conclude, editing this book felt analogous to what Yontef describes in his chapter (Chapter 11) as the four relationships in couples therapy (p. 124):

> the relationship of the therapist [editor][1] with each member of the couple [contributors and series editor], the relationship of the couple to each other, and the relationship of the therapist to the couple [book] as a whole. The four relationships are always going on simultaneously. Good therapy [editorial] work with couples requires picking an effective but shifting focus while establishing and nurturing all four relationships.

An essential part of editing requires multiple dialogic relationships between the editor and the writers, between the editor and editor of the whole series, and between the editor and the publisher. Most importantly of all is to ensure that the reader ends up with an inviting, coherent, and high-quality book.

Hopefully, the chapters speak for themselves, each with its own "now" (present) and "next" (future oriented) concepts, and together generate a direction into the future contribution of the Gestalt philosophy of being to the enrichment of other modalities as well as of the human race.

Note

1 All [ ] brackets are added by the editor.

Reference

Bar-Yoseph Levine, T. (ed.) (2005) *The Bridge – Dialogues Across Cultures*. Metairie: Gestalt Institute Press.

Chapter 1

Gestalt in the new age

Jay Levin and Talia Bar-Yoseph Levine

Gestalt-based therapy is too good to be reserved only for therapists. Its philosophical underpinnings bring into play a wide array of concepts in a novel way that combines radical ideas in a creative amalgamation. This unique coming together of different perspectives – a unique epistemological and ontological position that devolved from its adherence to three foundational sources, namely field theory, phenomenology and dialogue – has implications far wider than the field of psychotherapy and invites fresh and innovative viewpoints in the field of human activity. We have called this Gestalt-based approach the "Gestalt philosophy of being" in order to emphasize and affirm its breadth and depth in the area of human efforts. We believe it has been a reliable guide to understanding human concerns since its inception in the middle of the 20th century and into the 21st century.

Gestalt therapy based in a "Gestalt philosophy of being"

Currently the frequent and familiar term used to describe this approach is "Gestalt therapy." This is a commonly used generic term for addressing a wide variety of Gestalt-based thinking and practice, be it organizational consultancy, psychotherapy, or relationship in general. "Gestalt therapy" is used as an umbrella expression, an overall concept describing any application derived from Gestalt-based thinking. Indeed one might say that historically Gestalt was predominantly an approach to psychotherapy. Most training establishments and Gestalt practitioners identify themselves primarily as psychotherapists.

This stance, however, minimizes the breadth, the depth and the beauty of Gestalt as an overall "philosophy of being." The Gestalt philosophy of being can stimulate, inspire and encourage a different view of human nature – a more human vision of and for the future. The Gestalt philosophy of being traverses cultural restrictions and different languages and offers a healing through meeting in a diverse cultural universe as ours currently is (Bar-Yoseph Levine 2005). It is through the conviction of Perls, Hefferline, and Goodman (1971) that organismic self-regulation by way of Gestalt formation-and-destruction provides the basis of a coherent and significant understanding of living organisms in relations to their environment. As a philosophy of being, Gestalt therapy makes accessible this principle by which human beings can live their lives in a wide array of conditions and situations. In other words, the Gestalt philosophy of being is uniquely predisposed and ready to cultivate our humanity and humanize our culture in our new world.

Some of these implications have generalized Gestalt's original basic psychotherapeutic orientation into what Bar-Yoseph Levine suggests calling a "Gestalt philosophy of being" – an approach to maintaining and sustaining relationship. By philosophy of being, we mean that the Gestalt-based approach can contribute a unique understanding of living as autonomous beings in relationships. The concept "Gestalt philosophy of being" recognizes that persons use the same philosophical and practical guidance wherever they go, it contributes to who they are; it becomes part of their individuated make-up. Within the "Gestalt philosophy of being," we find every form of practice that deals with human relationships, for example, psychotherapy, organizational consultancy (Bar-Yoseph Levine 2008; Gaffney 2009; Melnick and Nevis 2010), educational critiques and initiatives (Goodman 1972; Neill 1962), the contribution of Gestalt therapy to a model of development (McConville 1995; Oaklander 1978; Stevens 1994), as well as the way people live in their community, and its value as a lens for viewing community work (Lichtenberg 2002; O'Neill 2009; Polster, in O'Neill 2009), in their family (O'Neill this volume) and with themselves. It guides the way people conduct their lives in a variety of capacities and contexts. For example, using the Gestalt philosophy of being, Bar-Yoseph and Zwikael (2007) take a refreshing view of dealing with change in the engineering profession. This is a welcome demonstration of the wide application that its theory of change offers.

One of the applications of the Gestalt philosophy of being is to further examine the notions of differentiation, difference, personal, private, community and coexistence. It contains much of the foundation needed to take the next step towards a better world. For example, its outlook indicates that investing in a meeting of differences leads to a contactful relationship which can lead to growth and healing. This is a perspective which overcomes a tendency either to ignore or even obliterate personal, national, cultural and social diversity and differences or exaggerate them into enmity (Lichtenberg 2002).

A process model of growth: the contact episode

In the 1950s what we are referring to as "the Gestalt philosophy of being" challenged established Western notions of normalcy and illness and proposed "organismic self-regulation" as an autonomous criterion of health (Perls, Hefferline, and Goodman 1971). From its beginnings in the 1940s (Perls 1969) this approach to existence has endeavored to articulate a fresh vision of what it means to be a person and what is entailed in living a human life. The authors suggest that the world and the person are in continuous relatedness and each is subject to influence, change and growth by the other. It is the primacy of field theory (in which we include the concepts of holism and organismic self-regulation); phenomenology and dialogue – the three pillars supporting the standpoint of the Gestalt-based approach – that is the basis for a comprehensive process model of growth (Resnick 1995).

The Gestalt philosophy of being is based on the immediacy of experiencing. "Here" refers to embodied sensory experience. "Now" refers to the temporal propinquity (closeness or immediacy) of contact. The "here" and "now" of Gestalt-based thinking refers to the occurrences and transformations of embodied sensory experience in which the non-personal environment is personalized and incorporated into support through contact.

Contact is an experience of difference that both separates and connects. The experience of difference is essential for connection. There is no sense of connectedness without a concomitant sense of difference. This touching of difference is called *awareness* in Gestalt-based therapy and the engagement of these differences is called *contact*. In other words, *movement* leads to *difference* which leads to *awareness* which leads to *contact*. Change and growth takes place in the contact (engagement of difference) between the organism and its environment.

Growth by way of relatedness becomes the epitome of personal and collective effect of experience. Growth initially evolves from and then builds on human experience, and returns repeatedly to confer unwavering power and authority on human experience. It is this unvarying *return to originality* that makes the Gestalt philosophy of being a blueprint for our times leading us into the future. The Gestalt philosophy of being introduces an epistemology that challenges the prevailing mechanistic, technical and outcome-oriented approaches of the 20th century. In other words, "Gestalt therapy" was not only advanced for the 1950s – it is still advanced in the new millennium.

The constant ongoing process of identifying and satisfying an organismic need is called self-regulation. Organismic self-regulation occurs at the point of contact between the organism and its environment. Polster and Polster (1974) refer to this process of organism/environment adjustment as a "contact episode." Contact provides meaning and context by "grounding" the organism in its historicity and situatedness (Perls, Hefferline, and Goodman 1971).

A contact episode is marked by situatedness, temporality, irreversibility, and growth (or stagnation). The level and quality of contact varies and can be adjusted when consciousness is heightened. The organism/environment contact boundary is marked by change and growth that incorporates the unknown into the known.

Typically, a contact episode has a beginning, middle, and an end. These temporal moments are discernible by 1) the initial experience of a need; 2) the accurate identification of the need; 3) recognizing and modifying the resources that will meet the need in an assimilable form for the organism; and 4) the organismic satisfaction of the need and its incorporation as support for further contact.

There are at least three illustrations of the contacting process that are described in *Gestalt Therapy* (Perls, Hefferline, and Goodman 1971), which have been used for heuristic purposes. For example, *Gestalt Therapy* (1971) uses the distinctions of pre-contact, contact, final contact and post-contact to describe the process of contact that occurs between initially experiencing an organismic need and its satisfaction. Of course, being on a continuum, these points are arbitrary. In addition, *Gestalt Therapy* (1971) offers another view to describe this process in terms of embodied transformations of excitement. The creative adjustments of id, ego, and personality describe procedural embodiments of the self as the organism progresses through a contacting event. Another perspective, this time from the standpoint of the ego, explores how interruptions to contact (anachronistic "creative adjustments") articulate disruptions in the continuum of awareness in a contact episode. These interruptions to contact are also portrayed on a continuum in *Gestalt Therapy* for describing the "layers" or stages of "resistance," called "boundary disturbances." They can be – and have been – described in other ways.

In addition, other formulations of the process of the contact cycle abound in Gestalt therapy. Burley (unpublished paper) has examined psychopathology in terms of interruptions of figure-formation utilizing a framework which has implications from neuropsychology – the undifferentiated field, emergence of need/interest, figure sharpening, scanning, completion, undifferentiated field. Gestalt formation and destruction has also been variously conceptualized by Smith (1994: 100), Zinker (1977), and Clarkson (1989) and others. Less formally, Perls (1974: 59ff) has identified five phases, or "layers of the personality," which are contacted and resolved in the process of identifying and satisfying organic needs: the cliché (or phony) layer; the synthetic (or phobic) layer; impasse; implosion; and explosion.

Irreversibility is another attribute of a contact episode. Change implies irreversibility – for better or worse. The process of Gestalt therapy is not a rehearsal for practicing what needs to be performed "outside" of the consultation room. The embodiment of organismic self-regulation in a contact episode is not a "dummy run" without consequences (for both therapist and client). In other words, the work itself is a therapeutic journey at the end of which the client has a new and aware behavior as part of being.

Growth or decay is the consequence of change. A contact episode can be more – or less – successful in identifying and satisfying a need. Successful identification and satisfaction of a need can be described as an ingathering and appropriation by the organism of the unknown aspects of the environment. Latner refers to this process of growth as "befriending the field":

> This is, in a way, a process of continually befriending aspects of the field. As we are involved in the coming figure and its resolution, we put parts of ourselves in an interaction with other parts of the field – other people, plants, animals, objects. In this interaction, they are inside our self-boundaries. We are identified with them. Our relationship with them is no longer (in Buber's terms) one of I and It; it becomes one of I and Thou. In this way, we assimilate the field, changing it by changing our relation to it.
>
> (Latner 1974: 78)

More successful contact episodes lead to growth while stagnation, and ultimately death, marks the outcome of less successful episodes. Each episode, leading to growth or stagnation, becomes incorporated (assimilated and accommodated) into the background for the next emerging figure of the need and imbues *that* (new) figure with renewed meaning and significance (Wheeler 1991).

Every contact, even of a poor quality, involves movement. Even a sense of stagnation includes the fact that something has occurred and (at least for a while) that there has been some movement, a "meeting." Addressing the process and exploring the sense of stagnation is an essential part of the therapeutic journey. It suggests that if the smallest movement exists, then change is possible and hence there is hope. Once movement/change is noticed, the question is of learning more and the development of good quality contact.

Contact and change

Since its inception over 100 years ago, psychotherapy has been hijacked by the narrow empiricism of the medical model. The authority of the medical model, with its cures for various illnesses and its place of prestige in the hierarchy of social values, is sanctioned by an epistemology that defends the mechanistic, technical and outcome-oriented approaches of the 20th century.

"Medical psychology," under the influence of positivistic science, embodied the conventional wisdom of 20th-century epistemology and ontology as "correct" theory and practice. This approach later came to be the benchmark of "good psychology," in concert with psychoanalysis, behaviorism and the "human potential movement" (also known as humanistic psychology). Under the auspices of this medical model, the goal of psychotherapy has essentially remained to provide relief, or change, through *cure by the "expert-practitioner"* (depth and behavior-oriented psychologies), or an understanding of *how to change oneself* with help/ direction from a therapist (humanistic psychologies) (Levin 2010).

The view that change can be controlled is placed in the modern psyche as an unassailable fact. Moreover, the concomitant idea that leadership is at its best in order to control, move forward, and be responsible for the process of change is being replaced slowly by the view of Gestalt principles that change simply is – its ontological significance is a "given" (Perls, Hefferline, and Goodman 1971). The Gestalt philosophy of being embraces the participatory nature of change, its characteristic to occur spontaneously, and the circumscribed role of leadership as facilitator of change – not originator. Nonetheless, a good number of "psychotherapists" still buy into the idea of being "change agents" rather than facilitators of self-regulation and growth.

Leaders need to be facilitators of change; encouraging participatory decision-making. Good leadership is at ease with this process of resourcefulness and creativity that leads to self-regulation and influence in relationships liberated from orthodoxy and conformity (Bar-Yoseph Levine 2008). This notion of change evokes a couple of thoughts; one is a reminder that "thinking leadership" in the context of the therapy room can enrich the therapeutic journey. The therapist could be supported by adhering to the thought that in some aspects he/she is a leader of a process of awareness by being the expert and, at the same time, the client is the existential leader of a journey of growth and change. The second thought is to consider that most organizational work contains components of a therapeutic journey. This illustration again highlights the connectedness between different areas of human efforts that hold fast to the same underlying principles of the Gestalt philosophy of being.

From the standpoint of Gestalt-based therapy, change is inevitable and leads to either organismic growth or stagnation. Change is a lifelong process. Organismic predilections and field conditions determine the result of change. This is a fundamental departure from prevailing conventional wisdom and assumptions underlying theories of change.

Rehabilitation and healing

The Gestalt philosophy of being is more than just an attempt at remediation and cure: it pursues the goals of *healing* and *rehabilitation* through *growth*. In a simple example of how advanced his thinking was in the last century, Perls challenged the medical model notion of sickness when he wrote in 1969, "I now consider that neurosis is not a sickness but one of several symptoms of growth stagnation" (Perls, in Perls, Hefferline, and Goodman 1971: 9).

Gestalt-based therapy's holistic approach avers that the whole is more/greater than the sum of its parts. The tendency for growth to include an emergent quality of contact and relationships precludes a reductionist perspective of the elements of healing. Gestalt therapy is ready to articulate these changes in approach from heroic utilitarianism to reverent hospitality. This involves a withdrawal of projections and a shift from telling to listening. Already in 1969 Perls addressed what is at present an evident need for the maintenance of global wellbeing:

> The "I'm telling you what you need" would be replaced by "I'm listening for what you want", and the basis for rational discussion would be opened . . . This applies as much to our inner conflicts as it applies to the world situation in general.
> (Perls, in Perls, Hefferline, and Goodman 1971: 11)

Gestalt-based therapy attaches importance to the insights of Buber (1965, 1970), particularly his contention that ontological priority is in and through the "I–Thou" relationship – i.e. it is only through this form of relatedness with a community of *others* that one's humanity can be fully realized. This "dialogic encounter" has become the touchstone for healing in Gestalt-based therapy (Hycner and Jacobs 1995). Buber contrasts this "I–Thou" engagement of two people with the everydayness of the "I–It" relationship that occurs between a subject and an object. The "I–It" relationship is purely instrumental, with an interest only in the outcome of the interaction. On the other hand, the "I–Thou" relationship is intrinsically valuable – not for any strategic outcome. Buber makes the crucial point that existential priority is in and through the "I–Thou" relationship – i.e. it is only through this form of relatedness with an-other that one's humanity is accomplished.

It is in the domain of community that the ontological foundation of a lived life is incarnated. The notion of "communitas" – that aggregate of people joined together by the values of immediacy and worth of each person without expectations – is central to the Gestalt approach. A healthy community is a precondition for healthy living and entails political and spiritual ethics (Goodman and Goodman 1960; Lichtenberg 2002).

The eclipse of political views and spirituality from the domain of mainstream psychotherapy has toughened over the years. Goodman (1991: 88) has long championed a political perspective integral with the Gestalt approach by pointing out that many human issues that recur may be deeply personal, but they are not private, being driven by forces "located in the institutions of society, the economic and political institutions, the moral, religious, educational and domestic institutions." His central observation and assertion is that the organismic need or "instinct" is *never* the problem, a perspective he gained from Reich (Perls, Hefferline, and Goodman 1971; Stoehr 1994). How relationships turn out to be bland when needs become obscured, repressed, shamed, guilt-ridden and fraught with anxiety through the actions of a repressive society and social institutions is a political issue (Perls, Hefferline, and Goodman 1971: 421), hence personal but not private.

Spiritual viewpoints have fared little better in mainstream psychotherapy and it seems as if efforts to include a serious discussion of the spiritual dimension of psychotherapy are met with derision at worst, or mild condescension based on reductionist arguments from empiricism at best (Naranjo 1980). Nevertheless, the Gestalt approach appreciates that the sense of "grace" that marks a genuine meeting between two people marks a sense of transcendent spirituality which is a creation of the encounter itself – rather than merely the collaboration of two people (Doubrawa 2006b; Pernicka 2008).

Malfunction or breakdown of the process of living is not a medical problem but, rather, one possibility of existence. The healer is present, with the client, in a mutually transformative passage of growth and individuation that incarnates both polarities of journeying and dwelling. Therapy can be likened to a pilgrimage undertaken in order to create-and-discover one's own place of dwelling after a journey in limbo and a return to community. It marks the subtle conversion of a "house" to a "home." "This going-home phase of pilgrimage is often overlooked, but it is the most important part. One cannot have made a pilgrimage unless one goes home afterward" (May 1980: 29).

Gestalt-based therapy invokes a place of habitation or, in some instances, rehabilitation. To rehabilitate is to restore someone to his/her rightful place in the community after some kind of disjuncture or relational rupture. Rehabilitation appeals to and summons up a place of belonging, a place to inhabit. However, this is not literally a geographical place, but a metaphorical location for the dwelling of one's existence in its transformative journey throughout individuation and growth. Rehabilitation provides a dwelling place together with a sense of belonging and of purpose in the world. Healing and rehabilitation are two sides of the same coin. There cannot be healing without rehabilitation and there cannot be rehabilitation without healing. In other words, *growth and rehabilitation include the ability of the organism to create (together with its environment) a place where organismic needs and the necessities for life converge to provide a place of human habitation.*

The practitioner as healer

In its unique view of change as well as its recognition that the "I–Thou" relationship is ontologically primary and foundational for community and human life, the Gestalt philosophy of being radically undercuts the individualistic paradigm of healing and change that pervades the older epistemologies of the previous century. Our post-modern society demands a revolution of perspective from that of the white-coated doctor immersed in the medical model which has failed so dismally to address the health needs of people, as well as the politics and spirituality of healing (Illich 1984). Healing has been reduced to cure, and rehabilitation reduced to a technological intervention (Kepner 1995). To interpret failure to thrive and grow as simply a medical problem, and to invoke the methods of inquiry and solutions proposed by modernistic approaches, is to overlook the vitality of the point of view embraced by the Gestalt philosophy of being.

The Gestalt practitioner is mandated – and equipped – to be both shaman and political champion. For example, the activity of psychotherapy is an invitation to sacred ground, to sanctify the secular as when the approach to the other encounters "the general human yearning, overt or hidden: for we are all second hand goods wanting to be appreciated as God's first sunset" (Schoen n.d.). As Naranjo (1980: 122) observes, "More than a Zen master, however, Perls resembled the earliest transpersonal individual and therapist, the shaman; and shamanistic, too, is the precedent of the gestalt therapist's role as an experience-guide, a consciousness conductor."

A healer for our times is also required to care for the surroundings and the community, addressing environmental issues and institutional reform, as much as issues involving the neurons of the brain. Although political work is more than therapy, therapy is certainly political (Doubrawa 2006a). "I think that when you are supporting somebody to become more authentic – in societies, which are more or less authoritarian or authority-orientated, it is always political work – in therapy, in education, in social work" (Laura Perls, in Doubrawa 2006a: 123).

Attending to both pre-personal (e.g. physiological, neurological, and maturational processes) as well as impersonal (e.g. cultural institutions and practices such as economics, education, child rearing, health care) aspects of the world is important for the successful execution of a process that supports healing.

A sick environment and community is just as disabling for the person as a sick body or brain. If, in the course of growth, we are to be seriously committed to "befriending the field" then we need to also be seriously committed to protecting and invigorating the field – both pre-personal and impersonal aspects of the field. As Doubrawa (n.d.) points out, "a healing therapeutic relationship is not all it takes to heal lives. It takes a healthy society where healing through meeting is intended and wanted." In addressing the psychopathology of social adjustment that permeates our current treatment and relational options, Goodman asks rhetorically, "Who can deny that the only practical mass method is to strike at the institutions and inhibiting mores and to give our sick generation, if not an era of peace, at least a war of liberation?" (1991: 45).

The ideas that sustain the Gestalt philosophy of being are far-reaching. From a Gestalt philosophy of being perspective, organismic growth is an aesthetic expression of values that attends to both the organismic needs and its relationships with its environment. Zinker observes that:

> there is an aesthetic side to all human interaction and every therapeutic style . . . Thus there is an "aesthetics of psychotherapy" as well as an "aesthetics of human interaction," since aesthetics is dedicated to the study of the expression of values.
>
> (Zinker 1994: 5–6)

The traditional lines separating healer from spiritual guide and from political advocate cannot be sustained in the face of the onslaught from economic and cultural imperialism and the scientific reductionism of community and human life. The contemporary healer has to accept this stance if there is to be integrity to his/her professional conduct. As Stoehr points out:

> It was part of the Gestalt attitude to regard each patient as a kind of trainee or apprentice, in a guild of everyday life if not literally in the therapeutic calling, to make community wherever one found oneself, working with the ordinary materials of experience rather than with schemata and protocols.
>
> (Stoehr 1994: 17)

The Gestalt philosophy of being has within its theory and methodology the means to address these requirements. This book is a hopeful contribution to exploring some of the options available.

References

Bar-Yoseph, B. and Zwikael, O. (2007) The practical implementation of the gestalt cycle of experience in project management. *Gestalt Review*, 11, 1: 42–51.

Bar-Yoseph Levine, T. (ed.) (2005) *The Bridge – Dialogues Across Cultures*. Metairie: Gestalt Institute Press.

Bar-Yoseph Levine, T. (2008) The organization as social-microcosm: Gestalt therapy oriented organizational practice. *Studies in Gestalt Therapy: Dialogical Bridges*, 2, 1: 69–80.

Buber, M. (1965) *Between Man and Man*. New York: Collier Books, Macmillan.

—— (1970) *I and Thou*. (W. Kaufmann, trans.) New York: Charles Scribner's Sons.

Clarkson, P. (1989) *Gestalt Counselling in Action*. London: Sage Publications.

Doubrawa, Erhard. (n.d.) The politics of the I–Thou: Martin Buber the anarchist. Retrieved August 5, 2008, from: *Gestalt Critique: The eMagazine for Gestalt Therapy, Politics and Spirituality*: http://ourworld.compuserve.com/homepages/gik_gestalt/doubrawa.html

Doubrawa, E. (2006a) Political Gestalt therapy. (Raphael Rapstoff, trans.) In E. Doubrawa (ed.) *Touching the Soul in Gestalt Therapy: Stories and More* (pp. 123–126). Cologne: Peter Hammer.
—— (2006b) Spirituality. (Raphael Rapstoff, trans.) In E. Doubrawa (ed.) *Touching the Soul in Gestalt Therapy: Stories and More* (pp. 117–121). Cologne: Peter Hammer.
Gaffney, S. (2009) Gestalt in society: the North of Ireland. In J. Melnick and E. Nevis (eds) *Mending the World – Social Healing Interventions by Gestalt Practitioners Worldwide*. Wellfleet, MA: Gestalt International Study Centre.
Goodman, P. (1972) *Compulsory Miseducation*. Harmondsworth: Penguin Books.
—— (1991) *Nature Heals: Psychological Essays*. (T. Stoehr, ed.) Highland, NY: The Gestalt Journal.
Goodman, P. and Goodman, P. (1960) *Communitas: Means of Livelihood and Ways of Life*. New York: Vintage Books.
Hycner, R. and Jacobs, L. (1995) *The Healing Relationship in Gestalt Therapy: A Dialogic/Self Psychology Approach*. Highland, NY: Gestalt Journal Press.
Illich, I. (1976/1984) *Limits to Medicine: Medical Nemesis – The Expropriation of Health*. Harmondsworth: Penguin Books.
Kepner, J. I. (1995) *Healing Tasks: Psychotherapy with Adult Survivors of Childhood Abuse*. San Francisco: Jossey-Bass Inc.
Latner, J. (1974) *The Gestalt Therapy Book*. New York: Bantam.
Levin, J (2010) Gestalt therapy: now and for tomorrow. *Gestalt Review*, 14, 147–170.
Lichtenberg, P. (2002) *Community and Confluence: Undoing the Clinch of Oppression*. Cleveland, OH: Gestalt Institute of Cleveland.
May, G. G. (1980) A pilgrimage of healing: personal thoughts of a transpersonal therapist. In S. Boorstein (ed.) *Transpersonal Psychology* (pp. 28–36). Palo Alto: Science and Behavior Books, Inc.
McConville, M. (1995) *Adolescence: Psychotherapy and the Emergent Self*. San Francisco: Jossey-Bass.
Melnick, J. and Nevis, E. (eds) (2010) *Gestalt and Social Change*. Cape Cod, MA: GISC Press.
Naranjo, C. (1980) Gestalt therapy as a transpersonal approach. In S. Boorstein (ed.) *Transpersonal Psychology* (pp. 116–122). Palo Alto: Science and Behavior Books, Inc.
Neill, A. (1962/1960) *Summerhill: A Radical Approach to Childrearing*. New York: Hart Publishing.
Oaklander, V. (1978) *Windows to Our Children: A Gestalt Therapy Approach to Children and Adolescents*. Moab: Real People Press.
O'Neill, Brian (ed.) (2009) *Community, Psychotherapy and Life Focus*. Wollongong, Australia: Ravenwood Press.
Perls, F. S. (1969) *Ego, Hunger and Aggression*. New York: Random House Inc.
Perls, F. S., Hefferline, R. F. and Goodman, P. (1971) *Gestalt Therapy: Excitement and Growth in Human Personality*. Harmondsworth: Penguin Books, Ltd.
Pernicka, M. (2008) The encounter phenomenon in psychotherapy. Paper presented at the first Czech and Slovak Gestalt Therapy conference, Ostravice, Czech Republic, 22–23 October.

Polster, E. and Polster, M. (1974) *Gestalt Therapy Integrated: Contours of Theory and Practice*. New York: Vintage.

Resnick, R. (1995) Gestalt therapy: principles, prisms and perspectives. (M. Parlett, ed.) *British Gestalt Journal*, 4, 1: 3–13.

Schoen, Stephen. (n.d.) Gestalt therapy and spirituality: psychotherapy as sacred ground. Retrieved April 6, 2008, from: *Gestalt Critique: The eMagazine for Gestalt Therapy, Politics and Spirituality*: http://ourworld.compuserve.com/homepages/gik_gestalt/schoen.html

Smith, E. W. (1994) Seven decision points. In E. W. Smith (ed.) *Gestalt Voices* (pp. 98–103). Norwood, NJ: Ablex.

Stevens, B. (1994) Reflections on unparenting. In E. W. Smith (ed.) *Gestalt Voices* (pp. 93–97). Norwood, NJ: Ablex.

Stoehr, T. (1994) *Paul Goodman and the Origins of Gestalt Therapy*. San Francisco: Jossey-Bass.

Wheeler, G. (1991) *Gestalt Reconsidered*. New York: Gardner Press.

Zinker, J. (1977) *Creative Process in Gestalt Therapy*. New York: Vintage.

—— (1994) *In Search of Good Form: Gestalt Therapy with Couples and Families*. San Francisco: Jossey-Bass Publishers.

Part I

Gestalt therapy and theory

Chapter 2

Flexibility in theory formation: point and counterpoint

Erving Polster

An illusion of clarity exists when therapy theories become identified with specific principles, reducing their flexibility and opening them to caricature. In the development of gestalt therapy there have been a number of such overstated positions. It was commonly said, for example, that gestalt therapy shunned "interpretation" because it had a depersonalizing effect, blurring direct experience. Yet, antithetically, another of gestalt therapy's key principles advocated good quality contact, which might call for relationally timely explanations. Or, gestalt therapy is often seen as a "process" therapy but there is no denying that "content" fills anyone's life. Or, some argue that gestalt therapy, as a "field" theory, does not recognize the independence of intra-psychic experience; yet, the human psyche naturally experiences its own self boundaries.

Whenever any single position is taken as the defining position, it is valid to say: not so fast. Gestalt therapy theory was implicitly remindful about this type of narrowing process when it gave special recognition to the Hegelian synthesis of thesis and antithesis. When the goal is synthesis, inclusion is required for the opposite end of any thesis. With that in mind I want to show how the theoretical dominance in gestalt therapy of *fluidity* of personal experience, as contrasted with *constancy*, has played a role in narrowing gestalt therapy's attention to personal identity, morality and a communal psychotherapy, each of which I shall discuss later in this chapter.

An increase in flexibility would be accomplished by the incorporation of point/counterpoint thinking. As the dictionary (American Heritage Dictionary 1978) tells us, counterpoint is "the musical technique of combining two or more melodic lines in such a way that they establish a harmonic relationship while retaining their linear individuality." There are key differences, however, between music and psychotherapy. In music, both point and counterpoint are heard simultaneously, making the exclusion of one or the other sound difficult to achieve. In psychological theory, however, the point and counterpoint relationship of principles may be more easily obliterated by selective attention to one or the other, making the connections optional, easily resulting in favoritism among principles. Furthermore, in music, the point and counterpoint may not be harmonic, possibly involving two dissonant experiences. That dissonance may be quite exciting and the ultimate unity of the melodies may be a function of a developed openness to both point and counterpoint. Such dissonance is more difficult for the psychotherapist to accept because there is a pressure for immediate clarity. But, difficulty notwithstanding, dissonance is a fact of life. Miller and From (1994: ix) highlight this reality when they observe about the seminal book, *Gestalt Therapy*, "Goodman had no more wish to thin out human complexity in order to make his formulations easy to digest than did, say, T. S. Eliot or Henry James."

Constancy and fluidity

Let's look at both fluidity and constancy. First, the constancy pole represents what we basically *are*: flesh and blood, parent, compassionate, extrapolative, searchers for ultimate truths, etc. The fluidity pole represents continuingly ongoing experience; it just flows, unclassified, released from the imagined givens of life. As Rollo May pointed out, existentialism derived its name and its character through its reaction against the western concern with "essence," which embodies constancy (May, Angel, and Ellenberger 1958). In hyperbolic emphasis, Jean Paul Sartre (1977) and the existentialist movement which he so heavily influenced have been widely represented by what is still a common attitude in our society – that people stand for themselves and that they are personally responsible for the creation of their life circumstances. As agents of their own existence they would presumably be released from the bondage so often felt – that people are wedded to the lives of their ancestors or geography or cultural priorities or even biology.

Sartre's "existence" cultivated fluidity, opening the future to the psychotherapeutic mission to create change. It was a freedom message, releasing people from many bands of circumstance which had immobilized them from becoming all they could actually become. His celebration of existence was inspirational but it also came back to haunt him and he, of course, never quite meant for people to take fluid existence as a lone beacon around which they could organize their resuscitated freedoms. He explained that existence *preceded* essence, not replaced it. Nonetheless, given the mid-twentieth-century reformulations of human possibilities and the widespread need to jettison many outdated behavioral and attitudinal givens, the emphasis on fluidity was timely and created the largest consequence.

Gestalt therapy took the shift in emphasis from constancy to fluidity as a cornerstone of its mind set. This new accent lit up an amplified existence, instrumented by concepts of "safe emergency," amplification of awareness and a sharp focus on the ever continuing, moment-to-moment contact between patient and therapist. These processes enhanced the flowing quality of ongoing experience and caught the attention of a large part of the psychotherapy profession, who resonated with the existentialist release from inhibitory expectations and habits. Nevertheless, the transformative value of fluidity notwithstanding, we are now in a new day, inviting us first for an increased need to a *secure and clear personal identity* and, second, for the development of a *therapeutically based morality*. I will try to show that each of these purposes would be better served by communal settings than the familiar private therapy sessions.

Personal identity

As inspiring as the spotlighting of fluidity became, there was a catch. Little room was left for what a person is "really" like. Misguided though many such classifications often are, there is, nevertheless, a human tropism toward this *constancy* of identity. We see it everywhere. People want to dependably identify with national, religious, professional groupings and often feel personally violated when these identities are threatened. They also identify with personal characteristics; their IQs, the color of their hair, the major sins they commit, the awards they receive, the books they read. For many people, this fixity was self defeating. For those who shunned such classificatory identity the essence of what any person dependably *is* became recognized more for its elusive quality in this world of fluidity, where, it was proclaimed, nothing could remain the same. Perls, Hefferline, and Goodman (1951: 373) have said, "The self is not to be thought of as a fixed institution; it exists wherever and when there is in fact a boundary interaction. To paraphrase Aristotle, when the thumb is pinched, the self exists in the painful thumb." Therefore, to favor fluidity became commandingly fundamental to gestalt therapy and this was, indeed, a propelling force for change. A paradoxical clash became apparent. Since fluidity is the very force which leverages change, excessive emphasis upstaged the constancy needed for a dependable sense of self. If I am what I am, will I still be what I was as I move through this fluid universe?

The challenge becomes softened for those who embrace the paradoxical qualities we all live with. Though fluidity is a commanding actuality in everybody's life every day, it is not all that difficult for people to find satisfaction for the need for constancy, a tenacious counterpoint. It is true that you can't catch Bus Number 22 twice. Yes, you call Bus 22 by the same name but it is not the same; even the color of the paint would be microscopically dimmed every moment. Still, people will insist that Bus Number 22 is "my bus" and it will get me to work every day. So, in my humanoid experience, the constancy of that bus exists for me, *approximation though it may be*. So, also, irrespective of ever-present change, my sense of a constant identity keeps me clear that I am a person who does the *same* job every day, or who is *dependably* kind, or *devotedly* studious, or *easily* confused or all the other personal approximations which I feel to be "me."

Gestalt Therapy has actually quietly long supported the constancy phenomenon with Beisser's (1970) paradoxical theory of change, which says that we must first be what we *are* in order to change. Now, constancy is further represented in the development of therapeutically oriented congregations, which I have called Life Focus Communities (Polster 2006). Membership in these large groups, which would meet for extensive periods of time, would be part of one's continuing life rather than the temporary ameliorative procedure, which is the model of private therapy. They bring people together, offering a life-time hospitality. They offer exercises, music, dancing, homework and psychologically based conversational exchanges which infuse its members with a sense of enduring belonging, irrespective of the irrepressible fluidity of life's experiences. The sustaining continuity of these settings would feed the development of each group's individual character, enhancing the feeling of belonging and dependable identity. Although these meetings would address a much wider range of concerns than personal identity, some elements which are directly relevant to personal identity would include:

- Familiarity of format, which would have certain repetitious characteristics: the large group framework, including members of long standing, the physical structure, rituals of beginning and ending, recognizable design characteristics, recurrent themes, inspirational music and dancing. These qualities would offer constancy but, always, each meeting would have its own uniqueness through the freshness of the experiences.
- Lectures introducing and elaborating the need for both constancy and fluidity, offering illustrations, discussion and inspiration.
- The ethos influenced by the paradoxical theory of change would guide people to realize that there is merit in the way people are already living their lives. Change would be portrayed as a natural partner to the recognition of life as it is, refreshing the familiar but not obscuring it. People in break-out groups would have thematically focused conversations, talking to each other about such matters as their personal priorities or the way they tell stories to their children or how they plan for the future or their feelings about forming continuing friendships.
- Communal idioms built into the design of meetings and in the forms of music and dancing together would offer a special identity to its members. Levels and content of humor, evolution of familiar language, ending meetings with a special song or a special way of dancing; all serve to recognize the dependability of the communal style, albeit always alert to the risks of cultish fixity.

Morality

Taking a fresh look at constancy opens a second avenue, the development of a therapy-based morality. Personal problem-solving, with which private therapy is identified, and a moral perspective, which is socially operational, are both relationship-based, but they are also quite different. The therapist is the client's agent of change, responsive to her best interests, keeping her focus on actual ongoing experience, whatever it may be. So prominent is the restoration of the integrity, vitality and happiness of this particular person that the relational perspectives of the community are only in the background. In contradistinction, morality looks beyond individual problem solving, offering a communal constancy of relational preferences. It provides a *socially evolved way for people to engage with each other*. Frequently this coalescence has resulted in narrow prescriptions, poorly geared to individual need and excessively strict. Though individual problem solving and morality are, therefore, often at cross purposes, in their roots they both hold a key charge, to find desirable ways for people to live with each other.

Such a kinship between problem solving and society's moral guidance notwithstanding, the divergence of purposes is more apparent than the commonality. Because of the priority of individual problem solving, therapists have done little to spell out the moral components of therapeutic procedure. Quite the opposite, in spite of the large range of writings by psychologists on the theme of morality, therapists, themselves, have avoided it. Freedom from the mandates of morality releases them to keep an open mind, tuned sharply into individual need, a key stance for solving individual problems. The communal counterpoint is always there but also – perhaps necessarily – set aside.

One of the basic realizations which became apparent early to therapists is that "right" behavior is an elusive concept. The damaging effects of moral generalizations are sad reminders that any fixed pathway to rightness will be booby trapped, life being too untidy for social fixities. Because of this ambiguity, moral standards are only *inconspicuously* apparent in therapeutic procedures. The quiet truth, however, is that the psychotherapy ethos has already been a social instrument in the formation of society's moral developments, irrespective of its concentration on individual need. While changes in morality influenced by psychotherapy are far from unanimously accepted, they are well known; loosened sexual prohibitions, lowered barriers among races and classes, expanded focus on ethics, increased attention to personal responsibility, recognition of the need for divorce, freer relationship with established authority, and other transformations in morality. Even though therapists were not paying direct attention to morality in their private sessions, their understanding of human relationships set a tone which heralded new moral perspectives. It is important to acknowledge this effect because the professional awareness may lead to greater motivation to become part of the moral social fabric. While there is a social dynamic which incorporates spontaneous contributions to new perspectives, there is a special leverage for change which is increased by articulated awareness. To heighten this awareness of therapy's effects on society's moral perspectives is one step further along the road we have been traveling.

First in line among these new understandings was the *contextualization of personal experience*. From Freud's explorations of every person's history to gestalt therapy's figure/ground formation, it became clear to therapists that everything the client does is part of a larger picture. This perspective offered a foundational model for *moral relativity*. This has been unsettling for society at large because it delays judgment and it challenges the community's insistent need for absolutist clarity. In the world at large, we run into moral judgments every day that rely on absolutist thinking. A lie is a lie; a sexual transgression is a sexual transgression; being late is being late. But contextualization blurs the usefulness of these truths, because circumstances can temper moral judgment. Uncertainty notwithstanding, relativity and its pluralistic consequences are making their mark. Religious pluralism, national pluralism, gender pluralism, political pluralism and moral pluralism: they are all realities which, in our age, society is commissioned by historical progression to tackle. As contributors in this social advance from absolutism to relativity, psychotherapists have shown that individuated truth can improve people's lives by freeing them to see their own selfhood as it is as well as how it should be. Seeing relationships through this prism of circumstance, psychotherapists have implicitly been contributing to moral relativity from the beginning and are well placed to influence its further advancement.

At first glance, the absolutist morality, unambiguous as it is, offers greater clarity than moral relativity. But it is an illusional clarity. Most people really do know that there is no blueprint for telling people exactly how they should live their lives. They count on moral relativity, not as a cop-out from the severity of absolutism, but because a sense of proportion is deeply imbedded in the human psyche, a generic counterpoint to the equally inherent need for absolutist clarity. We see the struggle moral relativity faces in diverse circumstances: in religious sermons the absolutist insistence which exhorts people to behave in prescribed ways; in political partisanship, where positions are sharply stated and narrowly fixed; in jumping to conclusions about specific statements friends make; in premature impressions of people because of their race, jobs or affiliations.

In spite of this common attraction to absolutism, it is a far cry from the other side of the way many people also live. Instead of absolutism, we see everyday that people offer rationale for errant behavior; love their roguish friends; forgive their prejudiced parents; make allowance for people under duress; humanize their own moral unevenness; cheer movie heroes who had temporarily gone bad. Even the law has different degrees of murder and distinguishes between felonies and misdemeanors. People who are appalled about moral relativity because of its ambiguity are failing to notice that it is a common part of living, even in their own circles.

This complexity is difficult to communicate to the public at large and consequently many people believe that moral relativity is a weak statement of good and evil. Worse, because relativity's loose standards are reckoned against the background of absolutist dominance, moral relativity is often mistakenly seen as the *absence* of morality. But it is not. It is just more complex, less incisive than what is compelling in much public communication. The psychotherapy session, therefore, has been made to order for the exploration of moral relativity because of its continuity, individuation, openness to examination, freedom from psychic fixity and generosity of spirit – all contributing to a vibrant and viable counterpoint to absolutist morality. However, because this largesse has been directed almost exclusively toward individual *problem solving*, the moral implications have been *inconspicuous*. Nevertheless, with a shift in attention, such inconspicuous morality becomes more evident as an underlying influence in ordinary therapy. To illustrate, what follows is a simplified simulation of a psychotherapy scenario, where morality is a factor even though there is no conspicuously moral statement.

> Alice and her husband, Franklin, came to therapy because Alice caught him looking at computer porn. She became furious; feeling personally insulted and betrayed. From a therapeutic perspective, there may be many contextual options. Possibly, the porn is an isolated experience and does not have to interfere with their normal relationships; possibly Franklin is addicted, watches porn at work and is in danger of losing his job; possibly Alice is unknowingly turning him away sexually; possibly there is unexpressed hostility in the insult to her; possibly he likes to take the easy way to satisfaction; possibly this, possibly that. Together, therapist and clients head toward a resolution of this faulty relationship.
>
> As the conversation evolves, Alice says what she has never said, that Franklin presses so hard against her when they are having sex that she feels invaded, she stiffens and becomes otherwise unresponsive to him. Then Franklin just gave up on her, let her stew in her own juice and took the porn route. He didn't get much satisfaction from the porn either because even in this isolated circumstance his own obscured morality about sex does not even allow him the full sensations he seeks but he continues doing it anyway, almost like taking medicine. Now, he is stunned to hear that he presses Alice

> too hard. She hadn't said anything before because she had a "don't complain" morality, out of sync with either of their needs. Rather than to communicate, she just didn't participate, satisfying her don't complain morality while violating another morality plank by abandoning her mate and herself.

These are relational failures which call for problem solving, but they each also have moral overtones. From a therapeutic standpoint, however, morality is not the point and may even be a distraction from the problem-solving mission. Nevertheless, therapeutic purposes notwithstanding, there are moral implications in failing to tell the truth, letting each other stew in their own juice, and distancing themselves from each other. When these individuated relational requirements are transformed into communal priorities about how people may best live with each other, we enter the realm of morality. When we consider optimal living in the communal world, we see other therapeutic issues in this illustration which also are suggestive of morality: forgiveness of those who have erred, moderation of criticism of vulnerable people, filling in generously to make up for the weaknesses of family and friends, willingness to change one's characteristic behavior in the service of others, kindness to those in trouble, or considering one's effect on family unity. Clearly there are many avenues of convergence between Alice and Franklin's therapeutic problem solving and the possible morality of our culture.

Entering the cultural stream

Such a convergence of therapeutic problem solving, on the one hand, and personal identity and communal morality, on the other, invites the therapist to step beyond the focus on individual needs into the society at large. While the therapy session has been well positioned to deal with the requirements of relativity, the communal setting is more unwieldy and calls for creative antidotes to its usual mandate for quick and simple articulation. With this in mind, I will portray two vehicles here for conveying a therapy-based morality into the community:

1. Life Focus Communities

I have proposed earlier in this chapter that the establishment of Life Focus Communities would serve to enhance personal identity. It would also be a hospitable ground for an evolving morality. There would be many possible themes, a few of which will illustrate the range of themes which could focus the group's attention to moral issues:

- Gratitude expressed and received.
- Memories of moral issues and dilemmas.
- Key people who were relevant to their morality.
- Behaviors through which people were harmed.
- Customary behaviors which only later seemed immoral.

Conversations framed around such themes would be designed for discussion in small break-out groups. Then, placed into the attention of the plenary group by reporting the substance of the conversations, these interactions among group members would develop an aura of the group's behavioral vista. Rather than to offer authoritarian indoctrination, these relational teachings would tap the diversity of individuated insights and form a communal understanding, sometimes very clear, sometimes splintered. Unanimity would not be required and the regularity of meetings, extended indefinitely over a lifetime, would magnify and solidify the lessons learned, providing inspiration, empathy, and belonging. In such assemblages, the recurrent messages over time, more or less integrated, would replace the fast track of absolutism, leaving room for differences in circumstance and values. Further, this format would have greater pertinence to the society at large than the private therapy experience. It would be a prototype for energizing a creative evolution of the community's understanding of their values emblematically encouraging a pluralism that would give human scale to moral considerations.

2. Instructional "shoulds"

The second vehicle is counterpoint to the open-ended evolution of moral sensibility. It would call for an explicit set of quickly understood moral values, set forth in the context of group interaction. This instructional route is tough for therapists who have a legitimate wariness about the value of any generalized "shoulds." They know that people yield too readily to authority, misunderstand instructions, or are unskilled in executing them. However, even though the communication of "should" creates these risks, it is important to recognize that, risky or not, "should" is inherent to living and people naturally seek it. Few people would disagree that you should go to college if you want to be a physicist or that you should fertilize certain plants if you want maximum growth. Comparably, from a morality standpoint, to form a good society, people "should" adhere to certain basic relational essentials, whatever the guiding principles of the moral framework may be. How, then, may we form the specific instructions so that they are more than stereotypes or autocratic edicts?

The major "shoulds" we are familiar with in western culture have been created by the Judeo-Christian religions, which have codified how people should live with each other. We see this in the Ten Commandments, in the behavioral priorities scattered throughout the New Testament and in the 613 Mitzvot (good deeds) of the Hebrew Torah. The Ten Commandments speak of faithfulness to God; honoring father and mother; not stealing, murdering or committing adultery, among other commandments. In the New Testament Luke says:

> How can you say to your brother, "Brother, let me take the speck out of your eye," when you yourself fail to see the plank in your own eye? You hypocrite, first take the plank out of your eye, and then you will see clearly to remove the speck from your brother's eye.
>
> (Luke 6:41)

Among the 613 Mitzvot we are told not to stand by idly when a human life is in danger, not to carry tales, not to take revenge and to relieve a neighbor of his burden and help to unload his beast. Psychotherapeutic instructions would surely have their own unique character, with considerable overlap with existing moral systems. Though most therapists have steered away from telling people how they should behave, there is nevertheless a psychotherapeutic ethos which is composed of preferences about relationships.

Some of these preferences would be to: develop empathy; listen to people; reciprocate good deeds; give people the benefit of the doubt; tell your story honestly; accept your own responsibility. These examples are only a small illustration of the many moral statements which psychotherapists might make. My own reaction to myself is how dare you declare those when there would be many times when any one of them won't hold water. Perhaps they are the wrong ones. Perhaps people are unskilled for doing these things. Perhaps this, perhaps that. Absolutism is not required for clarity and guiding principles to be alive.

These "shoulds" may be communicated to the group through writings, lectures, film, internet, music and word of mouth. There are already innumerable writings which address the community at large and which offer a wide range of instruction. Another key innovation that combines thematic specificity with an interactive process is that of Martin Seligman, a well-known psychologist whose work may serve as a tipping point in prescribing certain behaviors. On his web site (www.authentichappiness.org), where he has had almost 700,000 visitors, he has inaugurated an Authentic Happiness Coaching Newsletter and has suggested behaviors important to the development of happiness. Though he doesn't describe these as moral statements, many would qualify and he sets an important precedent for reaching out to the public. For one example, he teaches people to experience and express gratitude as a pathway to happiness. Further he says, "Understanding positive institutions entails the study of the strengths that foster better communities, such as justice, responsibility, civility, parenting, nurturance, work ethic, leadership, teamwork, purpose, and tolerance."

Perhaps it seems ingenuous to expect people to be capable of following such orientations. But there is boldness and clarity, as well as risk, in maxims, which offer a leverage for communal synchronicity, a leap away from resignation, a trust in the absorption of new perspectives. Therapists have learned humility in the face of the vast complexity of existence, perhaps excessively so, as we seek safety in familiar professional parameters, wanting never to create stereotypy, misunderstanding and failure. We are rightfully wary about the human attraction to quick and simple absolutism. Being wary though is not the same as giving up. Taming various forms of absolutism is what civilization has always done, perpetually repelling primitive behaviors which damage the community, such as killing, aggrandizing, stealing, unmediated sexual gratification and the prejudicial activities of a we/they mentality.

There is surely no way to obliterate these behaviors. But, there is hope in the counterpoint reality; that relativity is as primitive a reflex as absolutism, embodying the *context* of experience. In our developmental civilization, where we continuingly guide behavior to fit contemporary perspective, we are now swept into the advances of relativity, which has been growing as part of a general cultural sensibility. For psychotherapists to explicitly enter relativity of morality into a greater communal appreciation is a goal which would be no small contribution, a leg in the relay race of ideas. Difficult though it is to achieve a partnership between the clarity and precision of absolute morality and the contextualized relativity of morality, I believe the accomplishment of such a point/counterpoint relationship is pivotal in the mission to enhance the lives of people in their everyday living.

References

American Heritage Dictionary (1978) Boston: Houghton Mifflin Company.
Beisser, A. (1970) The paradoxical theory of change. In J. Fagan and I. Shepherd (eds) *Gestalt Therapy Now*. Palo Alto, CA: Science and Behavior Books.
May, Rollo, Angel, Earnest and Ellenberger, Henri K. (eds) (1958) *Existence*. New York: Basic Books.
Miller, M. V. and From, I. (1994) Introduction. In F. S. Perls, R. F. Hefferline and P. Goodman (eds) *Gestalt Therapy*. New York: Julian Press.
Perls, F. S., Hefferline, R. F. and Goodman, P. (eds) (1951) *Gestalt Therapy*. New York: Julian Press.
Polster, Erving (2006) *Uncommon Ground*. Phoenix, AZ: Zeig, Tucker and Theissen.
Sartre, Jean Paul (1948) *Existentialism and Humanism*. London: Methuen.
Seligman, Martin, www.authentichappiness.org

Chapter 3

Reconsidering holism in gestalt therapy: a bridge too far?

Charles Bowman

Reconsidering holism in gestalt therapy: a bridge too far?

Holism is identified repeatedly as a basic tenet of gestalt therapy. What does it mean? How does gestalt therapy meaningfully incorporate this concept? This chapter proposes that holism has lost utility for gestalt therapy and is mired in ambiguity. After exploring the history and development of the concept, this chapter concludes with a recommendation that "holism" has expired as a useful term. The maturing lexicon of field theory and the ongoing development of phenomenology in gestalt therapy provide the concise professional language necessary to advance gestalt therapy without reference to the speculative, metaphysical nature of holistic doctrine.

Any student of *Gestalt Therapy: Excitement and Growth in the Human Personality* (Perls, Hefferline, and Goodman 1951/1994) is familiar with ambiguity. This is not uncommon in works that synthesize ideas from diverse areas of thought and practice. The theory section of the manuscript is notably difficult to comprehend and at times ambiguous. Ambiguity is commonly introduced to students of gestalt therapy in understanding the concept of figure-ground through images such as the Rubin vase. Ambiguity – where more than one interpretation is verifiable based upon available data – could be dismissed as a hallmark of gestalt therapy praxis. Ambiguous terms such as holism could then be considered conventional, although this would be a wholly unacceptable outcome.

Of course, ambiguity is only an outcome of a long heritage and a complicated theory, not an intended consequence. Had the modern conception of the phenomenal field been fully developed, field theory would have been a superior choice for Perls in *Ego, Hunger and Aggression* when he identified one tool for improving psychoanalysis as "holism (field conception)" (Perls 1947: 7). A field theoretical approach was Perls' and Goodman's intention from the onset: "Our approach in this book is 'unitary' in the sense that we try in a detailed way to consider *every* problem as occurring in a social-animal-physical field" (Perls, Hefferline, and Goodman 1951/1994: 4–5).

But a bridge too far? Surely not. Holism is an endearing and oft-referenced term in gestalt therapy literature (Bloom 2000; Latner 1974; Perls 1969b; Yontef 1993). Gestalt therapy's connection with holism is confusing because it has been drawn from multifarious sources over time. Fritz Perls offers an explanation of how theory becomes errant over time, fully applicable to the loss of efficacy regarding holism:

> Theories are wholes, unifications of numerous facts. Sometimes a simple theory has to be corrected when new factors, not fitting into the original conception, are discovered. Sometimes so many additions have to be provided that we come to a confusing complexity instead of to a working hypothesis. When such a situation arises we have to pause and seek a reorientation, look for new common factors that can simplify the scientific outlook.
>
> (Perls 1947: 185)

A bridge too far, indeed! As the idiom implies, the term holism requires crossing too many contextual bridges in order to understand its application to gestalt therapy. Like stretching the allied troops too thinly across too many bridges over the Rhine in an overzealous attempt to march through Europe in World War II, stretching the meaning of the term holism to reference concepts in gestalt therapy restrains the advance of gestalt therapy theory as a result of the many meanings one must bridge to get to something useful from the term. Today, gestalt therapy's holistic attitude is attributed to the Gestalt psychologists, Jan Christian Smuts, Kurt Goldstein, Kurt Lewin, existential philosophy, Eastern spirituality or some quixotic combination of these sources. The term is further muddled when considering contemporary meanings in medicine, health, spirituality, ecology, and even New Age living. Gestalt therapists associate gestalt therapy with transpersonal, holistic, and spiritual meanings as much as with field theoretical, process-oriented, and scientific meanings (Bowman 1998).

Perls' close association with the human potential movement and the groundswell of alternative therapies in the 1970s contributed to this confusion. Today, holism has found new life in modern psychology, physics, philosophy, and bio-medicine through this diversification of meaning, but as a result it has lost the specific relevance originally intended in gestalt therapy. The term has evolved to an extent that disambiguation will not restore utility to the concept as it no longer references the ideas developed in earlier German philosophical or scientific thinking nor the developments of holistic thought by Kurt Goldstein, Wolfgang Köhler, Kurt Lewin or even Fritz Perls.

Wading through definitions of holism

One need look no further than a standard dictionary to glimpse the indistinct and vague nature of the term "holism." The *Cambridge Advanced Learner's Dictionary* (2008) defines holism as "the belief that each thing is a whole which is more important than the parts that make it up." The *Compact Oxford English Dictionary* (2008) defines holism as "the treating of the whole person, taking into account mental and social factors, rather than just the symptoms of a disease." *Merriam-Webster's Online Dictionary* (2008) identifies it as "a theory that the universe and especially living nature is correctly seen in terms of interacting wholes (as of living organisms) that are more than the mere sum of elementary particles." Is holism a belief? Is it a method of treatment? Is it a theory of the universe? Yes. Linguists refer to the consequences of this ambiguity (having multiple, indefinite meanings) as "pragmatic intrusion," occurring when it is necessary "to reason about the intentions of the speaker in order to determine what is said" (Korta and Perry 2007: 94). The level of pragmatic intrusion and the panoply of meanings inferable from the term render it exceedingly context-sensitive. Holism lacks the integrated utility necessary to add parsimonious value to gestalt therapy.

In *Ego, Hunger and Aggression* holism is a central notion, amassed significantly from Smuts' development of the concept, "which realizes that the world consists 'per se' not only of atoms, but of structures which have a meaning different from the sum of their parts" (Perls 1947: 28). Perls' initial use of "holism" was quite specific: "Organism-as-a-whole-embedded-in-environment. This becomes the Unit" (Perls 1969c). When Smuts wrote *Holism and Evolution* in 1926 he was developing a technical language to extend scientific and philosophical discussions that engaged the rubric of "life," such as Henri Bergson's *élan vital* (Smuts 1926/1996: 99). Smuts' holism was a replacement for the term life. "The vagueness and indefiniteness of the idea of life have proved a serious stumbling block and has largely influenced biologists to look for the way out in the direction of mechanism" (p. 99).

Citing what he labeled "abuse" of the term life, he continues,

> I suggest that the substitution, for scientific and philosophic purposes, of the concept of the whole for life would give far more precision to the underlying idea. Thus a definite concept, whose properties could be investigated and defined, would take the place of a vague expression, already ruined by popular use and abuse.
> (Smuts 1926/1996: 109–110)

The concept of holism yields no such precision today and has suffered the same ruination Smuts attributed to the term "life" in 1926. Namely, holism has become a vague expression, mired in popular connotations, and unsuitable for gestalt therapy theory development.

Aesthetic, philosophical criteria characterized Smuts' blend of philosophy and science (Benking and van Meurs 1997; Robine 1993). Smuts wrote of *Holism and Evolution*, "It is a book neither of Science nor of Philosophy, but of some points of contact between the two" (p. v). Similarly, Perls identifies in his autobiography that his creation "Gestalt therapy" is a "philosophy-therapy" (Perls 1969a: 264). This garbled definition is an important determinant for choosing the social science-based field theoretical approach superior to holism as a basis for modern gestalt therapy. Never the clearly developed concept Smuts intended, holism continues to reference disparate sets of ideas and there remains many context-sensitive interpretations that include metaphysical, aesthetic, epistemological, organismic, embodied or spiritual components, to name but a few. Holism is a term that is dramatically context-sensitive and spurious in gestalt therapy as a result of pragmatic intrusion.

Philosophical and organismic holism

Philosophical holism

Holism has been supported and opposed in philosophical discussions through the ages, pre-dating Plato to the atomism of Democritus and the holism of Parmenides. The European roots of gestalt psychology run deep in the Parmenidian philosophical tradition from the earliest works of Johann Wolfgang von Goethe and Johann Christoph Friedrich von Schiller. During the German epoch of Weimar Classicism Goethe's ideas of the planet-as-organism and of the world soul (*Weltseele*) were ubiquitous. Schiller's less prevalent work focused more succinctly on aesthetic holism, which contributed to Smuts' bewildering interpretations. Goethe laid the philosophical foundation for German holistic thinking, his work shepherding early phenomenological exploration and departing from the *methodology* of reductive science (Ash 1998).

In 1912, Smuts finished his initial treatise concerning holistic philosophy, *Inquiry into the Whole* (Benking and van Meurs 1997). That same year Max Wertheimer published his studies of perceptual grouping that distinguished perception as a holistic process (Bowman and Nevis 2005). In Europe holism was a canon ready to counter atomistic science and the mechanistic social order. The approaching storm of technology, industrialization and National Socialism would bastardize this advance. The canon, holism, failed to advance the fuzzy science of Smuts *or* the exactitude of Wertheimer to any appreciable degree but did provide justification for an advancing National Socialist party that provided intellectual support for Fascist totalitarianism. This application of holism to culture and government ultimately supported a vile practice in Nazi Germany – "Aryan Science" (Harrington 1996; Harwood 1998).

This history draws attention to category mistakes that occur when generalizing from philosophy to psychology, biology, and culture. Category mistakes are ontological/semantic mistakes involving the misascription of a thing into a category that is logically impossible (Ryle 1949). The notion of "state as organism" is one example of a category mistake since it is impossible for a living thing to be a polis or a politically organized body. This category mistake contributed to a devastating idealism in Nazi Germany. Smuts identifies a "progressive grading" of holism in a movement from physical mixture to chemical compound, organism, mind and personality (Smuts 1926/1996). Smuts predisposes holism to category mistakes in his attempt to connect substances, biological entities, mental traits or states of being. The admixture of holistic ideology, pragmatic intrusion and category mistake makes untangling the concept impossible. That is to say, holism has become a bridge too far.

Organismic holism

Goethe's early holistic work became a foundation for gestalt psychology and Goldstein's holistic biology. Goldstein, Wertheimer, and others developing gestalt psychology were interested in the scientific, clinical, and demonstrable implications of a holistic approach. Unlike Smuts' or Perls' adoption of a broad-spectrum holism – which Staemmler references as a "primarily undifferentiated monistic view" (Staemmler 2006: 73) – the gestalt psychologists took that which was particular to their respective field in order to maintain objectivity. Perls himself recommends closely examining Smuts' holism and mentions his support of only partial aspects of it, warning "I am not inclined to follow him in what I would call idealistic or even theological Holism" (Perls 1947: 29). Perls was remiss in adopting the term for gestalt therapy without further delimiting his specific objections to theological holism.

The holism of gestalt psychology references the organization of sensory experience which "demonstrates the operation of processes in which the content of certain areas is unified, and at the same time relatively segregated from its environment" (Köhler 1947: 17). The domain of gestalt psychology was clearly the scientific study of the dynamics of the nervous system. Holism referenced the integrative capacities of that system. This was the academic starting point for Perls' development of holism in gestalt therapy, pre-dating Perls' study of Smuts. A germinating gestalt therapy would be based upon perceptual holism and biological organismic functioning.

The praxis of the gestalt psychologists was empirical observation. Kurt Koffka and Wolfgang Köhler were familiar with Henri Bergson's efforts to reconnect scientific inquiry with lived experience. They disagreed with the metaphysical, non-empirical aspects of his foundation but were influenced by his conception of lived consciousness as a continuous experience – in league with Wilhelm Dilthey, John Dewey, Edmund Husserl and William James (Ash 1998). This dynamic concept of consciousness, explored via phenomenological observation, relegated holism in gestalt psychology to observable, measurable investigation. Holism was solidly, scientifically operationalized in gestalt psychology and was in no way dependent upon metaphysical assumptions.

Fritz and Laura Perls received training in gestalt psychology in Goldstein's laboratory. Here they were steeped in biological holism. Goldstein identified himself as an "organismic psychologist," developing a theory of the organism based on gestalt psychology's holistic understanding of perception (Sherrill 1986). Goldstein shifted from the laboratory science of the gestalt psychologists towards a phenomenal understanding of the organism and the total situation – Goldstein's "sphere of immediacy." "When we are in this sphere, subject-object experiences remain more or less in the background and the feeling of unity comprising ourselves and the world in all respects and particularly in relation to other human beings is dominant" (Goldstein 1939/1995: 20).

Goldstein's foundation was much broader than gestalt psychology – "the holistic relation of all biological phenomena" (Goldstein 1939/1995: 199). He soundly reintroduced biology to holism, proposing that the actualizing tendencies of the organism were always based in relation to others (Goldstein 1939/1995; Harrington 1996). A note found in his personal papers indicated an unpublished work in progress to be titled *From Anatomy to Philosophy: Late and Early Writings in the Holistic Approach*. This work was to organize material from neurology to sociology; that is, from an organismic paradigm to an environmental one (Harrington 1996). Had this developed, Goldstein's exactitude could have buffered the tendency towards category mistakes in the broad-spectrum application of holism in gestalt therapy. This work was not to be and Goldstein's legacy is that of biological holism.

Perls maintained Goldstein's concept of the organism-as-a-whole throughout his life (Perls 1969a) and it is a key contribution to gestalt therapy. Perls' later writing moves from Goldstein's biological approach through the epistemology of Smuts' holism to a developing phenomenal field perspective. By 1973, he was refining his notion of field to include "the *individual's* relationship to his environment" (Perls 1973: 18, emphasis added), not the biologically contained *organism's* relationship to its environment. This movement continues today as gestalt therapy theorists reclaim phenomenology and apply a more developed field approach to the discipline.

Kurt Lewin and field theory: a reasonable bridge

Field theory is a pillar of gestalt therapy (O'Neill and Gaffney 2008; Parlett 1991, 1997; Resnick 1995; Staemmler 2006; Wheeler 1991; Yontef 1993) and Kurt Lewin was the founder of field theory in the social sciences. He deviated from holistic biology in that he approached *behavior* and the field dynamics of human personality, not organismic functioning *per se*. His focus became action methodology using mathematical description in his topology (Eng 1978). This direction moved Lewin away from gestalt psychology and organismic biology but closer to Husserl in the final analysis, "[f]or when Lewin placed practical behavior in the context of a topological field, he saw that this field was not the physical field of science but the life-space of the experiencing organism" (Spiegelberg 1972: 81). This movement may account for Lewin's conspicuous absence in early gestalt therapy writing, especially the Perls, Hefferline, and Goodman text, and for being an expanding presence in current gestalt therapy literature.

In Lewin's 1997 collected works the term holism is not referenced in the index although his training in philosophical holism and holistic biology is unquestionable. Lewin's field theory deviates from holism extensively. It is not doctrinal. It is methodological. Whereas Smutsian holism is an evolutionary doctrine of a tendency towards whole making inherent in the universe, Lewinian field theory is a method for phenomenologically understanding a given, limited situation. Lewin's approach requires no metaphysical description, is grounded in phenomenological observation (Eng 1978; Marrow 1977; Wheeler 1998), and solidly places all behavior as a function of the person and the present field. Lewin wrote, "[t]oday we know that we do not need to assume a mystical Gestalt quality, but that any dynamical whole has properties of its own" (Lewin 1948/1997: 60).

Rosemarie Wulf (1996) summarizes Lewin's contribution to gestalt therapy succinctly:

> Lewin took the Gestalt model out of the laboratory and transferred it to the complex realm of everyday situations. His thesis was that the need organizes the perception of the field and the acting in the field. He considered human activity as interactive and at least partly a reaction to the perceived conditions of the field. He emphasized the dynamic interrelatedness of the elements in a field.
>
> (Wulf 1996)

This movement from biological holism to field theory differentiates gestalt therapy from organismic biology by narrowing the focus to the *actual situation*. Consideration of the actual situation provides a solid foundation for revisiting gestalt therapy without the metaphysical implications of holistic doctrine. This is not holism. It is consideration of the whole situation and is developed further in current works such as Dan Bloom's person-world model (Bloom this volume) and Talia Bar-Yoseph Levine's gestalt philosophy of being (Bar-Yoseph Levine 2009).

Beyond Lewin: revisiting the actual situation

The death knell for holism as a useful concept is post-Lewinian and found in the 1970s human potential movement, which had a major – and unfortunate – impact upon gestalt therapy. During this period medicine, physics, biology, and psychotherapy were reacquainted with metaphysics in varying degrees. Gestalt therapy was not immune to this New Age adaptation, in no small measure ushered in by Perls' practice at Esalen Institute in Big Sur, California (Anderson 1983). "New Age mysticism certainly found a nurturing environment in the humanistic therapies" (Wymore 2006: 135). While some gestalt therapists have adopted these New Age influences, they do not make for sound science or theory and have led to ungrounded, uninformed practice branded "gestalt therapy." The argument against this movement in gestalt therapy is the argument against Smutsian holism as well – "Smuts, then, has a teleological agenda that contradicts the phenomenological attitude" (Meara 2008: 35).

Current developments expand upon the field theoretical and phenomenological base of gestalt therapy, inadvertently highlighting the difference between holism and focusing on the actual situation while avoiding reductionism and metaphysics. Bloom (this volume) addresses Goldstein's concept of organism/environment as biological reductionism, in agreement with Frank Staemmler:

> Gestalt therapy originally proposed that all experience is a function of the organism/environment field. This remains the bedrock of gestalt therapy – and it should remain so. But it is an incomplete foundation. Human beings are animals; we are also persons. The organism/environment field fully accounts for our *biological* nature as the necessary fundament of life. The organism/environment field is not the phenomenal field; it is not the psychological field (Staemmler 2006). The organism/environment does not – and cannot – fully account specifically for us as persons. The meeting of an organism with its environment is a biological interaction, and although it is absolutely necessary for experience, it itself is not an *experiential* event.
> (Bloom this volume: 77–78)

Bloom proposes a chaste phenomenological approach to the actual situation, neither a biological reduction nor a metaphysical treatise.

In another approach to the totality of the actual situation, Talia Bar-Yoseph Levine proposes the broad application of gestalt therapy across cultures and disciplines, again without reference to holistic metaphysics. She posits a "Gestalt philosophy of being" (Levin and Bar-Yoseph Levine this volume: 1) that expands applications of gestalt therapy theory, maintaining Köhler's unification–segregation orientation and gestalt therapy's legendary "appreciation of differences."

> By philosophy of being, we mean that the Gestalt-based approach can contribute a unique understanding of living as autonomous beings in relationships. . . . One of the applications of the Gestalt philosophy of being is to further examine the notions of differentiation, difference, personal, private, community and coexistence. . . . For example, its outlook indicates that investing in a meeting of differences leads to a contactful relationship which can lead to growth and healing.
>
> (Levin and Bar-Yoseph Levine this volume: 2)

Although this is the application of gestalt therapy on a grand scale, it continues to hold the original unifying aspects of gestalt psychology and gestalt therapy while developing the scope of the actual situation: all without a foray into metaphysical, teleological, or holistic explanation.

The past 20 years can be characterized as a renaissance in gestalt therapy and these authors exemplify the meticulous work still needed to refine holistic and field theoretical concepts into tools germane to gestalt therapy praxis today. "The core idea of the field . . . has the capacity to force us to rethink nearly everything we do in therapy" (Latner 2008: 27). This work involves the further separation of field theory and holism and a number of gestalt therapists are undertaking this work today.

A reprieve and summary

Revisiting the charge of category mistake as applied to holism offers hope for those still enamored with the concept. Peter Philippson (2009) agrees with Smuts that there are levels of evolving wholes inherent in all matter. Meaning is a product of this organization and results from progressive awareness of the larger whole. From this perspective everything is process and perpetually unfolding. Holism, accordingly, is a necessary adjunct to field theory as an explanation of this process of interrelatedness. From this perspective there is no category error in movement from matter to self.

Advocacy for holism can also be found in Sylvia Crocker's identifying a central function of the self in gestalt therapy as the whole-making function. "All learning, whether cognitive or behavioral, is the result of the whole-making capacity of organisms" (Crocker 1999: 24). This is a less doctrinal version of Smutsian holism and more in line with the original ideas of the gestalt psychologists. Crocker maintains the vernacular of holism within gestalt therapy in a more discreet and delimited approach.

Will gestalt therapy's current renaissance in field theory and phenomenology mark the abandonment of holism and the colloquialism brought about with the New Age zeitgeist? If so, perhaps gestalt therapy will mature without the stigma of eastern-influenced metaphysical ideologies. Alternatively, will gestalt therapy continue on a path of integrating energy work, herbal medicine, shamanism, and *avant garde* expressive therapies? The term "holism" suggests this esoteric patois and moves gestalt therapy away from the serious study from whence it was born as a scientific-philosophical movement.

A shift away from holistic doctrine, ironically, promises to restore gestalt therapy as an encompassing philosophy. It also promises a precise system of psychotherapy with enough face validity to be a unifying framework for multiple cultural, scientific and psychotherapeutic schools of thought and practice. Time will tell if holism is an antiquated concept, lingering long enough to enable gestalt therapy to define differences and similarities in the world of philosophy, science, and psychotherapy.

References

Anderson, W. (1983) *The Upstart Spring: Esalen and the American Awakening.* Reading, PA: Addison-Wesley.
Ash, M. (1998) *Gestalt Psychology in German Culture 1890–1967: Holism and the Quest for Objectivity.* Cambridge: Cambridge University Press.
Bar-Yoseph Levine, T. (2009) Submitted and accepted by the Guest Editor, *International Gestalt Journal.* Publication of special issue delayed indefinitely.
Benking, H. and van Meurs, M. (1997) History, concepts and potentials of holism. Paper presented at symposium on holistic aspects in systems research, Baden-Baden, August 1997. On-line. Available at: http://www.ceptualinstitute.com/genre/benking/holismsmuts.htm (accessed 12 January 2009).
Bloom, D. (2000) Experience indivisible, preaching to the converted. Paper presented at the New York Institute for Gestalt Therapy, New York, April.
Bowman, C. (1998) Definitions of gestalt therapy: finding common ground. *Gestalt Review*, 2, 2: 97–107.
Bowman, C. and Nevis, E. (2005) The history and development of Gestalt therapy. In A. L. Woldt and S. M. Toman (eds) *Gestalt Therapy: History, Theory and Practice.* Thousand Oaks, CA: Sage Publications.
Cambridge Advanced Learner's Dictionary (2008) Cambridge: Cambridge University Press. On-line. Available at: http://dictionary.cambridge.org (accessed 15 November 2008).
Compact Oxford English Dictionary (2008) Oxford: Oxford University Press. On-line. Available at: http://www.askoxford.com (accessed 15 November 2008).
Crocker, S. (1999) *A Well Lived Life: Essays in Gestalt Therapy.* Cambridge, MA: GIC Press.
Eng, E. (1978) Looking back on Kurt Lewin: from field theory to action research. *Journal of the History of the Behavioral Sciences*, 14, 3: 228–232.
Goldstein, K. (1939/1995) *The Organism: A Holistic Approach to Biology Derived from Pathological Data in Man.* New York: Zone Books.
Harrington, A. (1996) *Reenchanted Science: Holism in German Culture from Wilhelm II to Hitler.* New York: W.W. Norton & Company.
Harwood, J. (1998) Holistic theories of mind in early twentieth-century Germany. *History of Science*, 36, 4: 485–497.

Köhler, W. (1947) *Gestalt Psychology*. New York: Liveright Publishing Corporation.
Korta, K. and Perry, J. (2007) Radical minimalism, moderate contextualism. In G. Preyer and G. Peter (eds) *Context Sensitivity and Semantic Minimalism: New Essays on Semantics and Pragmatics*. Oxford: Oxford University Press.
Latner, J. (1974) *The Gestalt Therapy Book: A Holistic Guide to the Theory, Principles and Techniques of Gestalt Therapy Developed by Frederick S. Perls and Others*. New York: Bantam Books.
—— (2008) Commentary I: relativistic quantum field theory: implications for Gestalt therapy. *Gestalt Review*, 12, 1: 24–31.
Lewin, K. (1948/1997) *Resolving Social Conflicts and Field Theory in Social Science*. Washington, DC: American Psychological Association.
Marrow, A. (1977) *The Practical Theorist: The Life and Work of Kurt Lewin*. New York: Teachers College Press.
Meara, A. (2008) Commentary II: relativistic quantum field theory: implications for Gestalt therapy. *Gestalt Review*, 12, 1: 32–39.
Merriam-Webster's Online Dictionary (2008) Springfield, MA: Merriam-Webster, Inc. On-line. Available at: http://www.merriam-webster.com (accessed 15 November 2008).
O'Neill, B. and Gaffney, S. (2008) Field-theoretical strategy. In P. Brownell (ed.) *Handbook for Theory, Research and Practice in Gestalt Therapy*. Newcastle, UK: Cambridge Scholars Publishing.
Parlett, M. (1991) Reflections on field theory. *British Gestalt Journal*, 1: 68–91.
—— (1997) The unified field in practice. *Gestalt Review*, 1, 1: 16–33.
Perls, F. (1947) *Ego, Hunger and Aggression*. New York: Vintage Books.
—— (1969a) *In and Out of the Garbage Pail*. Moab, UT: Real People Press.
—— (1969b) *Gestalt Therapy Verbatim*. Lafayette, CA: Real People Press.
—— (1969c) A life chronology. On-line. Available at: http://www.gestalt.org/fritz.htm (accessed 10 December 2009).
—— (1973) *The Gestalt Approach and Eyewitness to Therapy*. Palo Alto, CA: Science and Behavior Books.
Perls, F., Hefferline, R. and Goodman, P. (1951/1994) *Gestalt Therapy: Excitement and Growth in the Human Personality*. New York: Gestalt Journal Press.
Philippson, P. (2009) *The Emergent Self*. London: Karnac Books.
Resnick, R. (1995) Gestalt therapy: principles, prisms, perspectives. *British Gestalt Journal*, 4, 1: 3–13.
Robine, J. (1993) "Le holism de J. C. Smuts," paper presented at the conférence à l'Institut Français de Gestalt-thérapie, Paris, October. On-line. Available at: http://www.gestalt.org/robine.htm (accessed 11 September 2008).
Ryle, G. (1949) *The Concept of Mind*. New York: Hutchinson.
Sherrill, R. (1986) Gestalt therapy and Gestalt psychology. *Gestalt Journal*, 9, 2: 53–66.
Smuts, J. (1926/1996) *Holism and Evolution*. Gouldsboro, ME: Gestalt Journal Press.
Spiegelberg, H. (1972) *Phenomenology in Psychiatry and Psychology*. Evanston, IL: Northwestern University Press.
Staemmler, F. (2006) A Babylonian confusion: on the uses and meanings of the term "field." *British Gestalt Journal*, 15, 2: 64–83.

Wheeler, G. (1991) *Gestalt Reconsidered: A New Approach to Contact and Resistance.* Cleveland, OH: GIC Press.

—— (1998) Deconstructing individualism: an interview with Gordon Wheeler, Ph.D. G. Wheeler interviewed by M. Goodlander, *Gestalt!* 2, Fall: 1998. On-line. Available at: http://www.g-gej.org/2-1/wheeler.html (accessed 25 November 2008).

Wulf, R. (1996) The historical roots of Gestalt therapy theory. *Gestalt Dialogue: Newsletter of the Integrative Gestalt Centre*, Christchurch, New Zealand. On-line. Available at: http://www.gestalt.org/wulf.htm (accessed 17 December 2009).

Wymore, J. (2006) *Gestalt Therapy and Human Nature: Evolutionary Psychology Applied.* Bloomington, IN: AuthorHouse.

Yontef, G. (1993) *Awareness, Process & Dialogue: Essays on Gestalt Therapy.* Highland, NY: Gestalt Journal Press.

Chapter 4

The interactive field: Gestalt therapy as an embodied relational dialogue

Michael Craig Clemmens

The world we live in moves at an accelerated pace, sometimes as fast as our wireless connection and mobile phones seem to carry us. Thinking or *processing* faster than we can sense has become a way of life. Information, video representations of combat, sex, house designing, musical creation, etc., rush to us often before we can notice our sensory and bodily responses to them. Action swifter and more efficient has become the by-word of the Western world and the global culture that yawns before us all. Many clients coming for therapy feel "disconnected", "isolated" and complain of not having "relationships." My experience is that clients come to therapy to feel a sense of connection or coherence in themselves and in relationship to another. Given these field conditions, *our present challenge is to experience the whole of our selves at this moment in relation to others.*

Psychotherapy is a unique relationship where one person (the client) comes to another with a need and the other (therapist/consultant) attempts to help. In gestalt therapy, this "helping" occurs, not through advice giving, but through our presence (Jacobs 2006) and relating to our clients with the fullness of ourselves. This fullness includes our thoughts, feelings, sensations and movements as they emerge within the context of the relationship *and in service of the client's emergent needs.*

To clarify the embodied approach, we need to examine the embodied sense of presence and field. Presence is our grounded embodiment, the multitude of movements, structures and knowings that co-create our physical relationships within a contextual field. Field is "the contextual, interactive, energetic and interpersonal environment that supports a particular way of interacting" (Kepner 2003: 8). When these interactions are primarily desensitized, mechanical or disembodied our sense of our self and of the world we live in are diminished. We become, as Kennedy (2005) describes, "absent" in our interactions, going through the motions, not fully present to our own process or to others. This is the ennui of our present field context, where it is possible for an individual to commit suicide on the internet and have a multitude of observers observing as a disembodied audience. So our experience of our self is embedded in the surrounding context which we co-create. In contrast, the client–therapist relationship can be an alternative field in which to experience the meaning of our behavior and a greater range of interacting styles.

The emphasis in Gestalt therapy on present moment and process orients us to what is occurring between the client and ourselves. From a Dialogic perspective reality emerges between the therapist and client as we encounter and transform each other. This is dialogue and an inherently interactive process. By attending to *how* this "in between" emerges and can be directly known through our bodily experience, relational patterns become explicit for the client. Many Gestalt therapists attend to this "in between" through the dialogic verbal process (Hycner 1995; Jacobs 1995, 2006). What is being described here is an extension of that dialogic approach to include the emergent physical experience of the client/therapist field in the moment. The Gestalt therapist, by focusing on the immediate embodiment in the client and his/her own, allows a deeper dialogic resonance to become possible. Nowhere is this more salient than in the *pas de deux* of psychotherapy where minute movements, gestures, tone, and glances communicate and co-create meanings, the senses of wholeness and relatedness for the client.

It is important to distinguish between what we refer to as "the observer" perspective and embodiment. From the observer perspective, everyone "has a body." He/she is a body right before us; they take up space, move, breathe, vocalize their experience and seem to be "here and now". Frequently people "know" they are "here" through their thoughts or concepts of self. But this is not embodiment. This is thinking about or observing our self from previous experience, what we might refer to as "body as object" (Clemmens 1997). Another aspect of this observer mode is the sensate "feeling" our body like an athlete or performer. We can sense our body, stretch, perform sex and do many tasks but without experiencing my body as "me" in relation we are merely working the machine (Clemmens and Bursztyn 1997).

In contrast to this, embodiment is the sensate experience of my body as self in relation to others and the world about me. I know my arms as I reach my heart as I feel it/me beat together, my eyes as I gaze upon the other. Embodiment is a quality of presence, an ontological sense of "here and nowness," and the sense of being awake and fully engaged in the relational world. But my embodiment is not only how I experience myself (felt body), it is also how others experience and perceive me. That is, others experience me as a body that moves, speaks gestures and impacts them in many ways. As Kennedy (2005) points out, referencing Merleau Ponty, our body is the cohesion that allows us to experience the unity of the world. This coherence is reciprocal: the world comes to me and me to it, feels me and I feel the world or horizon. We make sense of our experience; we integrate our experience by including ourselves as others and with others through embodiment. It is through my embodiment that others experience me, know me. The contacts between mother and child in early development, the experience of being seen and noticed (or not noticed), the gaze of a lover, all of these and many more co-create a sense of being "some-body" and "somewhere." The relative absence of these contacts may be useful at any given moment, what we call a *creative adjustment* and/or reflective of an impoverished sensate field. An embodied relational therapy can explore a more impoverished relational field and offer an alternative experience embedded in a richer sensate field.

From a field perspective, two aspects of embodiment are inseparable. We experience ourselves through how we sense self through proprioception (alignment, internal tensions and muscular adjustment) (Frank 2003) and the experience of being seen, touched, and creating space with each other. It is not that we each have a separate field with the possibility of bumping into each other, but rather the embodied field we experience is interactive, a dynamic tension between us. Consider the image of two dancers. The movement they create develops between their individual proprioception. Yet this becomes fully activated at the boundary through their hands, arms and legs, in every contact point where they touch, adjust and interact. The pressing, pushing, yielding, feeling for the other, these "small" exchanges create the sense of "I/we." This is what occurs in the interaction between the client and therapist, an ongoing process of sensory adjustment, dances of affect, attunements of position in relation to each other, and meanings embedded in our experience often not yet verbalized. To try and separate what is mine and yours as if we were separating variables in a laboratory is as meaningless and impossible as separating out the effects of the experimenter in the same experiment. Who I am now, how I experience my body is never field independent. We are the shared context for each other's experience and development through our physicality.

If we fully abandon the myth of objectively observing to include our own sensate experience in response/relation to our clients, we can practice psychotherapy as a mutually embodied interactive dance. By learning to attend to this mutual dance and the relational and developmental themes that emerge from it, we can provide a forum for connection and reparation. This is the advantage of an embodied gestalt therapy.

Skills for attending to the embodied relational field

In attending to the embodied relational field there are four skills that support our process as facilitators. These skills are embodiment, attunement, resonance, and articulation.

Embodiment

As defined before, embodiment is experiencing my body as self in relation to the other and the field. So how do I maintain embodiment when sitting with my client? I can do this by noticing my breath, feeling my feet on the floor, my back on the chair and noticing my eyes and all of my sensing and orienting processes in this moment. All of this process needs to be an ongoing discipline and as figural as my thoughts or theories about the client and our process. Our embodiment as therapists is the fundamental condition to support the following other skills. Without experiencing our own embodiment we can not attend to the client/therapist field in this distinct manner.

The discipline of embodiment is to remain sensitized and curious when we become desensitized. Through sensitization we can orient to our mutual physical experience, as the significant organizing force the field. From this basic stance, what occurs in the embodied relational field becomes meaningful. It is as meaningful as the client's language and thoughts and is the cohesion or basis for these verbal and cognitive figures.

Attunement

Attunement is opening or reaching out with my senses to whatever "echoes" or shifts in the field (within us and our client). It is a receptive mode. In order to do this we must empty our task-oriented mind and allow our bodily experience to be part of the foreground. The guiding questions are how the client's content is embodied in this moment and, conversely, how my embodiment is in relation to their process. Thus, my attunement takes the form of noticing how my client moves, breathes, and gestures as he/she speaks. My goal is to have my client share this curiosity. I want to support my client to be attuned to their sensate experience in the relational field.

Resonance

The third skill in working with relational embodiment is to notice my own movements, breathing and posture in response to my client or in concert with him/her. Or how I can feel their voice, their tension resonating inside of me. This skill is what I call *resonance*, the process of sensing and attending to shifts in my own embodiment and that of my client like ripples in a stream of water.

Once I am attuned to the client and myself I can "stay with" and allow myself to experience what emerges in me in relation to become more developed. Resonance is the skill of noticing and amplifying my sensate response to my client in the moment. This experience is similar to being a bowl or resonant instrument (Clemmens and Bursztyn 2003), that is, how I vibrate in resonance with my client. I may chime at different tones or feel empty and soundless inside at other times in our encounter. This is the embodied experience of Inclusion (Hycner 1995) or what Kepner (2003) refers to as embodied empathy. For example, I might notice myself pressing my feet into the floor while listening to my client's voice float around the room and seeing their feet dangle above the floor. Or in concert with my client I might tighten my jaw as she does when talking. These behaviors, differentiation (doing some opposite of my client) and confluence (mirroring) are forms of my embodied responsiveness.

Articulation

Following with the process of allowing myself to experience resonance, the movement is to allow this resonance to form into thought or language. This skill is articulation, the point in the contacting process where I put into meaning through thoughts for myself and statements to my client. Articulation is the process of making known either to our self or the client the embodied shifts current in the field as we sense them. Of course, the timing and choice of articulating to my client about my embodied self experience or of their embodied experience needs to be bounded by considerations for their functioning, the stage of therapy and other field conditions. I also don't always have to comment of what I attune to and resonate with in this moment. I am also curious how his/her bodily supports relate to the cognitive and verbal themes he/she talks about in the session. Whether body is background (supporting and out of the client's immediate awareness) or foreground (the immediate focus of his/her awareness), my task is to remain interested in how these spheres of experience are intertwined and significant.

Case example: Thomas

The following is a description of an encounter between me and a client. It illustrates using these skills as a method to opening up the dialogue to the emergent embodied patterns.

> Thomas was referred to me by his father, an actor and a very charismatic man. "Tom" had a recent history of feeling depressed and suicidal following some professional disappointments. What struck me when we met was the economy of his movement. He sat on the couch across from me with little gesture, barely raising his head to speak. When I spoke, he would slightly smile and then drop his head again. I began to notice my own body movements in relation to him. I took up much more space in my chair, my legs widely set and my shoulders square. The contrast between us initially was like we were two ends of a continuum. This was the initial sense of attuning to the field and our relational embodiment.

I found myself trying to sit like Tom, narrowing my shoulders and dropping my head more as I spoke. I had begun to resonate with his way of organizing himself in relation to me (and possibly the world). Two changes occurred during this shift of me trying on his way of sitting. First, I experienced a sense of being smaller inside of myself. It was as if I was shriveling inside as well as taking up less space in the room. Secondly, he began to look up at me more frequently and even square his shoulders. My sense was that I was making more space for him and he was taking the space I offered. After a few minutes of this shift in our postures, I asked Tom if what he felt was significant in his life. To my excitement, he said: "I feel small, particularly with people like my dad who are talented. And sometimes I just give up because there doesn't seem to be enough room on the stage for him and me."

At this point I articulated to Tom what I had been experiencing in my body and how I saw him taking so little space. He was skeptical and a little curious about how what he was talking about could be "played out in our bodies." I invited him to experiment with using his body in different ways and notice how he felt about himself and his experience of me. "You mean I might sit like you?" he asked. Tom tried to sit as he saw me, with his shoulders, back and legs widely set and his head upright. He began to breathe more fully and his eyes widened much more. His experience was that of feeling more exposed and he was worried that he was being rude to me, "not respectful." At this point Tom and I were attuned to each other's posture and through resonance exploring the possibilities of our relationship.

Tom then went back to exaggerating his "narrowed" stance and said he could feel how much less space he inhabited. I asked him if he wanted to know about my experience when he was in the different positions. He was very interested but said he already knew that I wanted him to be like me, sit like me, be strong, and look confidant. I immediately narrowed my shoulders and my knees again while dropping my shoulders. I said "How about I will be Tom and you be Michael?" to which he said "No you be Tom and I'll be Dad." From there we had a dialogue of the big father to the lesser son, each of us starting in our postures but ending up both in a middle position. Tom was crying as he articulated (as his father) to me: "I see you are not me and I want you to be you, do things your way". I asked Tom what he would say in my position as the son; he lifted his head up a little more and said: "I can't be you . . . only me, I need to do things my way."

This session exemplifies the potency of attending. I embodied Tom's posture as I listened to his words and he assumed the position that he did when sitting with his father. Through dialogue, both physical and verbal, we were able to explore the meaning of the stance he took with me and in the world. My willingness to resonate with his posture allowed Tom to see how he embodies himself in relation to me and his father. His willingness to explore the range of his options led to a very important experience of his relationship with his father, a passage to manhood through his body. This embodied approach of Gestalt therapy emphasizes phenomenological experience without beginning with a verbal understanding or construct. What is unique here is the development of this experience from the resonance or embodied empathy emergent in the client/therapist field. We developed a figure through our shared embodiment, a fractal of his relationships with his father. My client experienced an important developmental field he was embedded in and was able to "dis-embed" himself from an adolescent field (McConville 1995) and to position him in the next developmental stance. I facilitated this development initially by attuning to our mutual embodiment in the moment and articulating this experience with him. The second movement of our dance developed as Tom tried on both his way of sitting and mine, as the stance of an adult. This led to his awareness of the embodied field and the meaning of the lived space for them as father and son. Tom's developmental theme was lived out in the interactive field created by our physical selves in relation.

Shame in the embodied field: a special case of an embodied relationship

From an interactive field perspective, shame is a lack of support and acceptance in the field for our basic needs and experience (Wheeler 1996). Shame is fundamentally a relational and bodily experience, relational in that we learn and perpetuate the sense of being "unacceptable" through our inter-subjective experiences, and bodily in that this learning and lack of support is experienced through our bodies. Through gestures, the ways we are looked upon/do not look upon each other, the tones of our voices, the sense of shame is co-created and perpetuated. The interactive dialogue can enable and perpetuate feelings of shame for either client/therapist or both of us. We can also create supports for the client to "have a new experience." One of the most significant components of support is our embodied interaction.

Long before we can articulate it, there may be a felt sense of shame as fundamental ground in our relationship. Shame often exists at what Kennedy (2008) refers to as "the pre-personal level" preceding verbal and cognitive levels of interactions. Shame can emerge when looking at or being looked at by another, in the tone with which we are spoken to, from the entire range of facial and affective responses from the other, all of these can contribute to our sense of shame. We can feel shame as frozenness in our face or as a holding back or tightening of our musculature. Shame is a physical withdrawal, aversion or disconnection when we have the experience that we are unacceptable, unlovable and bad (Wheeler 1996). It is a profound sense of kinesthetic separation in the relational field. We feel separated and repulsively different. Other embodiments of shame are a desire or movement to curl inward, inhibiting our movements or gestures out of fear that we will seem "too needy", nausea or feeling ill, heat or flushing in our face, a desire to flee or "get out of the room," anger or rage at being noticed or exposed, and dropping our eyes or looking away to manage the degree of intensity.

The following is an example of shame in the embodied field and the use of the skills of embodiment, attunement, resonance, and articulation to support working with shame.

> Jimmy is telling me about his prostitution for drugs during his addiction. He asked me if this was "okay" to talk about with me. He leaned his head in toward me when asking and when I responded pulled his head back as I answered. I took a deep breath and scanned my own body in order to give him an answer that was based on my felt experience, not just an immediate "of course." I told him that I was interested in what he was saying. As I said this I could feel myself as heavy in my chair, as if there was more gravity in the moment between us. I then asked him how he might know that I was remaining with him while he spoke about his behavior. I also suggested he try doing what I just had done, breathing and taking the time to feel himself. He was silent for a few minutes as he sat with his head down, eyes on my shoes and his body still. He finally looked up at me and said: "I need to see that you are not disgusted with me, I want to see in your face that you won't turn away from me." We devised an experiment that he would look at my face while he spoke. I felt excited by the clarity of his request. As he spoke of his experience of selling himself for drugs, I paid attention to my body and his, it was as if he was giving me his experience of shame and looking to see if I would cut off from him. At one point, I began to tear up and he said: "what is happening, are you feeling sorry for me?". I responded that I was remembering my own experience of embarrassment. He stopped and said "you too?" I said though soft eyes "yes". Jimmy continued to speak and he began to tear up. At this point his head was no longer swinging but steady on his shoulder. He looked at my face and said: "You do not look disgusted. . . . so I am not

> disgusting to you". I asked him how he could tell, and he responded that my eyes remained open and I did not turn away from him. I then asked Jimmy to try on his question as a statement while we looked at each other. He repeated "I am not disgusting". He stopped after two repetitions, and looking straight at me said: "I am not disgusting but I felt disgusted in my body when I did this".

This vignette illustrates the power of contacting through attention to shame as emergent in our relational field with emphasis on our embodied interacting. Jimmy's experience of "knowing I was not disgusted with him" (or that he was not disgusting) emerged through his attunement to my face. He was already attuning to me as he risked showing his "face." We explored how what he believed and felt about him was manifest in our interaction in the moment. By physically offering and including me in his shame experience, we were able to create enough support and context for him to both articulate his embodied shame and to experience himself differently. He did this through articulating what he feared and felt in relation to me in our embodied dialogue. The support offered to him was my attention to his physical pattern, my face, my own emotional resonance and a context to explore this with safety and mutuality.

Concluding thoughts

Through attention and dialogue based on our mutual embodied awareness we can explore relational patterns of our clients and create alternative experiences and supports for change and growth. In this chapter, I have focused on the therapy/consulting situation as an embodied interactive field co-created out of the client and therapist relationship. Our experiences are not unrelated isolates but constantly mutually influencing steps in choreography. If we accept the fact that we are our bodies in relation with each other (embodiment), then we can attend to the meaning of our client's experience through embodied resonance.

This approach has significance for the practice of gestalt (and all therapies). Mutual embodiment means that all themes and figures are supported and available through attention to our physicality. Our feelings, our dreams, our thinking are all supported and emergent in our bodies at this moment with each other.

Secondly, emphasizing embodiment as a focus in therapy requires that, as practitioners, we learn to pay more attention to how we create this interactive dance and how we can intervene with clarity and embodied awareness. The skills of attending to embodiment, attunement, resonance and articulation are not implicit but "practices" that contrast with our cultural and individual tendencies to intellectualize and desensitize. To practice Gestalt therapy in this way requires that we discipline ourselves to notice our own embodied presence, not as metaphor or idea, but as we are actual pulsing, gesturing, and breathing partners. It is through our resonance that we connect with our clients and help them fully articulate their experience in the process of change.

References

Clemmens, M. (1997) *Getting Beyond Sobriety: Clinical Approaches to Long Term Recovery*. San Francisco: Jossey Bass.
Clemmens, M. and Bursztyn, A. (2003) Culture and body. *British Gestalt Journal*, 12, 1: 15–21.
Frank, R. (2003) Embodying creativity, developing experience. In Margherita Spagnuolo-Lobb and Nancy Amendt-Lyon (eds) *Creative License: The Art of Gestalt Therapy*. Wien/New York: Springer-Verlag.
Hycner, R. (1995) The dialogic ground. In *The Healing Relationship in Gestalt Therapy; A Dialogic/Self Psychology Approach*. Highland, NY: The Gestalt Press.
Jacobs, L. (1995) Dialogue in Gestalt therapy. In R. Hycner and L. Jacobs (eds) *The Healing Relationship in Gestalt Therapy*. Highland, NY: Gestalt Journal Press.
—— (2006) That which enables: support as complex and contextually emergent. *British Gestalt Journal*, 15, 2: 10–19.
Kennedy, D. (2005) The lived body. *British Gestalt Journal*, 14, 2: 109–117.
—— (2008) The eclipse of dialogue. *British Gestalt Journal*, 17, 1: 15–26.
Kepner, J. (2003) The embodied field. *British Gestalt Journal*, 12, 1: 6–14.
McConville, M. (1995) *Adolescence: Psychotherapy and the Emergent Self*. San Francisco: Jossey-Bass.
Wheeler, G. (1996) Self and shame: a new paradigm for psychotherapy. In *Voice of Shame: Silence and Connection in Psychotherapy*. San Francisco: Jossey-Bass.

Chapter 5

Personality: co-creating a dynamic symphony

Carmen Vázquez Bandín[1]

Gestalt theory, rooted in field theory, offers a fundamental and radically original explanation of the self. The essential point of departure of its theory is contact, understood as a sequence of awareness and motor response towards assimilable novelty, and the rejection of unassimilable novelty; that is, the creative adjustment between the organism and the environment. The self is the function of contacting the real (if ephemeral) present if we view the activity as a temporal process. The self is present wherever and whenever an interaction exists at the boundary between the organism and the environment. The principal temporary structures of the self are: id, ego and personality.

In this chapter, we proceed deductively – moving from the general to the particular – to consider, within a filogenetic and ontogenetic paradigm, how personality functions, and how it permits us to be who we are, not simply as individuals but as a species.

The reader will naturally understand the difficulty of developing all the possibilities, nuances and implications of personality in limited space. By way of conclusion, we provide a brief exposition of personality as the culmination of an individual's life in "society." We underscore the fact that personality is continually changing even as a certain stability that is maintained.

We never cease being a mystery to ourselves. There are, however, awesome (i.e. inspiring awe) processes for gaining knowledge about the laws that govern the universe (cosmology, microphysics), about our terrestrial matrix (earth sciences), about the science of human and animal life (biology), about the origin and formation of the human species (prehistory), about the relation of human beings to their surroundings (ecology), and about our social and historical destiny. We also discover many other messages about our deeper selves as expressed through the languages of the human soul: literature, poetry, music, painting and sculpture.

The various branches of science and the arts elucidate, each from their own perspective, the fact of being human. Nevertheless, these moments of transparency are separated by areas of deep shadows, and we frequently lose sight of the complex wholeness of our identity. The convergence of the sciences and humanities, necessary for the restoration of the human condition, is not always achieved. In fact, the latter is more often than not uprooted from the environment, as though it were an intrusive force:

> It makes no sense to speak, for example, of an animal that breathes without considering air and oxygen as part of its definition, or to speak of eating without mentioning food, or of seeing without light, or locomotion without gravity and supporting ground, or of speech without communicants.
> (Perls, Hefferline, and Goodman (PHG) 1951: 230)

If the human being is deprived of knowledge of the physical world (even if she is a thermal machine), cut off from the world of life (even if she is an animal), or estranged from the environment (indivisible unit in the field of organism-environment), she is fragmented into isolated pieces within the human sciences. Indeed, reductionist and disjunctive – if not dehumanizing – principles that have dominated the field of science, including the human sciences, impede focusing on the human aspect. Once that which is human suffers disintegration, the capacity to sense wonder, and to interrogate aspects of human identity, is eradicated as well.

We are in need of a thought process that seeks to gather and organize the components – biological, cultural, social, individual – of human complexity and incorporate scientific contributions from anthropology. This is, at the same time, to refocus the concept of the "generic human being," complexifying and deepening it, by connecting its corporal being, the *psyche*, birth, death, youth, old age, woman, sex, aggression, love, health-sickness and codependence with the environment. We are constrained to apply the existential, holistic perspective that is endemic to our process,[2] thereby proffering a unique approach to the anguish, joy, pain, ecstasy we experience as human subjects. Moreover, as our radical theory bids, the environment is both a constituent element and an agent of our identity and of ourselves. Finally, we need to look to ourselves as both elements and agents of environmental stability and change.

The term "human" is rich, contradictory, flexible, and constantly changing. Knowledge of human identity ought to have a more scientific, philosophic and poetic base than it has been apportioned. The body of knowledge reflected by the theory of human identity is complex:

- because it recognizes that the human subject it studies is included in the object of study;
- because it conceives of human oneness and diversity as inseparable;
- because it conceives of all dimensions of human reality in holistic terms – physical, biological, social, mythological, economic, sociological,

historical, ethical and aesthetic – even though these aspects are in actuality separate and compartmentalized;
- because it cannot separate the individual from the environment, thereby making the individual, together with the environment, co-creators of reality;
- because it conceives of *homo* not only as *sapiens, faber* and *economicus* but also as *demens, ludens* and "*consumans*";
- because it allies the scientific dimension (i.e. the verification of data and the creation and refutation of hypotheses) with epistemological and philosophical (i.e. reflective) dimensions, as well as with ethical and the aesthetic factors;
- because it gives meaning to terms – cognitive and affective – often disparaged or rejected by the sciences: soul, mind, thought, feeling.

In search of identity

"Who are we" is inseparable from *where we are, where we come from, where we are going*, and *whom we are with*.

The mortal human being, as any living creature, carries within it a biochemical and a genetic unity of life – the unity of creation. She is a "hyper"-being whose life potential has evolved in unprecedented form. She expresses in extreme terms the egocentric and altruistic qualities of the individual. It is a dance, indefatigable and uninterrupted, of figures and grounds from the I to the We (Bloom 2008); as Bergson (1911/1985: ch. 3) once wrote, "Evolution is creative." The human being is hyper-alive in the sense that she develops life's creativity anew. As humanity evolves, so does the creative faculty.

The human being as a meta-alive being creates new forms of life – psychic, mental and social in accordance with her organizational and cognitive aptitudes – because all contact is creative and dynamic.

The human being is *sui generis* a vertebrated animal, of the class mammalia, and of the primate order. But the human being is a hyper-mammal given that she is marked by confluence and symbiosis with the mother (Bowlby 1969). Only upon reaching adulthood does she develop the affective side of mammals marked by love and tenderness, anger and hatred, preserving innocent connections in the form of mature friendships, intensifying commonalities and rivalries, increasing the power of memory, intelligence and feeling and pushing to the extreme the capacity to love, to experience pleasure, to suffer. Mammals are imbued with affective attachments, a childlike capacity for play and learning, and the experience and wisdom of old age; we maintain our primary mammalian condition when we go on being young even when we grow old; our theory states: "The childish feelings are important not as a past that must be undone but as some of the most beautiful powers of adult life that must be recovered: spontaneity, imagination, directness of awareness and manipulation" (PHG 1951: 297).

Humans are "hyper"-sexual animals because their sexuality has ceased to be temporal, as is the case with chimpanzees, for example, and it has ceased to exist only in the genitals: it has pervaded the entire being, and reproduction is no longer its sole *raison d'être*; sexuality permeates – *à la* Freud – all behaviors, dreams and thoughts. We have a complicated sexual apparatus, involving the senses as excitants, and motor responses such as kissing, embracing, all aimed at a climax.

Human beings are super-primates in whom passing or provisional traits have been transformed into permanent characteristics found amongst the higher class of simians: bipedality and the ability to deploy tools. The brain of their primate ancestors has undergone hypertrophy; with the development of their intelligence and curiosity, human beings have become creatures imbued with an aesthetic sensibility.

The poor physical equipment of humans with respect to other animals, however, has not impeded a great launch of humanity and its subsequent dissemination throughout the world of living beings. It is as if the ensuing development of individual intelligence and social organization has compensated for deficiencies in terms of musculature and sense organs. Moreover, out of such deficiencies (e.g. salt or vitamins) has come a need to seek, explore, discover, invent.

Culture as a human co-creation that creates and recreates

Since a human being cannot be seen except in relation to the environment – "no animal is complete in its own skin" (PHG 1951: 91) – an inseparable unity is created between the two. This co-creating intertwining makes for the correlation of nature and culture.

Interactions among individuals create society, and society reverberates upon human beings through its culture, allowing them to be fully human. Society lives for the individual, who in turn lives for society. Each of these elements is, in its own way, both a means and an end: culture and society enable the actualization of the individual, and the interactions among individuals are what permit the perpetuity and the actualization of culture and the reorganization of society.

This relation is at the same time dialogical; that is, its complementarity can become an antagonist. Society represses or inhibits the individual, and the individual in turn aspires to emancipate herself from the yoke of society; instead functioning as a social dynamic in which human beings can discover themselves, inventing themselves and others, we are perennially "forced to think of three warring abstractions: the mere animal, the harried individual self, and the social pressures" (PHG 1951: 87). Neurosis and other inhibiting symptoms are reactions against rigid social conventions.

That culture is the greatest emerging force of human society is a strong impression left with me after reading Bar-Yoseph Levine (2005). It is the patrimony of its memory and organization. This patrimony is first inscribed in the memory of people (oral culture) and later in laws, civil rights, sacred texts, literature, the arts. Acquired from one generation to the next, culture is continually regenerating itself. Culture trains and gives form.

Culture leaves its stamp on every individual who is born into its fold, often imposing its prohibitions, imperatives, educational system, dietary regime, models of behavior. Culture favors and stimulates, all the while that it represses, inhibits and overdetermines individual aptitudes, thereby exerting influence over brain functioning and mind formation. Thus, it intervenes to co-organize, civilize, socialize, control the gamut of personality. Society also provides other elements of support in order to stimulate creativity in the individual and instill in her a feeling of belonging, and so forth.

Individuals evolve mentally, psychologically, affectively in the bosom of culture and society. Culture is constituted of the combined habits, customs, practices, know-how, knowledge, rules, norms, prohibitions, strategies, beliefs, values, ideas, and myths which are perpetuated from generation to generation, reproduced in each individual and regenerated to form the social matrix in all its complexity. Culture accumulates what is preserved, transmitted, learnt, and it entails principles of acquisition and programs of action. Culture is basic human capital.

Words are left me

Speech is at the centre of human culture and society. Language keeps itself alive in amazing ways. Languages evolve, effecting changes in their lexicon and grammatical structures. The principal characteristic of language is often said to be poetry. Words accommodate to, delight in, drink up the connotations that they evoke and invoke: metaphors break forth, analogies take flight, phrases shake off their grammatical shackles and capture the freedom of good speech. The human being has created the language that has created the human being.

Whatever the language, in every enunciation there is an implicit *I*, a *You* whom the *I* addresses, and an *It* of the situation, all of which "speak" at the same time. In other words, language proffers the essential gyratory movement between connecting forces: biological, human, social, cultural. If language is part of the wholeness of every human being, the wholeness of every human being is contained in language. Without altering the syntax, and often with the same words, oral language contains within itself the possibility of expressing two human states: the prosaic and the poetic. In poetic language, words connote more than they denote; they evoke, they are converted into "words of fire" in the face of more prosaic "words of stone" of which Dan Bloom (2001) speaks: "In Gestalt therapy, words have two aspects relevant. They may be instruments or tools in the contact process. Secondly, they may assist in the interruptions in the creativity of that process. The latter are words of stone, the former, words of fire" (p. 36). Heraclitus put it this way long ago: "It always was and is and shall be: an everliving fire, kindling in measures and going out in measures" (in Geldard 2000: 11). The poetic state of "words of fire" is an emotional and affective state. It comes to us from the moment we reach a threshold of participatory intensity. It comes to us when we are present and reveal ourselves to ourselves (Vázquez Bandín 2008a). In this state one can exist in relation to another, in a community. This – contactful – poetic state is filled with attention, concentration, interest, concern, excitement and grace (PHG 1951: xxvi).

"Connected" individuality

To speak of an individual is to speak of a subject. A subject is an individual and an individual is a subject. An individual does not possess a stable physical or psychological identity; rather, her physiological cells and experiences change constantly and are continually being updated. She is a being immersed in time and her reality is to live along with the flow of experience. As James (1904/1912/1976) reminds us: "To experience one's personal continuum in the living way is to know the originals of the ideas of continuity and sameness" (p. 21).

What makes every individual unique is the quality of her subjectivity and not her individual characteristics. Consequently, her differentiation in relation to the other does not lie in her genetic, anatomic, psychological or affective singularity; it lies in her capacity as a subject to know her subjectivity (i.e. him/herself as I). This ego functioning is the identification with and the progressive alienation from various choices; the delimiting or enhancing of ongoing contact, including motor behavior, aggression, orientation towards and manipulation of the situation. Personality is born of experience; it is an outcome of contacting. Put another way, personality "is the created figure that self becomes and assimilates to the organism" (PHG 1951: 157).

The notion of the subject implies exclusion and inclusion, acceptance and rejection. The individual lives in a dialogical relationship with her environment and, in this way, actualizes herself. She gets to know herself at the same time that she influences and transforms her environment. When exclusive she is egocentric, centered on herself; when inclusive she is altruistic and makes of herself a "we." The individual lives for herself and for the other in a "beating" of the moment, in terms of how circumstances change the referent of figure/ground: I, You, We.

The relation to the other is original and inherent. The primordial relation to the other is "virtual," existing *in potentia* in each person and must be realized in order for each person to realize herself. What produces intersubjectivity is a living-togetherness. The capacity for understanding allows one to recognize the other as another subjectivity, and eventually to experience her in love as an *alter ego*, another I. On the other hand, as we know through Maslow (1943), the need for recognition is inseparable from the subjective need for self-affirmation. If the subject is unaware, she feels hurt, limited. Rousseau (1770) pointed appositely to one's need to experience the gaze of the other in order to exist in human terms. Hegel (1807) underscored the need for recognition, something which Maslow and Todorov (1989/2001) also emphasize. One's need of another is radical, as Gestalt's field theory maintains. An individual is shown to be incomplete when she does not take into account the other: for example, to speak is to speak *to* or *with*; to flee is to flee *from*.

Gestalt therapy's concept of the individual-subject surpasses the alternative choice of an egocentric vision as propagated by Descartes and Husserl; the Gestalt perspective is enriching in that it is defined in relation to the *other*, following Emmanuel Lévinas's ethics of the Other. Gestalt incorporates both poles – the self and the other – into a field theory where they are inseparable; it is a given that human functioning interacts within an animal, physical, and socio-cultural field.

Personality, the child of experiment

We are now in a position to assert, following PHG (1951), that "personality is the system of attitudes assumed in interpersonal relations . . . the assumption of what one is, serving as the ground on which one could explain one's behavior, if the explanation were asked for" (p. 382). This is perforce a partial structure of the self, created from early interpersonal relations and formed by incorporating a large amount of material from the environment.

Since every individual emerges in a social field, social and cultural elements, speech, early interpersonal relations form the sediment or background of the personality. If we speak of developmental processes, an infant's experience is the function of the field caregiver-infant (Tronick 2007). Moreover, the structural patterns established early on in these relations will continue to function within the adult individual and may be identified as styles of contacting (Frank 2001). An individual in isolation is not possible. Therefore, personality may be viewed as the figure into which we have transformed ourselves and the one with which we are identified, even though in each creative contact we grow as individuals, and we actualize ourselves personally, socially and culturally.

The functioning of personality is the field of activity of culture and society; as such, it is achieved, integrated, and remembered. This structure offers stability and coherence to identity, embedding the subject in a social and cultural framework and conferring responsibility on her. Such responsibility is understood as an "agreement," insofar as coherent behavior emerges within whatever framework has been agreed upon; the result of creative, social contact is *personality*.

At the same time, the field of activity of culture and society as it impacts each individual has particular characteristics. The elements that can be considered determining and formative of identity include, among others, identification, dependency, communicative skills, imitation and learning, love choices and keeping company, sympathy, antipathy in the affective sphere, mutual assistance and rivalry. These elements provide stability and coherence to the personality, enabling it to maintain and actualize itself by dint of three acquired "habits": loyalty, morality, and rhetorical attitudes.

"Group-identification that has fulfilled needs and powers and is a source of strength for further action is the *habit of loyalty*" (PHG 1951: 423, emphasis added); such a habit is incorporated when we adopt behaviors by imitating others or identifying ourselves with them. G. Santayana (1942) referred to this "habit" as one of identifying with the "realms of our being." Language, individual turns of phrase in our speech, customs, forms of dress, culinary habits, etc. are preserved as a result of group loyalty. Loyalty, by definition, is an action of permanence; it defines consistent behavior of attachment, choice or preference for something or someone. Loyalty implies faithfulness and creates a feeling of belonging. But we cannot forget that loyalty is merely a quality of the personality function; it is not the full functioning of the self.

Loyalty must work in conjunction with prudence in a determined situation in order for experience to be assimilated. A balance must be created between the two in order for change to occur without the production of undue conflict. In the majority of cases, when needs change the reference group also changes, and prudence gains strength over loyalty, allowing the group to experience change without having any conscious awareness of conflict (Vázquez Bandín 2008b). But at other times, forcefully felt conflicts arise between two background actions that exist in relation to an individual's identification with a group. This is where morality comes into play. Only by supporting conflict can a new – creative – solution be produced, which is a basic tenet of Gestalt therapy's "paradoxical theory of change" (see Beisser 1970). Conflict must be resolved through the interplay of loyalty and prudence. Generally, two other forms of evaluation are deployed which do not result from any form of assimilation: learned moral choice and self-domination. Before abandoning one habit of loyalty, however, another must be found, insofar as "sociability of some kind is always part of one's needs" (PHG 1951: 204).

Rhetorical attitudes, that is, one's personal and particular form of speech, constitutes the third so-called habit that provides stability and coherence to the personality. Through these attitudes – voice, syntax and verbal manners

– human beings have learnt to manipulate personal relations and create their individuality. Rhetorical attitudes "can be observed by concentrating on one's voice, syntax, and manners. Such attitudes are complaining, bullying, being helpless, shiftiness, or forthrightness, give-and-take, fairness, etc." (PHG 1951: 205). Children acquire these kinds of techniques of manipulation early on, for they need to have a limited and concrete audience for their activities; they discover immediately which resources work and which do not. Later, when these techniques are taken out of awareness, we continue to use them without consciousness of having created them (see Vázquez Bandín 2008a). Personality, in this sense, is radically a creative structure of speech habits.

The foregoing discussion leads us to affirm that if individual personality, like organized society, changes continuously, it nonetheless maintains a certain stability by dint of "identity" understood as a framework of attitudes; attitude here is a learnt response to someone or something and relatively permanent. In other words, the personality function is the responsible, autonomous, prudent, loyal, sure, reasonable part of ourselves that allows us to know ourselves and, at the same time, knows what we have already learnt and are by now practised at.

Gestalt therapy, whose primary objective is the expansion of a person's *awareness*, is characterized above all by its use of *experiments* (as opposed to exercises, the difference here being teleological). If, in exercises, the therapist or facilitator expects, *a priori*, to bring about a particular outcome, in the experiment we know what we are proposing, but we know neither the process (how each person will work through it), nor the end result. What matters in Gestalt therapy is not the completion of actions *per se*, but what *interferes* with the successful completion of a task; it is esssential for the client to become aware of how she reacts throughout the process.

The experiment is rendered possible because it is a workable undertaking based on a number of factors: self-regulation of the individual who is experimenting, the facilitator's knowledge, the freeing of anxiety, and the creative, formative power of every human being. The awareness gained through the use of the experiment contributes to self-knowledge; it enables the human subject to feel alive in the fullest sense. Personality, in the final analysis, can be construed as a fuller reading of experience itself, insofar as it produces awareness *in this moment* of the totality of "my life" which, as we know all too well, is more than the sum of its parts.

Notes

1 Translated by Susan L. Fischer.
2 "Gestalt therapy takes its bearing from what is here and now, not from what has been or what should be. It is an existential-phenomenological approach, and as such it has to be experiential and experimental" (L. Perls 1992: 137–138).

References

Bar-Yoseph Levine, T. (ed.) (2005) *The Bridge: Dialogues Across Cultures*. Metairie, LA: Gestalt Institute Press.
Beisser, Arnold (1970) Paradoxical theory of change. In J. Fagan and I. Shepherd (eds) *Gestalt Therapy Now* (pp. 77–80). Palo Alto, CA: Science and Behavior Books.
Bergson, H. (1911/1985) *Creative Evolution* (Arthur Mitchell, trans.). New York: Henry Hold and Company.
Bloom, D. (2001) The song of the self, language and Gestalt therapy. *The Gestalt Journal*, 24, 2: 31–44.
—— (2008) In pursuit of Gestalt therapy group process: group process as a self process. In B. Feder and J. Frew (eds) *Beyond the Hot Seat Revisited: Gestalt Approaches to Group* (pp. 53–66). Metairie, LA: Gestalt Institute Press.
Bowlby, J. (1969) *Attachment and Loss*. New York: Basic Books.
Frank, R. (2001) *Body of Awareness*. Cambridge, MA: Gestalt Press.
Hegel, G. W. F. (1807/1977) *Phenomenology of Spirit*. London: Oxford University Press, Galaxy Books.
Heraclitus. Fragment 30, Clement Strom. V, 104, 1. In R. Geldard (2000) *Remembering Heraclitus*. New York: Lindisfarne Books.
James, W. (1904/1912/1976) A world of pure experience. In F. Burkhardt, F. Bowers and I. Skrupskelis (eds) *The Works of William James*, Vol. 3. (pp. 21–44). Cambridge, MA: Harvard University Press. Originally published as James, W. (1912) A world of pure experience. *Journal of Philosophy, Psychology, and Scientific Methods*, 1: 533–543, 561–570.
Maslow, A. (1943) A theory of human motivation. *Psychological Review*, 50: 370–396.
Perls, F. S., Hefferline, R. and Goodman, P. (1951) *Gestalt Therapy: Excitement and Growth in the Human Personality*. New York: Julian Press.
Perls, L. (1992) *Living at the Boundary*. Highland, NY: Gestalt Journal Press.
Rousseau, J. J. (1770/2008) *The Confessions*. New York: Penguin.
Santayana, G. (1942) *Realms of Being*. New York: Scribner's.
Todorov, T. (1989/2001) *Life in Common*. Lincoln, NE: University of Nebraska Press.
Tronick, E. (2007) *The Neurobehavioral and Social-emotional Development of Infants and Children*. New York: W. W. Norton.
Vázquez Bandín, C. (2008a) ¿Cantan las sirenas? (Are the sirens singing?) In *Buscando las palabras para decir* (*Searching for Words to Tell*) (pp. 257–293). Madrid: Sociedad de Cultura Valle-Inclán.
—— (2008b) Cuando la lealtad se convierte en un ancla. (When loyalty becomes a burden.) In *Buscando las palabras para decir* (*Searching for Words to Tell*) (pp. 295–326). Madrid: Sociedad de Cultura Valle-Inclán.

Chapter 6

Critiquing projection: supporting dialogue in a post-Cartesian world[1]

Lynne Jacobs

One of the most remarkable things about gestalt therapy theory has been its leadership in developing a post-Cartesian set of ideas about what it means to be human: about human functioning and psychology. The birth of gestalt therapy, with its avowedly post-Cartesian aims (Perls, Hefferline, and Goodman (PHG) 1951: viii), included a radical reconfiguration of many extant psychological concepts, most drawn from the world of psychoanalysis. The notions of Self, Id, Ego, Personality, and Unconsciousness were reworked to become more compatible with the gestalt shift in the ways in which we understand experience.

Projection has escaped similar scrutiny until recently (Sapriel 1998). Perhaps it has escaped scrutiny because it has held such a central place in our clinical theory and verbal culture since our beginnings (Smith 2006: 101, 188). In fact, an ironic twist in the development of my own critique of projection is that it was triggered by reading a critique of projection in a contemporary psychoanalytic treatise (Stolorow et al. 1987: 34)! I will argue that the word and the concept of projection is weighted so much by its birth and long association with the Cartesian world of dualisms, objectivity, the correspondence theory of truth, and mind as container, that we are better off developing more phenomenological and dialogical means to understand the phenomena we are tempted to think of as projection.

My critique of projection occurs at two levels of abstraction. I will first illustrate problematic uses of the concept. That alone would not be a reason to rethink the concept *per se*. But it does establish the ethical problems that arise from what I believe is an epistemological problem. The exploration of the underlying epistemological problem leads to a suggestion to reject projection *per se*, not just a suggestion to reject its misuses.

Misuses of projection

1. I offer a thought experiment: Try to remember the last few times you thought that a patient was projecting. I will make a guess that such a thought occurred to you when your patient made an attribution about the

reality of a situation that was disturbingly at variance with your own sense of reality.

This use of the idea of projection establishes a hierarchy of truth. The implication is that the patient's assessment of reality is distorted by some disturbance of contact function and awareness, whereas the therapist's own assessment is not (for if the therapist is projecting, then he or she cannot "know" that the patient is projecting). Hence, there is an implicit establishment of a power imbalance, in which the therapist is claiming to have a more "accurate" view of reality.

Already the epistemological problems are manifold. What ground do you stand on when you decide that the patient is distorting and you are not? Surely this cannot be the ground of gestalt therapy's field theory with its emphasis on the idea of multiply valid realities, or the horizontalism of phenomenology, nor the dialogical maxim that requires that we meet patients with an effort to understand them from within their perspective, without the assumption that our own perspective is more "objective" than theirs. I will elaborate on the incompatibility of this use of projection later in the chapter.

2. I often overhear gestalt therapists say, "Perhaps I am only projecting here, but . . ." I cringe when I hear that entry phrase. The speakers are simultaneously saying that they need not be taken seriously, and the "but" asks to be taken seriously despite the fact that they are "*only* projecting." At times one can decipher, in this phrase, the invalidating power of this common usage of the term, "projection." If the speakers are "only" projecting, then their reality can be dismissed as a distortion. Why does the speaker not say, instead, "I have an *idea*"? Sometimes speakers say they are projecting when they are concerned that their opinions may create disharmony in their conversational group. Saying they are "only" projecting can perhaps soften possible conflicts. On the other hand, they immediately disempower themselves, and the "but" seems to reflect some discomfort with their self-negation.

These two examples speak to my ethical concerns about our use of "projection" without giving much thought to the implications of its use (such as the creation of unearned imbalances of power). In fact, I began to develop my critique because of my discomfort with the frequency with which we therapists seemed to use (or mis-use?) the concept of projection in a way that pathologized the patients' experiential truths. I see it as a dangerous use of the concept, one that compromises our commitment to phenomenological dialogue. In fact, I think the concepts of projection and projective identification are often used, in gestalt therapy and elsewhere, as a support for therapists' defensiveness in the face of threats to our emotional equilibrium.

This ethical danger has also propelled me to develop an epistemological critique; I assert that projection is a decidedly Cartesian concept, to a post-

Cartesian worldview. If we can rid our theory of a concept that is so easily used in the service of our defensiveness, we might develop other ideas to replace the concept of projection, ideas that will be more consistent with our post-Cartesian direction, and that will provide us with stronger conceptual supports for remaining in a dialogical/phenomenological exploration even when we were engaged in conversations that challenge our emotional equilibrium by challenging our view of reality.

While the examples above can be said to represent misuses of the concept of projection, are there not circumstances in which projection might be used in the service of dialogue? My colleague Frank M.-Staemmler offers just such a possible example:

> After a difficult conversation with a colleague last week, I entered my therapy room to see one of my clients again for the first time this year. My immediate impression was that he looked troubled, which I said to him. He responded with surprise: "Not at all, I am really fine. How do you come to think I was troubled?" I thought about it for a minute and said: "When I came into the room, you seemed to frown." – "Oh, yes," he said, "the sun was blinding me." And with an expression of mischievousness he added: "Maybe you are projecting?" I felt both caught and seen, so I admitted: "You are right, I am having some trouble."
>
> Obviously, my mood (one part of my phenomenal field) had colored my spontaneous perception/interpretation of his facial expression (another part of my phenomenal field). One might as well say that I had "projected" this "color" onto that latter aspect of my experiential world. Through the dialogue with my client I became aware of this process. His question had helped us to establish a joint attribution of meaning with respect to both his facial expression and my experience of it. In my view, this was a nice little piece of dialogue, because his question, friendly and funny as he had put it, had helped me and us to make sense of our actual situation. As a result of this dialogue we agreed that I had been projecting, and this agreement formed the shared basis for our subsequent conversation.
>
> (Staemmler, personal communication)

Theoretical problems

Correspondence vs. coherence as truth statements

This example gives rise to the epistemological problem, which I shall now address. First, let me be clear what I am *not* saying. I am *not* trying to argue against the idea that our moods, our history, our needs of the moment do not color, or shape, or play a large part in the gestalt of our first impressions (as well as our next impressions, and so on). I am *not* saying that ultimately those first impressions will prove to be more adequate for addressing the current situation than the impressions that develop over time, and that include greater complexity born of flexible reflexivity and openness to dialogue.[2]

In a dialogue we take our first impression *only as a starting place* for exploring our shared situation, not a final statement. And then, as the conversation continues, some of the factors that predominated in our initial impression move to the background as other factors – such as the patient's differing self-report – come to predominate in shaping our next gestalt. There is a continual process of shifting from an initial gestalt that is shaped more by the immediacy of one's own state of mind, toward *gestalten* that are continually more complex, and shaped additionally by experiences in conversation, by self-reflection, by broadened access to one's awareness and one's reflective awareness. These continually emergent *gestalten* become increasingly adequate to address the shared situation, as both partners in the dialogue contribute to the shaping and re-shaping of each other's experience.

In the re-shaping, we ordinarily assume that an initial projection has been corrected. Here the reader can see how easily the concept of projection is linked with distortion or inaccuracy. However, accuracy is a concept embedded in the correspondence theory of truth (a Cartesian theory of truth). Instead, I am arguing here that although Staemmler's first impression was amended in the ensuing dialogue, we cannot actually make a correspondence truth claim about his first statement (that it was either "objectively" true or not true), since although the patient's awareness did not include distress, one can never know what one does *not* know about one's situation. What can be said is that Frank's openness to the patient's different experience, and the patient's willingness to share it, were supports for a "joint attribution of meaning" that seemed to both of them to be adequate for continuing a dialogue. They needed no further exploration of the difference in their experiences once a satisfying explanation had been achieved. The most we can say about the truth-value is that it has an experiential resonance, a felt rightness that rendered their differences coherent to them. This is a coherence theory of truth, a post-Cartesian, dialogical theory of truth.

The contradiction in our founding text

In *Gestalt Therapy* (PHG 1951), there are two quotes relevant to our discussion of projection:

> A projection is a trait, attitude, feeling, or bit of behavior which actually belongs to your own personality but is not experienced as such; instead, it is attributed to objects or persons in the environment ... The

projector, unaware, for instance, that he is rejecting others, believes that they are rejecting him; or, unaware of his tendencies to approach others sexually, feels that they make sexual approaches to him.

(p. 211)

Projection: something of the organism in the environment.

(p. 462)

These definitions of projection exhibit three aspects of the Cartesian worldview:

1   dualistic categorizing, making a sharp distinction, organism and environment
2   viewing mind as a bounded container with a sharp distinction between inside and outside (something of the organism in the environment)
3   hewing to the correspondence theory of truth that holds that what is real depends on building "internal" representations "in" our minds of the "external" world.

PHG fall prey to this particular Cartesian fallacy when they assert that a particular phenomenon, "*actually belongs to your own personality.*" They claim a knowledge of "what and where" that matches Cartesian objectivism, but is incompatible with gestalt field theory.

The contradiction is that PHG critiqued these very dualisms in much of their writing in *Gestalt Therapy*. They argued that experience emerges at the boundary of contact, and that boundary is not the "bounded" mind as container, but is rather a *moment* in time in which a differentiation of self/other emerges phenomenally, and the boundary has the quality of "reversibility" (Merleau-Ponty 1964), belonging neither wholly to the subject nor wholly to the other. In much of *Gestalt Therapy*, their ideas break out of dualistic and objectivist thinking, but in the two quotes cited above, the dualism and objectivism that are two foundations of Cartesian thought stand out strongly, and have, in my opinion, misled many a gestalt therapist.

The quotes above pose at least a few theoretical problems for the post-Cartesian thrust of gestalt therapy:

1   Reality, especially interhuman experience, is inherently ambiguous and cannot ever be fully known. Thus, when patients and therapists have discrepant views on their shared situation, or on each other's personal processes, the most patient and therapist can do together is have a conversation about how each experiences their being-together, and their various interpretations about the "who/how" each of them is. But whatever they might say remains provisional (and hopefully continually evolving) at best. In fact, neither the therapist nor the patient can ever "know" reality, although, as in the Staemmler example above, they can

certainly arrive at satisfying and useable shared descriptions of their actuality (their senses of their shared situation).
2   The gestalt therapy theory of phenomenology horizontalizes – at least as a starting point – statements of experience (McConville 2001; Spinelli 2005). Whereas deciding that a patient is projecting treats one kind of experience (non-projected) as more valid than another kind of experience (projected) and thus violates this basic phenomenological rule.
3   The field theory and phenomenological theory used in gestalt therapy eschew the rigid demarcation between self and environment, or between "inner" and "outer." The boundary between self and other is always a momentary, ever-shifting, highly fluid, emergent moment-in-time, and a clear demarcation is impossible to find. Thus it is impossible to say with any certainty that something is experienced as in the environment when it actually belongs to the organism. Such a statement is too sharp of a demarcation between person and their experiential world, and also means that the therapist's description is being privileged over the patient's perspective.

Theoretical solution

I believe there are much more experience-near ways to understand phenomena in which the patient's perspective is discrepant from the therapist's. I offer one example below, drawing on the perspectivalism of phenomenological field theory.

The patient says to the therapist, "you are angry with me again." Let us assume that the therapist has no sense of him or herself as angry. And let us also assume this particular therapist has never encountered the notion of projection, but finds the idea of an inherently ambiguous, fluid and only partially knowable reality to be congenial (this therapist would be embraced by our pragmatist forbearers!). The therapist's and patient's realities are understood to be perspectives, potentially expandable through dialogue.

This therapist might wonder, "In what experiential world is this a true statement?" (Orange 2008: 189). The therapist will undertake the task, along with the patient, of making sense of the comment and its implications. We might wonder what sedimented expectations might be at play, and how our participation has activated those expectations again.

Various approaches to the exploration are possible; I offer two examples. In one, the therapist may say, "I am not aware of such. But tell me, what are you noticing? And how is it for you to have that experience of me? And, how is it for you that I seem not to find what you speak of?" (Obviously, this is not all said at once, but is being used to point to an approach that simply attempts to understand and expand upon the immediate experience together.)

In another approach the therapist might respond with, "Oh, yes. I think I understand. This is familiar between us. When I say the word, 'you,' rather than speaking of 'we,' or 'us,' I have removed myself from the picture and I am blaming you, as if your feelings are bad and wrong and have nothing to do with my participation."

One understanding of patients' repetitive alertness to particular configurations such as, "you are often angry with me," is that their experiential horizons are quite narrowed and fixed (usually consequent to trauma), and they do not have the supports to recognize their experience as a perspective. They may assume that the part (their perspectives on the shared situation) can account for the whole of the situation. Openness to dialogue, and ability to contextualize one's first impressions by reflecting on one's own awareness process, is relatively common in ordinary situations, but becomes increasingly difficult as situations are more emotionally charged, and are all but impossible when one has been triggered into a traumatized state of mind.

Patients who have gone without the necessary supports – such as attuned responsiveness to their emotional states – for the development of emotional resiliency, must necessarily be alert for the emotional conditions that pose a threat to their experiential coherence. They must be careful about exposure to conditions that destabilize self-regulation. Thus, instead of "projecting" their own anger, for instance, they are simply following the adage, "safety first." They are sensitive to aspects of the situation that are potential threats. These threats to the patient's equilibrium may not be noticeable to the therapist. We know from gestalt studies of perception that danger is perceptually vivid and paramount. And the mere fact that therapists are free agents means they are capable of getting angry. That is dangerous. If one's self-cohesion is threatened by experiences of anger – anyone's anger – their own or others, then one must be alert for its presence everywhere.

Only after some degree of emotional resilience has developed might one have the supports to look beyond sources of potential danger to sources of potential nourishment and enrichment as well. Only then might one be able to risk recognizing that "you are often angry with me" is a part of a larger whole that also includes the therapist's compassion, wit, intention to help, clumsiness, stupidity, brightness, etc. It takes its place amidst a variety of capacities and inclinations that we all have.

Clinical problem

In my opinion, the greatest clinical problem of the concept of projection is that it often stops dialogue. An exploration may continue, but it cannot be a dialogue once one person's experience has been treated as having less truth-value than another's. Patients cannot use their experiences to offer corrections to therapists' ideas if their experiences do not stand on an equal footing with the therapists' experiences. Dialogues are mutual.

I seek to develop the most radically dialogical stance possible, one in which the mutuality and reciprocity of emotional influence is taken for granted, one in which it is understood that both parties in the therapeutic process are embedded in their shared situation, which includes the experiential history of them both, and in which it is understood that any experience that either person has is a co-emergent phenomenon of the shared situation. Neither has a "God's eye view" (Nagel 1974) of the contacting process in which they are both engaged.

When one assumes that projection is occurring, one has stopped trying to understand the patient's experience from the patient's perspective. One can no longer learn from, be changed by, the patient. One has already decided the nature of the experience. What hermeneutic philosopher Georg Gadamer referred to as "undergoing the situation" has ended (Gadamer 1975/1991).[3] An analysis has begun. Gadamer (1975/1991) also averred, about conversation, that we fall into conversation, or become involved in it, and that true conversation is unpredictable. "Projection" ends a dialogue *with* the other, and becomes instead a conversation *about* the other.

A danger of the emphasis on projection is it presumes there is an experience the patient is supposed to be having, a more appropriate one than the one the patient professes (a decidedly anti-phenomenological stance for a gestalt therapist to take!). The therapist's ideas about what a patient ought or ought not be experiencing carry more weight than the patient's actual experiences. Obviously, a simple safeguard against the "ought" is to engage in a dialogue about our different experiences, especially if we can engage with an intention to learn something new, even if it challenges us.

I am reminded of a patient about whom I wrote, during an earlier stage of our work together (Jacobs 2004: 51). Her negative and mistrustful attitude towards others was quite disconcerting to me. I found many ways to decide that her perspective was just simply wrong, motivated by various defenses, and I tried to keep my distance from the horrors of her world-view. Only when I rededicated myself to appreciating the perspectival truth of her world-view was I able to ask myself what was interfering with my ability to undergo our situation together. I learned how much my own emotional well-being was predicated on a more "innocent" view of people and their intentions, and I wanted her world-view to be false so as not to have to broaden my own world-view to encompass the evil to which her world-view pointed. We began to learn more readily from each other at that point, as I spoke of my personal dread of her perspective, and she of her longing for and dread of my perspective. Both of our world-views have become more richly textured through our work together.

Suggested solutions

Perhaps my suggestion for a way forward without projection has become obvious by now. I will elaborate using a paragraph drawn from earlier writing (Jacobs 2005: 44).

Perls et al. (1951) write that neurotic process includes that "attention is heightened to meet the danger, even when there is no danger" (p. 264). This interests me because they also make the case that "There is no indifferent, neutral reality" (p. 233). In that case, how does the therapist decide that there is no danger to the patient? One can only say that for the therapist there is no sign of danger. But that reality is not the patient's reality. In fact, later Perls et al. walk us through some imaginary therapeutic work with a patient who they apprise as being in a "non-existent" chronic low-grade emergency (p. 65). Even though they say that the emergency is non-existent, they point out that, for the patient, only later was the situation "felt as safe because the patient is at a stage adequate to invent the required adjustment" (p. 65). In contrast to the assertion by Perls et al. – of a "non-existent" danger – it seems to me that if a patient does not yet have the access or the adequacy to draw on self and environmental supports for a creative adjustment, then for that patient the danger is real!

Frank-M. Staemmler (2007) has written about the value of engaging in hermeneutic dialogue informed by Gadamer's thoughts on undergoing the situation together toward a fusion of horizons of experience. Hycner and I (1995), drawing on Buber, emphasize that this includes surrender to a dialogue in which the interaffective influence expands the experiential horizons of both participants. In this way of thinking, the gestalt therapy focus on awareness might be the attention to the perspectival constraints on the expansion of our experience. All experience has limiting horizons, and as Gadamer pointed out, becoming aware of a horizon simultaneously transcends it (Gadamer 1976: xxi).

Our pragmatist roots also provide guidance – the insights and attitudes about "knowledge" and "truth" that emanated from James, Dewey, and Pierce (Menand 1997, 2001) and that Goodman put to good use in developing gestalt therapy theory. If we start with the perspectival truths that Gadamer and Buber and the pragmatists emphasize, we structure the therapeutic conversation as a dialogue along the lines that Buber and Gadamer draw out, we only need add here that the pragmatists remind us that the initial face validity of each statement undergoes revision in the course of conversation (for instance, James 1903/1997: 95). So an initial statement, "you are often angry," might evolve into a statement, "I am frightened when I think you are angry with me," and later, "I used to flinch when I saw you get angry. Now, either you don't get angry as often, or I am not concerned enough to notice it!"

The dialogue through which such an expansion occurs depends on the supports for emotional skill acquisition that come through attuned responsiveness in dialogue. The skills are hard won skills, and often require of therapists that they suffer alongside patients rather than try to change patients' perspectives. The changes come from being well met and understood as a fellow traveler rather than from having the adequacy of the contacting process evaluated from a supposedly neutral perspective. So if our patients find themselves in a low-grade emergency situation, as per the example above, our task is to find out together just how this situation is for them an emergency, rather than to challenge them to see that no emergency exists, that they are projecting their anger onto us. By entering into the ways we constitute an emergency situation the patients may feel supported enough, not to "invent" a more useable adjustment, but to allow the emergence together of a creative adjustment.

Notes

1 I am grateful to Dan Bloom for useful comments on an earlier draft of this chapter. And I am especially grateful to Frank M.-Staemmler who was generous in helping me organize and clarify my thoughts. I do not wish to speak for them, so I remind the reader that their help to me does not imply agreement with my opinions.
2 See Fairfield (2010) for a good description of the process of, and supports for, staying in contact under difficult conditions.
3 See especially Staemmler (2009) for an introduction to Gadamer's perspective on understanding and dialogue.

References

Fairfield, M. (2010) Dialogue in complex systems: the hermeneutical attitude. In L. Jacobs and R. Hycner (eds) *Relational Approaches in Gestalt Therapy*. Cleveland, OH: Gestalt Press.
Gadamer, H. (1975/1991) *Truth and Method*. New York: Crossroads.
—— (1976) *Philosophical Hermeneutics* (D. Linge trans. and ed.). Los Angeles: University of California Press.
Hycner, R. and Jacobs, L. (eds) (1995) *The Healing Relationship in Gestalt Therapy: A Dialogic/Self Psychology Approach*. Highland, NY: Gestalt Journal Press.
Jacobs, L. (2004) Ethics of context and field: the practices of care, inclusion and openness to dialogue. In R. G. Lee (ed.) *The Values of Connection: A Relational Approach to Ethics* (pp. 35–56). Cambridge, MA: Gestalt Press/Analytic Press.
—— (2005) The inevitable intersubjectivity of selfhood. *International Gestalt Journal*, 28, 1: 43–70.
James, W. (1903/1997) What pragmatism means. In L. Menand (1997) *Pragmatism*. New York: Vintage.
McConville, M. (2001) Husserl's phenomenology in context. *Gestalt Review*, 5, 3: 195–204.
Menand, L. (ed.) (1997) *Pragmatism: A Reader*. New York: Vintage.
—— (2001) *The Metaphysical Club: A Story of Ideas in America*. New York: Farrar, Straus and Giroux.
Merleau-Ponty, M. (1964) *Sense and Non-sense*. Evanston, IL: Northwestern University Press.
Nagel, T. (1974) What is it like to be a bat? *Philosophical Review*, 83: 435–450.

Orange, D. (2008) Recognition as: intersubjective vulnerability in the psychoanalytic dialogue. *International Journal of Psychoanalytic Self Psychology*, 3, 2: 178–194.

Perls, F. S., Hefferline, R. F. and Goodman, P. (1951) *Gestalt Therapy: Excitement and Growth in the Human Personality*. New York: The Julian Press.

Sapriel, L. (1998) Can gestalt therapy, self-psychology and intersubjectivity theory be integrated? *British Gestalt Journal*, 7, 1: 33–44.

Smith, E. (2006) Projection in depth. *International Gestalt Journal*, 29, 1: 101–128.

Spinelli, E. (2005) *The Interpreted World: An Introduction to Phenomenological Psychology*. London: Sage.

Staemmler, F.-M. (2007) On Macaque monkeys, players, and clairvoyants: some new ideas for a gestalt therapeutic concept of empathy. *Studies in Gestalt Therapy: Dialogical Bridges*, 1, 2: 43–63.

—— (2009) *Aggression, Time, and Understanding: Contributions to the Evolution of Gestalt Therapy*. Cleveland, OH: Gestalt Press.

Stolorow, R. D., Atwood, G. E. et al. (1987) *Psychoanalytic Treatment: An Intersubjective Approach*. Hillsdale, NJ: The Analytic Press.

Chapter 7

Sensing animals/knowing persons: a challenge to some basic ideas in gestalt therapy

Dan Bloom

Gestalt therapy is the psychotherapy of awareness[1] (see, for example, Yontef 1993). From the simplest activity of the cellular membrane to the complex achievements of a human being, awareness is the thread that knits the sequence of contacting[2] into a whole experience, culminating in an actual moment of integration – itself also called awareness. We are human animal organisms (Isadore From, personal communication, 1985) – biological creatures with awareness. This description expresses our need for a theory of holism. It may even be gestalt therapy's unique identifier in the world of psychotherapy. It might be folly for me to ask us to reconsider this.

Awareness served gestalt therapy well. I will argue here that as it has been used, it limits gestalt therapy's ability most fully to address human experience. Consciousness is being studied in many different disciplines. "Consciousness [is] just about the last surviving mystery" (Dennett 1991: 21) and it is one of the central concerns of contemporary psychology, cognitive neuroscience, and philosophy. Sometimes in the literature consciousness is called conscious awareness. Sometimes awareness is not even mentioned at all. And sometimes no distinction is even made between the two. But according to gestalt therapy, consciousness is *only* a functional hesitation within human experiencing. Awareness is *the* transformative process of experience. Since gestalt therapy gives its own meanings to Awareness and consciousness, contemporary discussions of consciousness in psychology and philosophy are not readily understandable within gestalt therapy's terms – and vice versa. So long as we gestalt therapists speak our own language, we speak only to ourselves. Unnecessarily private terms ought to be redefined to enable a broader conversation between gestalt therapy and other approaches. When redefined, Awareness and consciousness more effectively can be used experientially and be more valuable phenomenological tools in our psychotherapy practice than they are now.

Even more problematic for us as clinicians than our relationship to the larger world is that we reach the limit of the usefulness of Awareness when we try to address relationship and dialogue, or consider existential questions of meaning, freedom, and responsibility *within* gestalt therapy itself. Of course we are animals biologically coupled to our environment in our embodied functioning. Yet, using Aristotle's classic phrase, human beings are *zoon logon politikon echon* – reasoning, speaking, social animals. Of course, self emerges at the contact-boundary of the organism/environment field. Yet human *beings* – as *existential-phenomenal* beings – are persons in a social world of values and meaning who know the finitude of their own lives. Humans are socially related persons with bonds of trust and love, not only instinctually driven organisms. Awareness and the "organism/environment field" are insufficient concepts to address these further dimensions.

In this chapter, then, I challenge the primacy of Awareness in gestalt therapy. I question the sufficiency of Awareness to account for our *human animal's* fullest nature and offer alternatives. I ask that Awareness share its central position with consciousness so that the "awareness continuum" (L. Perls 1992: 13) may become the "awareness-consciousness continuum" of experience. Further, I propose that the organism/environment field be *supplemented* with another field, the self/world field, which I will describe below, so that the fullest measures may be taken of the human *knowing* animal organism.

An historical expedition

But where did gestalt therapy's "awareness alone" model originate? This is easy to answer: Gestalt therapy's founding text, *Gestalt Therapy: Excitement and Growth in the Human Personality* (Perls et al. 1951), which remains the most influential presentation of gestalt therapy's metatheory to this day. It establishes the centrality of awareness. In the following section, I will critically examine Perls et al.'s treatment of consciousness and awareness. Perls et al. unnecessarily exaggerated the split between awareness and consciousness, leaving us with a theory that insufficiently accounts for such significant matters such as intersubjectivity, relationship, responsibility, dialogue, and the fullness of being human – of being a person.

Gestalt therapy begins

In developing their own modality, the founders of gestalt therapy were understandably eager to establish their alternative to psychoanalysis. They had a specific dragon to slay, which was the central place of *the* conscious and *the* unconscious mind in psychoanalysis. Consciousness denoted the "conscious mind." They had to find a more distinctive concept than "consciousness." They needed a concept to announce gestalt therapy as different – without the seemingly cerebral and abstract connotations of the psychoanalytic model. That concept was "awareness." Perhaps they thought Awareness fitted perfectly within the biological holism of Gestalt theory or of Kurt Goldstein's theory of the organism – although Goldstein himself apparently did not use that term. Or perhaps Awareness "consciousness" appealed to Paul Goodman's Aristotelian holism, in which the soul and body constitute a single substance. (Crocker 1983/2008; Kitzler 2007).

Whatever the reason, they chose "awareness." Perls et al. describe it expansively: "[A]wareness is characterized by *contact*, by *sensing*, by *excitement*, by *Gestalt* formation" (Perls et al. 1951: x). "It is orientation, appreciation and approaching, choosing a technique; and it is everywhere" (Perls et al. 1951: 385), and "every contacting act is a whole of awareness, motor response, and feeling" (p. 258). Continuing to build their concept, they write, "[T]he contact-boundary is the specific organ of awareness" (p. 259), and "Aware response in the field . . . is a creative integration of the problem" (pp. 230, 232) – not a thought about it.

Consciousness? It is a functional delay in the sequence of contact to solve a problem of adjustment (Perls et al. 1951: 259). Or, when referring to the "conscious mind" in psychoanalysis, it is a *passive* associator, rationalizer, or talker (Perls et al. 1951: 239). Was Perls et al.'s unique distinction between awareness and consciousness well founded?

At the time that *Gestalt Therapy* was written, the study of introspection was supplanted by the dominance of behaviorism (Güzeldere 1999). Yet in continental Europe, the study of consciousness and subjectivity continued to flourish (Spiegelberg 1972). Except for references to Gestalt psychology and psychoanalysis, Perls et al. ignore these developments since, I argue, this served their goal of founding their own method. Despite some brief references to the Harry Stack Sullivan's Washington School, it was as if psychoanalysis was the only game in town.

The authors claim that from the beginning psychoanalysis was hampered because it neglected Gestalt psychology's "adequate" theory of awareness (Perls et al. 1951: 239). Gestalt psychology for its part failed to make a "rapprochement" with psychoanalysis. "The lack of daring to do it must be attributed to the Gestaltists, for the psychoanalysts have not lacked daring" (Perls et al. 1951: 398). But gestalt therapy *will* have the courage to do what the gestalt psychologists lacked courage to do: to take an "adequate theory of awareness" from Gestalt psychology and integrate it into their new psychotherapy. Yet on what basis can the authors claim that Gestalt psychology concerned itself with Awareness at all?

The English translations of the Gestalt psychologists exclusively use the word "consciousness" – not awareness. German has different words for Awareness (*Bewusstheit*) and consciousness (*Bewusstsein*). Evidently Awareness was *not* of interest to Gestalt psychologists – consciousness was. On what basis can the founders rest their claim of psychology "having an adequate theory of awareness"? Looking at our founders' sources for another possible reference, Awareness does not appear anywhere in Jan Smuts' *Holism and Evolution* (1926) either, although here, too, there are discussions of *consciousness*.

Perls et al. then proposes a definition of consciousness:

> [C]onsciousness is the result of a delaying of the interaction at the boundary.... [C]onsciousness is functional.... [I]f the interaction at the contact-boundary is relatively simple, there is little awareness ...; but where it is difficult and complicated, there is heightened consciousness.
>
> (Perls et al. 1951: 259)

Consciousness *emerges from* awareness when functionally necessary. This seems to be a casual point to the authors; it is a significant point here since I propose that awareness and consciousness are *inseparable* within the sequence of contacting as the *awareness-consciousness continuum*. I go further: *contact, not awareness, is the creative integration of experience*. Contacting is the process that includes *both* awareness and consciousness as phenomenal elements of the emerging figure/ground within the flow of experience. Contact, not awareness alone, is the basis for gestalt therapy's theory of self. Contact is the heart of gestalt therapy. The awareness-consciousness continuum is the sequence of contacting. I will return to this shortly.

Consciousness is more than a delay, it is knowing

But if consciousness is *just* a practical delay, it has not much use in an uncomplicated world. Its function is to solve problems and in simple worlds there are simple problems. Small problems, little difficulties: minimal delays, barely any consciousness – but without much consciousness there is not much knowledge. Does gestalt therapy seriously propose a model of human functioning where knowledge would be superfluous? Or where knowledge is only "a delaying of interaction," rather than that which enables and enhances human interaction, or the basis for interest or curiosity? To be sure, "delay" has practical advantages. Matters come to our consciousness, we notice what we need, get it, and then go on our way.

Awareness, that which guides a plant to light, a bee to a flower, rules the biological domain. Yet this world for a biological organism is different from that for a human being. Consciousness as a functional delay must be from William James's (1983) *Principles of Psychology*. His insight was a watershed contribution to philosophy that reverberated through American pragmatism and Continental philosophy (Heidegger 1927/1962). Later, in "Does 'consciousness' exist?" James added some further considerations: "*[T]here is a function in experience which thoughts perform. That function is knowing.* 'Consciousness' is supposed necessary to explain the fact that things not only are, but ... are known" (James 1987: 1142, emphasis added).

Consciousness is a function and this function is *knowing*. Human beings thrive on knowing. Knowledge is our species' achievement. Consciousness is human knowing. Our sense of ourselves as persons in relationship to one another would be impossible without consciousness – as knowing. Our being in relation to one another is on the basis of our knowing one another – with hesitations and interruptions as well as grace and satisfactions. More radically, consciousness as knowing constitutes our being amidst one another since understanding – knowing, consciousness – is a function of our being-in-the-world (of others) (Heidegger 1927/1962). Understanding is an element to intersubjectivity (Orange 1995). It is a good deal more than delay. Yet, awareness has been the cornerstone of gestalt therapy from Perls et al. onward (Klepner 1995). The goal of gestalt therapy is the heightening of awareness (Yontef 1993), so that the sequence of contacting may proceed without unaware interruptions.

Reconfiguring awareness and consciousness

By the continuing use of Perls et al.'s definition of consciousness without critical examination, gestalt therapy is missing an opportunity to address more finely the nuances of lived experience. So long as awareness alone is the template for the gestalt therapy process, gestalt therapy is locked in the organism/environment field model, which implies *individual* animals driven to satisfy biological needs. Yet awareness and consciousness can be understood as different yet integral components of gestalt therapy – unified by the crucial concept of contact. By reconfiguring consciousness as a function of the human knower, gestalt therapy opens to wider notions of the person situated in a world of other persons. An *awareness-consciousness continuum* integrates awareness with consciousness within the sequence of contacting and self. Further, it has the advantage of opening the barriers of gestalt therapy's private language so that gestalt therapy might join other contemporary inquiries into consciousness, subjectivity, and intersubjectivity – in which gestalt therapy has a good deal to contribute.

To this end, I suggest the following reconfiguration of awareness and contact. Awareness is our sense of the situation. It is the sensible ground of our experience, the *incarnate* domain of self, or the "id of the situation" (Robine 2003), without which we would be disembodied specters. Awareness is our felt ground as our "sense" of the social field (Spagnuolo Lobb 2007). Awareness is our *sense of one another*, as the ground for whole "intersubjective" experience. Awareness can also be thought of as "embodypathy" (*Einleibung*) (Staemmler 2007: 53).

Awareness is our initial awakening to what is, from the first barely focused seeing of our waking eyes, to the background throb of a sore limb in our dim awareness, or the background as we attend to figural concerns of which we are conscious. It is the fringe around the focus of our consciousness. Awareness can shift in and out of consciousness with the direction and re-direction of our attention. Awareness "could be described as the fuzzy twin of attention. Awareness is more diffuse than attention – it implies a relaxed rather than a tense perception by the whole person" (Perls 1973: 10). Consciousness emerges from awareness within the sequence of contacting (Perls et al. 1951: 403). We act with conscious deliberateness. We draw on knowledge to guide us and to widen our perspective of the world. Without consciousness, awareness is empty sensation. Awareness and consciousness develop across the sequence as a continuum, remaining connected in the developing figure/ground process.

Often awareness functions without consciousness, as many of our activities do not need conscious attention. But awareness is the scaffold upon which consciousness rests. It is its ground, as in figure/ground. Consciousness cannot stand securely without this foundation. Awareness, to some degree, is always present. But if dim, a person would then be on insecure ground. Consequently, contacting might become more fixed than fluid; hollow abstractions of egotism might develop and these might increasingly become distant from lived experience. A person might become rigid, and stiffen as against the unaware ground. With diminished awareness, consciousness is short-sighted, lost in a dark world. This is one of different possibilities when consciousness is separated from awareness.

Consciousness with awareness is, of course, embodied consciousness – an experience of contact, which brings the fullness of human knowing and the possibilities of personhood and intimate relatedness. We approach one another with conscious knowledge gained from previous contact, not just with isolated aware sensation. We knowingly form relationships and forge bonds of community. The more seamlessly awareness and consciousness are connected, the more solidly – the more contactfully – these are built. Of course, we often approach one another with knowledge that limits the possibilities for creative new experience. Our experiences enrich our future powers of contacting as well inhibit us from necessary risk taking. The figure of contact is at its brightest to the extent it is unfettered by unnecessarily restricting prior "knowledge." Of course everything we do is not a result of conscious deliberation. We act skillfully in the world with a familiarity most often transparent to us. We know how to do things without being conscious or aware of how we do them (Heidegger 1927/1962). This "understanding" is neither phenomenally aware nor conscious, but available to either in the sequence of contacting.

Familiar concepts "re-tooled"

Consciousness

I now offer a brief review and modification of gestalt therapy's core theory that, I suggest, enables it to more suitably address the fullness of human experience.

"Experience is ultimately contact," and "self . . . [is] the function of contacting the actual transient situation" (Perls et al. 1951: 229), and or as formulated more recently, contacting the other (Philippson 2001: 20), "Self[3] . . . is aware and orients, aggresses and manipulates, and feels emotionally the appropriateness of environment and organism" (Perls et al. 1951: 373). It is both aware and conscious. Self emerges as the awareness-consciousness continuum from aware sensed id functioning through conscious deliberate, knowing ego and personality functionings. Self is contact in its immediacy and contacting in its entire process.

As a process, self develops within the temporal sequence of contacting as three partial elements functions: id functioning, ego functioning, and personality functioning. This is significant since awareness and consciousness are aspects of these functions. Id functioning is the sentiency of the situation – sensations, urges, and tensions. This is awareness par excellence. Ego functioning is the process of self exercising conscious choice, agency, taking meaningful actions – with consciousness, par excellence. For ego functioning to function, so to speak, the "I" must know what to choose, how to orient, with what to identify. Awareness and consciousness go hand in hand as qualities of self functioning – the awareness-consciousness continuum.

Personality functioning is the consequence of previous contacting. It is the self function for what we have learned from prior contacts and now know, including – and importantly – what we have learned from social contacting. Through continuing social contacting, interpersonal knowledge increases. We acquire personal and shared history, values, culture, and so on. Personality functioning is the responsible structure of self. Personality functioning allows for personal continuity. It is the basis upon which further contact intelligently can be made. Were it not for our having an identity, remembering our likes and dislikes, how could we make choices? At the risk of invoking homunculi, how could ego functioning function without being able to "consult" the results of previous contacts while also trusting the felt senses of id functioning? *Self functions are inseparable.* Contacting, then, is of the actual indivisible situation (Bowman, this volume).

Organism/environment field and self/world field

Gestalt therapy originally proposed that all experience is a function of the organism/environment field. This remains the bedrock of gestalt therapy – and it should remain so. But it is an incomplete foundation. Human beings are animals; we are also persons. The organism/environment field fully accounts for our *biological* nature as the necessary fundament of life. The organism/environment field is not the phenomenal field; it is not the psychological field (Staemmler 2007). The organism/environment does not – and cannot – fully account specifically for us as persons. The meeting of an organism with its environment is a biological interaction, and although it is absolutely necessary for experience, it itself is not an *experiential* event. To the extent that gestalt therapy is a psychotherapy that focuses on human *experience*, it ought to address the phenomenal field – which is not the organism/environment field, though inextricably coupled to it. The exclusive use of the organism/environment field in gestalt therapy is biological reductionism (Staemmler 2007). It is time to consider a supplemental "field."

Criticism of the organism/environment model's sufficiency is not new. For example, in 1928, the Hamburg professor William Stern proposed specifically that the gestalt theorists' emphasis on the interaction of the organism and the environment was insufficient to account for human experience, including meaning-making and personality. Stern proposed the "person" as a solution (Ash 1998).

We ask, "Who are you?" A person answers

"Person" bears self's temporal continuity, carries knowledge and memory, and enables personal responsibility. Without personhood, we would be unable to enter into relationships. "In the conscious living of human beings," writes gestalt therapist Sylvia Fleming Crocker, an advocate of organismic holism, "one of the major ways in which affectivity shows itself is in the personhood of the person, since persons both originate and bestow value upon certain things and events and strive to realize their desire for them" (Crocker 1983/2008: 131). Gestalt therapy's self is emergent of the organism/environment field; and as a structure and function within the stream of experience, self is of the phenomenal field as well. The person/world might be this phenomenal field. Person usefully may be understood as the human being as rational, knowing agent (Sokolowski 2008). And "world" may be understood as the phenomenal world of which the person is a part: *lifeworld* (Gallagher and Zahavi 2008), *Umwelt* (May, Angel, and Ellenberger 1958: 54), *lifespace* (Lewin 1951: 43 ff.) or World (Heidegger 1927/1962; Buber, Rosenzweig in Friedman 1955), each of which is different yet sufficiently similar not to require further discussion here. Each describes a world constituted by and constituting the human being. The word "person" carries the further weight of no less of authorities than Martin Buber, Kurt Goldstein, and Kurt Lewin. Person/world field, then, is a candidate for the phenomenal field emergent of the organism/environment field.

Yet there is a better gestalt therapy alternative. Since self, not person, is the *immediately* emergent phenomenal structure of the organism/environment field, *self/world field* is a better name for the human being's phenomenal field. Self as a phenomenal structure is always in-the-world since, in gestalt therapy terms, self is constituted by contact. "World" is that "other" whose meeting at the boundary is the phenomenal contact-boundary of self emergence: Philippson's (2001, 2009) self/other. "World" is simultaneously constituted by self as its world of experience and constitutes self as contract. Self is in-the-world and this is the self/world field.

"Person" then emerges of the self/world field as a result of *social* contacting as self accumulates its own "personality" through experiencing its relational history. This is the personality functioning, functioning. Self emerges. Person develops. "Person" is not a split-off "entity," but remains integral to the self/world field. "Person" is not gestalt therapy's version of "the subject" in a subject-object social field.

Awareness in the biological and phenomenal fields

Every living cell adjusts to its environment with *biological* awareness. But do humans directly experience cellular activity? For the most part biological awareness is beyond our possible experience. The human being as *sensing* organism perceives and adjusts to its environment in *phenomenal* awareness. The human being as *knowing* person also adjusts to the world with consciousness. However, biological awareness and phenomenal awareness are different yet inextricable. Phenomenal awareness is a function of the *lived body* (*Leib*) (Welton 1999); biological awareness is a function of the physical body (*Körper*). Awareness, then, is actually a concept that can cross domains. It is a quality of the biological and phenomenal fields. That is, *in contact* the environment of the organism/environment field also becomes the phenomenal world of the self/world field. Said differently, the experiential world that gives "breath" to the person emerges from the natural environment that provides oxygen to the cells of the organism. The natural body of homo sapiens becomes the phenomenal lived body of the human person. These are coupled by awareness and contact.

Contact, with its consummation through the sequence of contacting, is the transformative experience central to gestalt therapy: the reconfiguring of new wholes of feeling, thought, and action. Contacting as a biological process and as a phenomenal event is of the *awareness-consciousness continuum* that crosses two domains of one whole human process (Kitzler 2007). It is inconceivable that contacting can proceed without the accumulation of knowledge. Contact is not merely awareness, but a whole experience integrating awareness with consciousness – and action. In contact, awareness as a biological process of the organism/environment field becomes a felt, *aware* sensation of phenomenal self/world field. *Contact is the hinge within gestalt therapy; contact enables awareness to cross the organism/environment to the self/world fields and thereby establish a unity of the human animal organism.* The person is emergent of this process and gives contacting its human face.

When gestalt therapy supplements the organism/environment field with the self/world field, awareness and consciousness may be re-defined to become more precise descriptors of experience. Awareness (first as biological responsiveness and then as sensing) and consciousness (now as embodied knowing) are experienced as the *awareness-consciousness continuum* in the developing sequence of contacting. These terms are more fitting a relational, dialogical, and field-emergent self perspective than awareness taken alone.

Let me take this further. Social contacting transforms the human animal's environment into the world of the person, the world of personal *experience*. This *"world is the structure of meaningful relationships in which a person exists and in the design of which he [/she] participates"* (May 1958: 59).

Self/world field and the organism/environment field, then, are aspects of one another, two sides of the same coin. Whatever occurs in one occurs in the other, yet they are *different*. Self/world field can neither separate from self nor can self, as contacting, separate from the organism/environment field. Self is always in-the-world and always a function of contacting – *a process of the organism/environment and self/world fields*. We human beings are biologically aware creatures and simultaneously phenomenally aware *and* conscious beings for whom own being is of concern to us (Heidegger 1927/1962). We are existential-phenomenal beings: persons.

> A person is not a substance or an entity that we perceive as a thing. A person is like an eddy in a stream, a vital locus of centering in the flow of all that enters a human's system: the physics and chemistry, the biology, the psychology, the culture that enters into each of us, and their relevant history as well.
>
> (Hefner 2000: 76)

Personhood crowns our humanness.

We are sensing/animals knowing/persons alive in the organism/environment *and* self/world fields: the indivisible world of the human being in which awareness (biological as well as phenomenal) and consciousness have central roles. The organism/environment field and the self/world field are unified by contact across the awareness-consciousness continuum.

Conclusion

Gestalt therapy has an important theory relevant to contemporary phenomenology and psychology that can contribute to in those fields. But so long as we unnecessarily use a private language with idiosyncratic definitions we discourage communication with those outside our "hideout." We keep our treasures hidden. I have attempted to show how the awareness-consciousness continuum and contacting are important phenomenological concepts. I hope they can be exported from gestalt therapy to the wider world. Our usage of awareness and consciousness, on the other hand, is idiosyncratic and serves to reinforce our isolation as a modality.

I have also proposed that the basic organism/environment field is insufficient to account for the wealth of human experiences. I have offered a supplemental field for consideration: the self/world field. This supplemental field brings to gestalt therapy more of the depth of phenomenology.

This cannon shot across the bough of mainstream gestalt therapy thinking will not likely have much effect. Even if my points are well founded and my argument strong, to budge the weight of tradition takes great effort. But if I've given some readers cause to pause or question, I will have succeeded sufficiently to have warranted this effort.

Notes

1 This chapter does not discuss consider "mindfulness" in gestalt therapy, which would be another matter altogether. Definitions of "mindfulness" vary and often use awareness, consciousness, conscious awareness, and attention in differing ways. See *Studies in Gestalt Therapy: Dialogical Bridges*, 3(2), specifically dedicated to "Attention, Mindfulness, and Awareness."
2 As used here, "contacting" refers to an entire process-sequence of contacting (Perls et al. 1951: 403), while "contact" refers to a moment in that sequence.
3 By no means do all gestalt therapists accept this theory of self. Lynne Jacobs, for example, is a major critic (Jacobs, personal communications, and in press).

References

Ash, M. G. (1998) *Gestalt Psychology in German Culture, 1890–1967*. Cambridge: Cambridge University Press.
Crocker, S. F. (1983/2008) A unified theory. In P. Brownell (ed.) *Handbook for Theory, Research, and Practice in Gestalt Therapy* (pp. 124–153). Newcastle, UK: Cambridge Scholars Publishing.
Dennett, D. (1991) *Consciousness Explained*. Boston, MA: Little, Brown, and Co.
Friedman, M. S. (1955) *Martin Buber – The Life of Dialogue*. Chicago: University of Chicago Press.
Gallagher, S. and Zahari, D. (2008) *The Phenomenological Mind: An Introduction to Philosophy of Mind and Cognitive Science*. London: Routledge.
Güzeldere, G. (1999) Approaching consciousness. In N. Block, O. Flanagan and G. Güzeldere (eds) *The Nature of Consciousness* (pp. 1–68). Cambridge, MA: MIT Press.
Hefner, P. (2000) Imago dei: the possibility and necessity of the human person. In N. H. Gregersen, W. B. Drees and U. Görman (eds) *The Human Person in Science and Theology* (pp. 73–94). Edinburgh: T & T Clark Ltd.
Heidegger, Martin (1927/1962) *Being and Time* (J. Macquarrie and E. Robinson, trans.). New York: HarperSanFrancisco.
James, W. (1983) *Principles of Psychology*. Cambridge, MA: Harvard University Press.

—— (1987) Does consciousness exist? In *William James Writings 1902–1910* (pp. 1141–1158). New York: Library Classics of the United States.

Kitzler, R. (2007) The ambiguities of origins: pragmatism, the University of Chicago, and Paul Goodman's self. *Studies in Gestalt Therapy: Dialogical Bridges*, 1, 1: 41–65.

Klepner, P. (1995) Awareness, consciousness, interpretation. Paper presented at the New York Institute for Gestalt Therapy, January 5.

Lewin, K. (1951) Defining the "Field at a Given Time." In K. Lewin and D. Cartwright (eds) *Field Theory in Social Science* (pp. 44–59). New York: Harper & Row.

May, R. (1958) Contributions of existential psychotherapy. In R. May (ed.) *Existence* (pp. 37–91). New York: Basic Books.

May, R., Angel, E. and Ellenberger, H. (1958) *Existence*. New York: Basic Books.

Orange, D. (1995) *Emotional Understanding*. New York: The Guilford Press.

Perls, F. (1973) *The Gestalt Approach & Eyewitness to Therapy*. Palo Alto, CA: Science & Behavior Books.

Perls, F. S., Hefferline, R. F. and Goodman, P. (1951) *Gestalt Therapy: Excitement and Growth in the Human Personality*. New York: The Julian Press.

Perls, L. (1992) *Living at the Boundary*. Highland, NY: Gestalt Journal.

Philippson, P. (2001) *Self in Relation*. Highland, NY: The Gestalt Journal Press.

—— (2009) *The Emergent Self*. London, UK: Karnac.

Robine, J.-M. (2003) Intentionality in flesh and blood. *International Gestalt Journal*, 26, 2: 85–110.

Smuts, J. (1926) *Holism and Evolution*. New York: Viking Press.

Sokolowski, R. (2008) *Phenomenology of the Human Person*. Cambridge: Cambridge University Press.

Spagnuolo Lobb, M. (2007) Being at the contact boundary with the other: the challenge of every couple. *British Gestalt Journal*, 16, 1: 44–52.

Spiegelberg, H. (1972) *Phenomenology in Psychology and Psychiatry, a Historical Introduction*. Evanston, IL: Northwestern University Press.

Staemmler, F.-M. (2007) On Macaque monkeys, players, and clairvoyants: some new ideas for a gestalt therapeutic concept of empathy. *Studies in Gestalt Therapy: Dialogical Bridges*, 1, 2: 43–64.

Welton, D. (1999) *The Essential Husserl*. Bloomington, IN: Indiana University Press.

Yontef, G. (1993) *Awareness, Dialogue, and Process*. Highland, NY: The Gestalt Journal Press.

Chapter 8

Mind and matter: the implications of neuroscience research for Gestalt psychotherapy

Peter Philippson

Introduction

Human psychological functioning can be described in two ways: through a theory of how the mind or consciousness works (including theories of human development), and through formal research into the functioning of the brain or the activities of young infants. We are currently in a period of major expansion of both of these areas of research, and my interest in this chapter is the assimilation of this new knowledge into Gestalt Therapy. I will argue that Gestalt Therapy has a very close fit with modern research in both these fields, while some aspects do need modification, in particular the paradoxical theory of change (Beisser 1970).

This also has implications for discussions about the research base for Gestalt Therapy. There are two kinds of research validation. One kind, outcome research, has not been engaged with sufficiently by Gestaltists, although that situation is changing now with the development of research projects and the publication of Gestalt-oriented books on research. The other kind is where more general research provides support for the theoretical or clinical assertions of a psychotherapy. This has been quite strongly the case for Gestalt Therapy.

Relational theory of self-in-contact

The central aspect of Gestalt theory that is supported by neurological and developmental research is the relational theory of self, well expressed by Fritz Perls in his 1957 Cooper Union lecture:

> Now the "self" cannot be understood other than through the field, just like day cannot be understood other than by contrast with night. If there were eternal day, eternal lightness, not only would you not have the concept of a "day", you would not even have the awareness of a "day" because there is nothing to be aware of, there is no differentiation. So, the "self" is to be found in the contrast with the otherness.

> There is a boundary between the self and the other, and this boundary is the essence of psychology.
>
> (Perls 1978: 55)

Or, as I put it in my own book:

> To put it simply, I experience myself as the one who sees the sunlight coming through the window, who loves my family, who types on the computer. My focus is on the window, the family, or the computer, not on the seeing, the loving, or my wanting to type. As I move from the computer to my son, my self-experience changes, as does his.
>
> When self is thought about in this way, its primary characteristics are fluidity and relationship. Whereas an "inner" self, characterised by stability and independence, raises questions of "How does self change?" and "How does self relate to the world?", relational self raises the question "How does self stabilise itself?"
>
> (Philippson 2001a: 1–2)

From this follows the whole edifice of classical Gestalt theory and practice, the idea that contacting *is* the process of self actualization, the co-formation of experiencing self and experienced other. The task of therapy is to explore the functioning of this process in the relationship of the therapy situation, rather than to work with the self of the client as an objective reality to be changed.

It is important to notice that Perls was coming to this from a research background, assisting the German psychologist and neurologist Kurt Goldstein (1878–1965) at his Institute for Brain-Damaged Soldiers in Berlin in the 1920s. Goldstein's findings while researching the impairments caused by various wartime brain injuries led him to his major work *The Organism* (Goldstein 1939), whose major assertions were 1) that the human organism functions as a whole, and impairment in one area of functioning affects many other areas, and conversely the brain can to some extent replace damaged brain areas with healthy areas reallocated to new functions; 2) that the organism "actualizes" in the world rather than merely responding to environmental stimuli. It is worth quoting this in full since it links to well to Gestalt theory and modern discussions of consciousness:

> The environment of an organism is by no means something definite and static, but is continuously forming commensurably with the development of the organism and its activity. One could say that the environment emerges from the world through the being or actualization of the organism. Stated in a less prejudiced manner, an organism can exist only if it succeeds in finding in the world an adequate environment

– in shaping an environment (for which, of course, the world must offer the opportunity).

(Goldstein 1939: 88)

Another researcher in the social sciences at that time, much influenced by Gestalt psychology, was Kurt Lewin. To quote from his writings at a similar time:

As far as the content is concerned, the transition from Aristotelian to Galilean concepts demands that we no longer seek the "cause" of events in the nature of a single isolated object, but in the relationship between an object and its surroundings.

(Lewin, Heider, and Heider 1936: 11)

Compare this with the much more recent writing by the child development researcher Daniel Stern, the researcher into infant development who has recently worked closely with Gestaltists.

It's very clear that human beings are constructed to read other people's minds . . . Our nervous system is constructed to do that . . . The conclusion . . . is that our minds are not so independent. Indeed, they are very interdependent. Our minds are not separate or isolated, and we are not the only owners of our own mind . . . Minds get created by virtue of being in constant interaction and dialogue with other minds, so that the whole idea of a "one person psychology" ought not to exist, or at least it must be incomplete.

(Stern 2004: 23)

As well as his own work with mothers and infants, Stern is bringing to this statement his knowledge of recent neurological researches into the *mirror neuron system* in primates including human beings (Rizzolatti and Craighero 2004):

When observers see a motor event that shares features with a similar motor event present in their motor repertoire, they are primed to repeat it. The greater the similarity between the observed event and the motor event, the stronger the priming is . . .

Mirror neurons represent the neural basis of a mechanism that creates a direct link between the sender of a message and its receiver. Thanks to this mechanism, actions done by other individuals become messages that are understood by an observer without any cognitive mediation.

(op. cit.: 180/183)

Thus we can see that there is a strong link between Gestalt psychotherapy and the cutting-edge neurological studies of the time of its initial development, and that the most central intuition of the therapy emerged directly from that research and has been even further supported by the most recent developments in the field. There is no contradiction between the neurology and the psychology, nor would we expect there to be in a therapy that always emphasized its holistic credentials: "Every contacting act is a whole of awareness, motor response, and feeling – a cooperation of the sensory, muscular, and vegetative systems – and contacting occurs at the surface-boundary in the field of the organism/environment" (Perls et al. 1994/1951: 34).

(We will look later at a missing aspect of this statement, about neurological structures.)

Healing splits in the personality

But Gestalt Therapy says something more: that we do not stay with our whole relational self-functioning. Rather, we polarize away from areas that cause us more anxiety than we can support. Fritz Perls spoke about "holes" in the personality, areas we do not identify with ourselves, but tend to project onto others (Perls 1992/1969: 56). He developed techniques such as two-chair dialogues to support the integration of the disowned aspects. What might be the neurological underpinning of this idea?

Part of the answer is in the understanding that memory and behavior are *state dependent*:

> Affect-state dependent recall refers to a tendency exhibited by subjects in either a positive or negative affective state to remember information that had been learned under the same affective state (congruent conditions) better than that learned under a different affective state (incongruent conditions).
>
> (Revelle and Loftus 1992: 138)

A materialistic but not reductionistic approach

There is still the question to be faced whether there is an incompatibility between the scientific sensibility represented by neurological research and the experience-near approach of Gestalt Therapy. This is the viewpoint taken by Kennedy (2008):

> The world of dialogic therapy is presently operating in a culture . . . where the amazing advances of neuroscience are in vogue amongst therapists. The scientific talk that people engage in, and of which

Ramachandran is an example, is forgetful of the fact that it is dependent for its meaning upon this original experience of the world . . . They become complicit with the tendency to medicalise psychotherapy.

(Kennedy 2008: 19)

My understanding is that this argument in itself limits experience. Our engagement with the world through brain scans and other methods can inform our experience of ourselves and our world in a way that is not inherently different from our experiencing with our unaided eyes. Who would say that the incriminating ash that Sherlock Holmes saw through his magnifying glass was less valid than his unmagnified view, or that someone with spectacles never has valid experience? But the real question is whether the neurological approach, as Kennedy suggests, reduces humanity to the actions of neurons.

Fortunately, due to comparatively recent understandings, we are in a good position to see that this need not be so. The work of Kauffman (1995), Prigogine and Stengers (1984) and others have shown the significance of emergent orders: more complex systems which emerge out of simpler systems under certain circumstances. These emergent orders obey the rules of the simpler order, but are not reducible to nor predictable from it. Nothing a car engine does, for example, is incompatible with the physics of its component parts, but the running of the engine has its own characteristics that cannot be derived from the characteristics of the parts. Indeed, the engine can support both an engine that is running and one that is not, in a way that I would say is similar to how a human body can support life and death.

The arrows only work one way: if a car has sufficiently faulty parts, it will not run. If a human body is sufficiently damaged, it will not live. If a human brain has certain kinds of damage, as Goldstein showed, consciousness will be limited in particular ways. But there is no necessary correlation between the functioning of a single aspect of a car, a body, or a brain and the functioning of the higher level. A thought is not the action of a single neuron, and the dynamics of thought are not reducible to the dynamics of neurons.

With this understanding, we can hold onto a unified understanding of mind and body, and at the same time not fall into a clockwork reductionism. The whole is truly not merely the sum of the parts (Smuts 1996/1926). We can be open to the effects of neurological impairment while emphatically not saying that all psychological problems are reducible to such impairment. And we can ask questions about the limitations of a non-medical approach in working effectively with specific neurological impairments without giving up our assertion that our approach can be extremely effective in other circumstances where a medical intervention would not, and that there are many situations where our work can support the development of new neurological structures which support growth towards psychological health. I will look at both aspects of this here.

Relational neurological development

There has been a great deal of research in recent years about the impact of the young infant's caring and parenting environment on his/her neurological development. The work of Allan Schore (1994) has been of particular importance:

> The child's first relationship, the one with the mother, acts as a template, as it permanently molds the individual's capacities to enter into all later emotional relationships. These early experiences shape the development of a unique personality, its adaptive capacities as well as its vulnerabilities to and resistances against particular forms of future pathologies.
>
> (Schore 1994: 3)

He notes that a human baby, uniquely among animals as far as we know, is born without its brain being anywhere near fully developed, most notably in terms of the higher organizing functions. The human brain continues to develop these functions up until the teenage years (which explains a lot!). But Schore's primary focus is the first eighteen months to two years of life, where something quite extraordinary happens. There is a vast overproduction of neural connections during those months, many more than the person can use. Then those connections which are not used disappear while those that are used remain. In this way, the infant's brain is sculpted into an image of its caring environment! That is, if the infant is surrounded by loving and playful touch, along with small amounts of inevitable frustration and pain, they will come through this period with rich neural connections to process pleasure and relatively sparse connections to process pain. They will be geared towards experiencing life in a positive way, not because of any act of figure/ground formation but because they are "wired" that way. Conversely, if they are brought up in those early years with a weight of pain or neglect and little bits of pleasure, they will bring to later life a neurological bias towards experiencing pain and frustration, and sparse capacity for experiencing pleasure. Once again, this is not a psychological orienting, but a result of neurological shaping in the earliest years. (I use the term "sculpting" to emphasize that the image is formed by taking away, like a sculptor carving stone, rather than by adding, as a painter adds paint to a canvas to make the image.)

After this earliest period, this process of overproduction and sculpting ends for ever. What replaces it is a slow ("painting") addition of new neural pathways in response to the changing environment. If the neglect or abuse and consequent impairment are too severe, as in the case, for example, of the babies abandoned in Romanian orphanages with minimal care, the impairment cannot be remedied in any meaningful way. In other less terrible circumstances, a relationship with someone who can supply the loving and caring the person was missing can allow for a reshaping of the person's neurological possibilities.

Implications for Gestalt psychotherapy

In many ways, this research is highly compatible with and extends the holistic and relational theory of Gestalt Therapy. Not only is the self relational psychologically, but its neurological development is also relational, and the deficits can be worked with in a relational therapy which leads to physical changes in the functioning of the client's brain.

The research raises questions about the simplistic concept of the therapist *attuning* to the client, as if the self of the client was some objective entity that could be attuned to. Even a baby and its mother both work to achieve an attunement, so that the baby the mother sees is the baby as it actualizes to her in the co-attunement, and vice versa. Rather, the mode of change is that both therapist and client attune as best they can to their here-and-now relating (hopefully the therapist bringing more flexibility and openness from his/her own training and therapy), avoiding the defensive fixed relational patterns that the client brings and finding new possibilities for being together. The experience of the therapist is a vital part of this, as the fixed patterns rely on others to pick up and take on their parts in the interactions. This capacity for direct engagement, and the disruption of "fixed gestalten" has always been central to Gestalt Therapy. However, although it is clear from our theory of relational self that the fixed patterns are relational, and the therapist is pulling both parties out of the pattern, it has generally been spoken about as if the fixed gestalt belongs only to the client, and "interrupting the interruptions" is something the therapist does *to* the client. This is one of the ways in which the new research provides a corrective to our cultural, rather than our theoretical, heritage.

The other significant learning which we need to assimilate relates to the "Paradoxical Theory of Change" (Beisser 1970). This states that "change occurs when one becomes what he is, not when he tries to become what he is not" (p. 103). While this is a beautiful summary of much of Gestalt theory, it is also a simplification of that theory. It relies on our capacity for *organismic self regulation* (Perls et al. 1994/1951: 137), and this in turn relies on our ability (even if we are not enacting that ability) to make flexible contact with the environment. There are several situations where this condition is not met (see Philippson 2005), but for the purpose of this chapter I will focus on the implications of Schore's work (op. cit.).

Put briefly, the paradoxical theory requires that the client has the neurological capacity to move flexibly into new perceptions and relations to the environment. However, Schore has shown that this is not true for those whose caring needs were not adequately met during the first vital two years of life. Rather, the emotional tone with which they experience their world will be skewed by what they can neurologically process. Their capacity for mutuality will be limited in a way that can only be remedied by slow accretion from a caring relationship, not by merely giving attention in a new way. The therapist needs to have that outcome in mind, while the client needs to engage with the therapist and others in a way that his/her whole neural functioning says is wrong and unnatural (and useless). It is only once the new functioning, allowing caring and being cared for, has "bedded in" neurologically that the paradoxical theory can function.

I do a lot of work with clients with a highly abusive or neglectful history. Knowing this information has helped me to help these clients in a much more focused way. In the past I have been guilty of trying to help create the conditions in the moment which would support growth, not knowing that the kind of relational growth I was trying to support was not possible for them at their present level of neurological development.

What can the therapist know about the client?

The other important corrective for Gestaltists from neurological research is the challenge to the statement "I cannot know anything about you: I can only guess and project. Only you can know about you." This statement, supporting Fritz Perls' prohibition on interpretation, was very prevalent in early Gestalt Therapy, and is still around today. It clearly never did fit well with the relational theory of self, and was a statement of the individualism that is being strongly challenged today (Wheeler 2000). I would say that the anti-individualism goes too far (Philippson 2001b: 120), and in fact goes further than the research supports to deny that an individual can actualize and make a difference to and in the world. Stern (2004: 82) writes about the "gating" mechanisms by which a person can distance the mirror responses and can come to his/her own position, and points out that there is even a condition of brain damage (echopraxis) where a person automatically mirrors the actions of others. The characteristics Stern points to for such gating – selective gating of attention, moving away from confluent imitation of action and inhibition of confluent emotional resonance – are all a very good fit with the Gestalt understanding of *awareness*.

What is inherent in Gestalt Therapy theory and also in the neurological research is that self and other are *so* emergent from the situation that the fact of a human being saying "I will do this, not that; I will believe this, not that" is a remarkable one. To the existentialist understanding, it is such moments that define the individual, rather than the individual defining the moments. From our current perspective, we can put it this way: the individual who makes these choices is not a fixed entity *in* a fixed environment, but a field-emergent individual making choices in a field-emergent environment. As Lewin says, "In answering this question it could be pointed out that the 'self' is experienced as a region within the whole field" (Lewin et al. 1936: 167).

However, the findings about mirror neurons show that we can often get a good "implicit" sense of the intentions of others. Of course we can get this wrong, misreading the situation, being blinded by our fixed assumptions, or being purposefully misled by the other. However, it is important to realise that all these distorting situations can equally apply to our awareness of ourselves!

With this awareness, we can look again at the pros and cons of interpretation, and can clarify that an intervention that asserts the therapist as having *extra* understanding of the client's situation, understanding that is *per se* not available to the client, and moves the client into being a cognitive recipient of the therapist's wisdom, does not fit with a therapy based round a mutual exploration of self actualization. The therapist's statement of an intuition *as* an intuition, a phenomenological event in the field, rather than as a truth to be believed by the client, is not in itself problematic, though it may become so in a particular field of a client who confluently agrees with the therapist.

Conclusion

I have attempted in this chapter to give a flavour of the psychological and neurological landscape described both by Gestalt psychotherapy and researches into neuroscience, both those researches which were assimilated into the therapy at its beginning (Goldstein, Lewin) and in recent years (Stern, Rizzolatti, Schore). I have made suggestions about the implications of these assimilations for Gestalt theory and clinical practice, and pointed out what a good fit there is between all these formulations, based round a field-relational theory of self and other.

References

Beisser, A. (1970) The paradoxical theory of change. In J. Fagan and I. L. Shepherd (eds) *Gestalt Therapy Now*. New York: Harper & Row.
Goldstein, K. (1939) *The Organism*. New York: American Book Company.
Kauffman, S. (1995) *At Home in the Universe*. London: Viking Books.
Kennedy, D. (2008) The eclipse of dialogue. *British Gestalt Journal*, 17: 1.
Lewin, K. (1936) *Principles of Topological Psychology* (G. Heider and F. Heider, trans.). New York: McGraw-Hill.

Perls, F., Hefferline, R. and Goodman, P. (1994/1951) *Gestalt Therapy: Excitement and Growth in the Human Personality*. New York: Gestalt Journal Press.
Perls, F. S. (1978) Finding self through Gestalt therapy, *Gestalt Journal*, I, 1: 54–73.
—— (1992/1969) *Gestalt Therapy Verbatim*. Highland, NY: Gestalt Journal Press. First published 1969.
Philippson, P. (2001a) *Self in Relation*. Highland, NY: Gestalt Journal Press.
—— (2001b) On existence and emotion. *British Gestalt Journal*, 10, 2: 119–122.
—— (2005) Paradox – strategic, naïve and Gestalt. *International Gestalt Journal*, 28, 2.
Prigogine, I. and Stengers, I. (1984) *Order Out of Chaos*. London: Flamingo.
Revelle, William and Loftus, Debra A. (1992) The implications of arousal effects for the study of affect and memory. In S. Christianson (ed.) *The Handbook of Emotion and Memory: Research and Theory* (pp. 113–141). Hillsdale, NJ: Lawrence Erlbaum Associates.
Rizzolatti, G. and Craighero, L. (2004) The mirror-neuron system. *Annual Review of Neuroscience*, 27: 169–192.
Schore, A. N. (1994) *Affect Regulation and the Repair of the Self*. Hillsdale, NJ: Lawrence Erlbaum Associates.
Smuts, J. (1996/1926) *Holism and Evolution*. Highland, NY: Gestalt Journal Press. First published 1926.
Stern, D. N. (2004) *The Present Moment in Psychotherapy and Everyday Life*. New York: W. W. Norton.
Wheeler, G. (2000) *Beyond Individualism, Toward a New Understanding of Self, Relationship, and Experience*. Cambridge, MA: GIC Press.

Chapter 9

Spirituality in gestalt therapy

Philip Brownell

Something rather than nothing – that is a dividing line between those who believe in God and those who do not. If, for instance, you start with the cosmological argument for the existence of God, and you say that the design inherent at every level of the universe points to an intelligent designer, then someone who does not believe in God might say that it is not necessarily so. They might claim that something just *is* or that one cannot know how it came about, or they might say that "design" is simply an artifact of particle and wave, that is, of thing and action, of noun and verb. They might say that when we see the way widgets operate in the world, and we contemplate the intricate, interdependent nature of the way widgets both depend on other elements of the world operating in their respective ways and provide a base for still other things to emerge and to function as they do, that the appearance of design is simply a mirage shimmering at a distance on a hot, summer's day. That is not satisfying, however, because then the question becomes, "How did the 'way' something functions in the world come about, and where did these 'things' come from in the first place?" The infinite regress of cause-and-effect culminates in the a priori commitment to there either being something (the creation from an uncaused cause) or there being nothing (the mirage and the fantasy). Are we all simply *happenings* – and there are actually no "things" (just waves appearing as particles) – or are we objects in relationship?

I am starting with the assumption that God exists, and I want to explore the implications that we are in relationship, one way or the other, with divine Being. The focus of this chapter is not to prove that God exists, but to explore the implications of the immanence of God for the practice of gestalt therapy.

Books abound on the subject of spirituality and journal articles on spiritual and religious issues are simply too numerous to list. People are interested in ways "to acknowledge and integrate religious and spiritual beliefs within ordinary therapeutic work by tapping into, instead of ignoring, these beliefs and practices" (APA 2008: np). The place of spirituality in gestalt therapy fits in this more general context of interest; therefore, a secondary purpose of this chapter is to show how spiritual concepts are relevant to evolving gestalt therapy praxis.

An orienting perspective

Various writers have characterized spirituality in gestalt therapy as transpersonal (Freeman 2006; Naranjo 1978; Starak 2008; Williams 2006), mystery (Crocker 1999, 2001), mystical (Ingersoll and O'Neill 2005; Snir 2000), pastoral care (Norberg 2006), or simply as gestalt process (Withey 2008). Some have maintained there is no need to consider spirituality in gestalt therapy (Feder 2001), and others have simply observed that gestalt therapy and spiritual disciplines are two different things (Au 1991).

Although gestalt therapy is not considered a spiritual system, the founders of gestalt therapy included eastern spirituality and religion (sometimes simply referred to as "eastern thought") in their theoretical formulations (Crocker and Philippson 2005; Eynde 1999; Ingersoll and O'Neill 2005; Schoen 1978, 1984; Wolfert 2000). The experiential focus, attending to awareness's moment-by-moment cyclical process – to "what is" – and appreciation for the impasse as holding potential for creation and growth are all rooted in Buddhist mindfulness (Eva Gold, personal communication, November 10, 2008). They are *process-oriented elements*.

It is far less well known that western, theistic spirituality has also been influential in the formation of gestalt therapy and continues to be important to its evolution (Crocker 1999; O'Neill in Ingersoll and O'Neill 2005; Norberg 2006; Brownell 2006, 2008a, 2008b, 2009b, 2010a, 2010b, 2010c, 2010d). Therefore, I will address a current western, theistic spiritual perspective that tends to be more *relationship-oriented*.

Theism is directly concerned with the "intersubjective encounter inherent in a relationship with an objective Being who is God (as opposed to mysterious, impersonal forces and the excitement of human encounter alone)" (Brownell 2006: 27).

Transcendence and immanence

A chapter on spirituality that addresses theism must deal with the concepts of transcendence and immanence. For the purposes here, transcendence means *distinct from* and immanence means *involved with* (Feinberg 2001), or present in the dialogical sense.

How a Being can be both transcendent and immanent, simultaneously, would make for a fine meditation. Of these two constructs Martin Buber (Buber 1952/1988) asserted that a complete inclusion of the divine within the sphere of the human would effectively abolish its divinity. Levinas would say that it would make the divine Other the "same" as oneself, confining God to one's thematization (Levinas 1998, 2000). Buber further claimed that if a person were to dare to turn toward God, in a face-to-face meeting, and to call out to Him, then "Reality" would meet him. Levinas would say that this sentient meeting constitutes the enjoyment of God, experienced directly and immediately in the course of embodied living, as opposed to an objectification of God through intentional representation (Critchley 2002). With such a perspective, if a person refuses to limit God to the transcendent, he will have a fuller conception of God than the one who does so limit Him; conversely, if a person limits God to only the immanent, then it is not actually the divine Being one is talking about (Buber 1952/1988).

Both Friedrich Schleiermacher and Soren Kierkegaard emphasized personal experience of God. Kierkegaard emphasized passionate, authentic faith, based in subjective experience rather than recitation of static, propositional assertions (i.e., fixed gestalts) (McDonald 2006). Schleiermacher described that as a starting point in understanding religious life (McGrath 2004). He was a student of Aristotle and understood religious experience as the feeling (Crouter 2005) of absolute dependence on God, "identical with the consciousness of being in relation with God" (Feinberg 2001: 112). Rudolph Otto (1923/1958) described that experience as one of God being an actually present entity and the encounter with God as having two features: fear (*mysterium tremendum*) and attraction (*mysterium fascinans*). Together, they constituted contact with the *Wholly Other* – experience of the *numinous*. The impression that God speaks (Wolterstorff 1995; Willard 1999), that God says, "I am," is part of codified theology, under the term *revelation*, but what is in view here is the simple experience that one has, in this contact, *personally heard from God*. One knows by experience that *God is – God is for, to, and with me*. The greatest implication of the possibility that God is present – involved in the situation – is the give and take that is then possible between oneself and God, inducing the actions that reveal one's self in turn (Wojtyla 1979). In Levinas the experience of the immanence of God calls for the response, "Here *I* am!" to one's neighbor (Levinas 1998: 75, emphasis added).

One can see many of these elements in the story of Isaiah's meeting with God:

> I saw the Lord sitting on a throne, lofty and exalted, with the train of His robes filling the temple. Seraphim stood above Him, each having six wings . . . one called out to another and said, "Holy, Holy, Holy is the Lord of hosts, the whole earth is full of His glory." Then I said, "Woe is me, for I am ruined! Because I am a man of unclean lips, and I live among a people of unclean lips; for my eyes have seen the King, the Lord of hosts." . . . Then I heard the voice of the Lord saying, "Whom shall I send, and who will go for Us?" Then I said, "Here I am. Send me!"
>
> (Isaiah 6:1–13)[1]

The implications of God's immanence, then, are threefold: the *sense* of God's presence, the *impression* that God speaks, and the *obligation* to respond through action of some kind that is often expressed as an ethical imperative in respect to one's neighbor.

Psychology and spirituality

A worldview is a system of assumptions and frameworks about the nature of reality that any given people use to organize their lives (Hiebert 2008; Brownell 2010a). Phenomenologically, it can be thought of as the sum of a person's worlds and the integration of his or her attitudes (Luft 1998). It is a thematic expression of one's field.

Attitude organizes a person's ground, bringing forward what accords with the attitude and leaving behind what does not. Attitudes, then, contribute to worldviews, and they are also shaped by them.

There is a difference between a largely psychological and a primarily spiritual worldview such that holding one or the other sorts a person's spirituality.

One of the assumptions in a worldview intrinsic to gestalt therapy is that human beings are whole organisms who are physically, psychologically, and socially embedded in overlapping situations involving diverse, interpenetrating dimensions (Crocker 2008). Since people manifest spiritual concerns or interests, spirituality is also a form of such embeddedness, and it needs to be accounted for (Copsey and Bar-Yoseph Levine 2005).

A theistic understanding of "natural" and "spiritual"

Roughly 2000 years ago Paul of Tarsus addressed the difference between a psychological worldview and a spiritual worldview. He contrasted the *psychikos* and the *pneumatikos* (the natural and the spiritual). He said, "We are talking about things not taught by human wisdom but taught by spirit, interpreting spiritual things by means of spiritual words. But an unspiritual man does not receive the things of the spirit of God, for they are moronic to him and he has no power to know, for they are spiritually investigated."[2]

Writing to a different group of Christians and describing a spiritual way of life, he said, "Do not be conformed to this age, but be transformed by the renewal of the mind, so that you might be able to discern what is the will of God . . ."[3]

Here, then, are the concepts in question:

- *Mind* is a facet of a person viewed psychologically.
- *Age* (in this context) is a segment of time in the course of world events.
- God is discovered by means of a spiritual capacity.

- *Spirit* is the medium of a *transorganismic relationship* tapping the larger realities, the ultimate mysteries of life resolving in the person of God.

These concepts have histories of meaning. In Old Testament Hebrew *ruach* (spirit) meant "air in motion" and by extension came also to stand for the consciousness of a person (Payne 1980), including his or her disposition and moral character (Brown, Driver, and Briggs 1907/1978). In New Testament Greek *pneuma* (spirit) was conceived of as wind, the breathing out of air, the breath-giving life of the body, and by extension part of the personality – the immaterial aspect of an individual. As such it was the source and seat of insight (Bauer, Arndt, and Gingrich 1957: 680–681). Greek *nous* (mind), on the other hand, was regarded to be "the faculty of physical and intellectual perception" (Bauer, Arndt, and Gingrich 1957: 546) – one's ability to think – an *intraorganismic capacity*.

These are constructs by which to sort capacities. The terms *psyche* and *pneuma* were considered functional. As such, they do not indicate substances or entities nor point to something external to a person (Anderson 1998).

In terms of psychological function mind is an emergent property. It comes forth or arises from the action of the physiology of the brain at work as a person interacts in the world. "Mind," in this discussion, is synonymous with "self," and the emergent self exerts a downward, causal influence over the brain, as the entire person is stimulated through contact in the environment (Brown 1998; Brownell 2009a; Gregersen 2000; Murphy 1998, 2002, 2006). So, there is transorganismic relationship involved, because we are all connected and related to what is other than ourselves in our physical and social environments, and "mind" emerges as the brain engages, but at that level alone (the level of *psyche*) it is simply *pscyhikos* – psychological (or natural). At that level alone it is not *pneumatikos* (or spiritual).

In terms of spiritual function, spiritual experience emerges through transpersonal contact with God (Brownell 2006; Pargament 2007); thus, spirit is a relational capacity. Spirit calls to, and calls forth, spirit, and that in turn excites, renews, and informs the mind in the person who is *pneumatikos*. In a theistic worldview the important things of life, what Paul Tillich (1987) called the ultimate concerns – even what some call mystery or still others identify as epiphanal beauty in an aesthetic sense of form – point past the immediate, visible and obvious to the Artist whose creativity produced them (Yancey 2003), and it is the relationship with that Person that organizes one's being in the world (Tillich 1959).

The pneumenal field

In the quote above from Romans 12, the writer's admonition was not to be conformed, or molded by "this age." An age (*aeon*) is a segment of time, and in this context refers to the course of world events within a given segment of time (Bauer, Arndt, and Gingrich 1957: 27). It can be likened to Lewin's construct of the situational unit. Thus, the translation for a gestalt therapy audience could be "do not be determined by the field, but be transformed by the renewal of the mind . . ."

From a theistic perspective, however, God is involved with and *part of* the field; so, one cannot avoid being influenced by the field if one is attempting, in spirit, to move in step with God. The admonition actually reflects the tension between the psychological and spiritual attitudes, for the age, the course of world events, is a natural category. Consequently, the admonition confronts the field as simply psychological. A better understanding might be, "do not be molded by the *psychikos aeon* (the unspiritual attitude in the field) . . ."

In a theistic worldview God intervenes in our lives in the medium of spirit. Thus, the *pneumatikos* is the one who is sensitive to the things that enter the field in such a way, and his or her mind identifies spiritual experience for what it is, but the *psychikos* is not sensitive in that way (the spiritual horizon is empty of such possibilities), and he or she cannot make sense of spiritual experience, crediting it instead to facets of mind or systems – theories in keeping with the psychological aspect of the natural attitude.

A current example of this is the work of Erving Polster (2006) in his book, *Uncommon Ground*, in which he examines religious communities and redefines the sacred. It is a masterful deconstruction of western spirituality from a psychological and natural perspective. For such people, mystery remains enigma, a cognitive oddity, rather than a catalyst for spiritual wonder.

Martin Buber (1952/1988) described these two approaches, the natural and the spiritual, when he publicly exposed Carl Jung as being *psychikos* – for extracting God from his version of spirituality and for making God's existence contingent upon the unconscious working of the human soul. Buber claimed that philosophy is mistaken in thinking of religion as originating in a noetical act, thus consigning religion to the knowledge of an object that is indifferent to being known. Rather, he understood the meeting with God to be mutual contact – the reciprocal meeting in life between one existence and another – and he regarded faith to be the entrance into such reciprocity, setting up a relationship with a knowable Being from whom all meaning comes (Buber 1952/1988).

Application to practice

At the beginning of this chapter I referred to an assertion that people want to know how to integrate religious and spiritual beliefs by tapping into those beliefs and practices. In an approach integrating theistic spiritual beliefs and practices this will include in-session episodes in which the *sense* of God's presence, the *impression* that God speaks, and the *obligation* to respond through action are included and accounted for. It will also include discussion of how the pneumenal field (with a "God-in" perspective) affects and supports both the client and the therapist in and out of session.

I am not asking the reader to believe as I do, but I am asking people to entertain that working in gestalt therapy from a theistic spiritual perspective includes people doing just these kinds of things that I am describing (which likely feel foreign or objectionable to someone who does not believe in God).

With a client for whom God is relevant, a gestalt therapist might suggest experiments that resemble "homework" but that include God, realizing that for the client God's presence and discourse do not cease when the client leaves the room. A gestalt therapist might choose to include in dialogical history questions about the client's spirituality. The therapist might pray for God's guidance and help in meeting with a client. There are times when I, for example, sense God's hand in bringing someone to me, and the sense of God's presence refers to that feeling that God is there with us both. He has brought this person to *me*, not just to a therapist, and He has convened a three-person field in the process. It frequently occurs that the client says exactly this: "I feel God brought me to you." To that I could add, "And I feel God is with us here now."

I practice God's presence by being sensitive to what He is doing, for God is at work not only in the client, but also in the therapist. I speak to God, I listen for God, and I often ask the client pointed questions that allow him or her to exercise a spiritual attitude.

The impression that God speaks refers to the experience of God actually speaking. One of my clients is an alcoholic. He is also a Christian. He told me about once being on a business trip and flying back through a terminal on Saturday night. Somewhere inside himself he was determined to drink, but he realized that where we live, alcohol is not sold on Sunday. So, he walked deliberately into the duty free store and picked up a bottle. He said that as he was walking to the checkout, with the bottle in his hands, "A thought came to me, 'This cannot lead to any good.'" As soon as he told me this, I realized it had been God speaking to him. Then, he said, "I think this was God." He later told me that this same "voice" had said the same thing to him during similar relapses.

Again, I understand that this will sound strange to people who do not know God experientially, do not sense His presence, and do not recognize His discourse. However, any given gestalt therapist is bound to meet clients who do.

Conclusion

Spirituality is an ultimate concern and a central capacity of the human person. Its processes and relationships need to be accounted for in gestalt therapy. Western spirituality includes the concept of relationship with a personal deity and the disciplines that organize such a relationship. By contrast, eastern spirituality includes the processes of life that attend to the qualitative and subjective experiential aspects of one's living. Eastern thought and western spirituality together provide an overall ground for a more complete spiritual gestalt: spirituality as process and spirituality as relationship. This is a general way of conceptualizing so that the integration of spirituality into gestalt therapy praxis might be facilitated, and it is a matter of emphasis rather than of strict and absolute separation of categories.

Notes

1 Scripture taken from the New American Standard Bible, copyright 1960, 1962, 1963, 1968, 1971, 1972, 1973, 1975, 1977, 1995 by the Lockman Foundation. Used by Permission.
2 Original translation of 1 Corinthians 2: 13–14, from the Greek New Testament, United Bible Societies, 3rd edition, 1983, Biblia-Druck GmbhH Stuttgart, West Germany.
3 Original translation from Romans 12:2, from the Greek New Testament, United Bible Societies, 3rd edition, 1983, Biblia-Druck GmbhH Stuttgart, West Germany.

References

American Psychological Association. (2008) APA psychotherapy videotape series – spirituality. Downloaded October 4, 2008 from: http://www.apa.org/videos/series6.html. Washington, DC: American Psychological Association.

Anderson, R. S. (1998) On being human: the spiritual saga of a creaturely soul. In W. Brown, N. Murphy and H. N. Malony (eds) *Whatever Happened to the Soul? Scientific and Theological Portraits of Human Nature* (pp. 175–194). Minneapolis: Fortress Press.

Au, W. (1991) Gestalt therapy and the spiritual exercises of St. Ignatius. *Studies in Formative Spirituality*, 12, 2: 197–213.

Bauer, W., Arndt, W. and Gingrich, F. W. (1957) *A Greek–English Lexicon of the New Testament and Other Early Christian Literature*. Chicago: University of Chicago Press.

Brown, F., Driver, S. R. and Briggs, C. (1907/1978) *A Hebrew and English Lexicon of the Old Testament*. Oxford: Clarendon Press/Oxford University Press.

Brown, W. (1998) Cognitive contributions to soul. In W. Brown, N. Murphy and H. N. Malony (eds) *Whatever Happened to the Soul: Scientific and Theological Portraits of Human Nature* (pp. 99–126). Minneapolis: Fortress Press.

Brownell, P. (2006) This I what I know – a response to "Spirituality and gestalt: a gestalt-transpersonal perspective." *Gestalt Review*, 10, 1: 26–32.

—— (2008a) Faith: an existential, phenomenological, and biblical integration. In J. H. Ellens (ed.) *Miracles: God, Psychology, and Science in the Paranormal, vol. 2, Medical and Therapeutic Events* (pp. 213–234). Westport, CT: Praeger Publishers.

—— (2008b) Personal experience, self report and hyperbole. In J. H. Ellens (ed.) *Miracles: God, Science, and Psychology in the Paranormal, vol. 3, Parapsychological Perspectives. Psychology, Religion, and Spirituality* (pp. 210–229). Westport, CT: Praeger/Greenwood.

—— (2009a) Executive functions: a neuropsychological understanding of self-regulation. *Gestalt Review*, 13, 1: 62–81.

—— (2009b) Gstalt-L, a virtual, electronic community. In B. O'Neill (ed.) *Psychotherapy, Community, and Life Focus: A Gestalt Anthology of the History, Theory, and Practice of Living in Community* (pp. 173–191). Wollongong, Australia: Ravenwood Publishing.

—— (2010a) *Gestalt Therapy: A Guide to Contemporary Practice*. New York, NY: Springer Publishing.

—— (2010b) Healing potential of religious community. In J. H. Ellens (ed.) *The Healing Power of Spirituality: How Religion Helps Humans Thrive, vol. 2, The Healing Power of Religion* (pp. 10–24). Westport, CT: Praeger/ABC-CLIO.

—— (2010c) Intentional spirituality. In J. H. Ellens (ed.) *The Healing Power of Spirituality: How Religion Helps Humans Thrive, vol. 1, The Healing Power of Personal Spirituality* (pp. 19–40). Westport, CT: Praeger/ABC-CLIO.

—— (2010d) Spirituality in the praxis of gestalt therapy. In J. H. Ellens (ed.) *The Healing Power of Spirituality: How Religion Helps Humans Thrive, vol. 3. The Psychodynamics of Healing Spirituality and Religion* (pp. 102–125). Westport, CT: Praeger/ABC-CLIO.

Buber, M. (1952/1988) *Eclipse of God: Studies in the Relation Between Religion and Philosophy*. Amherst: Humanity Books.

Copsey, N. and Bar-Yoseph Levine, T. (2005) An experiment in community. In T. Bar-Yoseph Levine (ed.) *The Bridge: Dialogues Across Cultures* (pp. 120–131). Metairie: Gestalt Institute Press.

Critchley, S. (2002) Introduction. In S. Critchley and R. Bernasconi (eds) *The Cambridge Companion to Levinas* (pp. 1–32). Cambridge: Cambridge University Press.

Crocker, S. (1999) *A Well-Lived Life: Essays in Gestalt Therapy*. Cambridge: GIC Press.

—— (2001) Spirituality, dialogue, and the phenomenological method. *Gestalt!*, 5, 3. Downloaded October 4, 2008 from: http://www.g-gej.org/5-3/crocker.html

—— (2008) A unified theory. In P. Brownell (ed.) *Handbook for Theory, Research, and Practice in Gestalt Therapy* (pp. 124–150). Newcastle: Cambridge Scholars Publishing.

Crocker, S. and Philippson, P. (2005) Phenomenology, existentialism, and eastern thought in gestalt therapy. In A. Woldt and S. Toman (eds) *Gestalt Therapy: History, Theory, and Practice* (pp. 65–80). Thousand Oaks: Sage Publications, Inc.

Crouter, R. (2005) *Friedrich Schleiermacher: Between Enlightenment and Romanticism*. Cambridge: Cambridge University Press.

Eynde, R. V. (1999) Buddhism and gestalt. *Gestalt Journal*, 22, 2: 89–100.

Feder, B. (2001) Letter to the editor. *Gestalt!*, 5, 3. Downloaded October 4, 2008 from: http://www.g-gej.org/5-3/letter.html

Feinberg, J. (2001) *No One Like Him: The Doctrine of God*. Wheaton: Crossway Books.

Freeman, D. (2006) Response to "Spirituality and gestalt: a gestalt transpersonal perspective." *Gestalt Review*, 10, 1: 22–25.

Gregersen, N. H. (2000) God's public traffic: holist vs. physicalist supervenience. In N. H. Gregersen, W. B. Drees and U. Gorman (eds) *The Human Person in Science and Theology* (pp. 153–188). Grand Rapids: William B. Eerdmans Publishing Co.

Hiebert, P. (2008) *Transforming Worldviews: An Anthropological Understanding of How People Change*. Grand Rapids: Baker Academic.

Ingersoll, E. and O'Neill, B. (2005) Gestalt therapy and spirituality. In A. Woldt and S. Toman (eds) *Gestalt Therapy: History, Theory, and Practice*. Thousand Oaks: Sage Publications, Inc.

Levinas, E. (1998) *Of God Who Comes to Mind*. Stanford: Stanford University Press.

—— (2000) *Alterity and Transcendence*. New York: Columbia University Press.

Luft, S. (1998) Husserl's phenomenological discovery of the natural attitude. *Continental Philosophy Review*, 31: 153–170.

McDonald, M. (2006) Soren Kierkegaard. In Edward Zalta (ed.) *Stanford Encyclopedia of Philosophy*. Stanford: Metaphysics Research Lab, Center for the Study of Language and Information (CSLI), Stanford University. Downloaded October 25, 2008 from: http://plato.stanford.edu/entries/Kierkegaard

McGrath, A. (2004) *The Science of God*. London: T & T Clark/Wm. B. Eerdmans Publishing Co.

Murphy, N. (1998) Non-reductive physicalism: philosophical issues. In W. Brown, N. Murphy and H. N. Malony (eds) *Whatever Happened to the Soul: Scientific and Theological Portraits of Human Nature* (pp. 127–148). Minneapolis: Fortress Press.

—— (2002) Supervenience and the downward efficacy of the mental: a non-reductive physicalist account of human action. In R. Russell, N. Murphy, T. Meyering and M. Arbib (eds) *Neuroscience and the Person: Scientific Perspectives on Divine Action* (pp. 147–164). Vatican City State: Vatican Observatory; Berkeley: Foundation and Center for Theology and the Natural Sciences.

—— (2006) *Bodies and Souls, or Spirited Bodies?* Cambridge: Cambridge University Press.

Naranjo, C. (1978) Gestalt therapy as a transpersonal approach. *Gestalt Journal*, 1, 2: 75–81.

Norberg, T. (2006) *Consenting to Grace: An Introduction to Gestalt Pastoral Counseling*. Staten Island: Penn House Press.

Otto, R. (1923/1958) *The Idea of the Holy*. Oxford: Oxford University Press.

Pargament, K. I. (2007) *Spiritually Integrated Psychotherapy: Understanding and Addressing the Sacred*. New York: Guilford Press.

Payne, J. B. (1980) Ruach. In R. L. Harris, G. L. Archer and B. K. Waltke (eds) *Theological WordBook of the Old Testament*, vol. 2 (pp. 836–837). Chicago: Moody Press.

Polster, E. (2006) *Uncommon Ground: Harmonizing Psychotherapy and Community to Enhance Everyday Living*. Phoenix: Zeig, Tucker, & Theisen, Inc.

Schoen, S. (1978) Gestalt therapy and the teachings of Buddhism. *Gestalt Journal*, 1, 1: 103–115.

—— (1984) A note on gestalt responsibility and Buddhist non-attachment. *Gestalt Journal*, 7, 2: 70–75.

Snir, S. (2000) A response from a kabbalistic perspective to "spiritual dimensions of gestalt therapy." *Gestalt!*, 4, 3. Downloaded December 1, 2008 from: http://www.g-gej.org/4-3/kabbala.html

Starak, Y. (2008) A transpersonal search for meaning. *Inner Sense, A Journal of Australian Spiritual Life*, 1, 2: 8–11.

Tillich, P. (1959) *Theology of Culture*. New York: Oxford University Press.

—— (1987) Our ultimate concern. In F. F. Church (ed.) *The Essential Tillich: An Anthology of the Writings of Paul Tillich* (pp. 32–38). Chicago: The University of Chicago Press.

Willard, D. (1999) *Hearing God: Developing a Conversational Relationship with God*. Downer's Grove: Intervarsity Press.

Williams, L. (2006) Spirituality and gestalt: a gestalt-transpersonal perspective. *Gestalt Review*, 10, 1: 6–21.

Withey, L. (2008) Gestalt therapy and spirituality. *Inner Sense, A Journal of Australian Spiritual Life*, 1, 2: 12–18.

Wojtyla, K. (1979) *The Acting Person, Analecta Husserliana: The Yearbook of Phenomenological Research, vol. X*. Dordrecht: D. Reidel Publishing Company.

Wolfert, R. (2000) The spiritual dimensions of gestalt therapy. *Gestalt!*, 4, 3. Downloaded October 4, 2008 from: http://www.g-gej.org/4-3/spiritual.html

Wolterstorff, N. (1995) *Divine Discourse: Philosophical Reflections on the Claim that God Speaks*. Cambridge: Cambridge University Press.

Yancey, P. (2003) *Rumors of Another World: What on Earth Are We Missing?* Grand Rapids: Zondervan.

Part II

Aspects of Gestalt practice

Chapter 10

Creating an embodied, authentic self: integrating mindfulness with psychotherapy when working with trauma

Lolita Sapriel

Introduction

Certain patients, who learned as infants that emotions, arousal, and action are dangerous, come to therapy as traumatized adults. They established relational patterns requiring them to adapt to a caregiver's vulnerability and limitations in order to preserve the bond, often at the expense of the developing self. Self experiences had to be kept out of awareness and could not be used to develop a sense of agency and authenticity. These protective mechanisms were creative adaptations to a pervasive absence of attunement. Under those conditions, affect integration could not take place. Mindfulness and a focus on body awareness, embedded in a safe and secure therapeutic relationship, are critical tools to help such patients develop a sense of agency, contain previously uncontainable affect, and become capable of nourishing contact. Gestalt therapy has always emphasized the importance of the body and both Gestalt therapy and intersubjectivity theory value the therapeutic relationship as an essential healing agent to help the patient risk and grow. Recent findings in infant research and neurobiology provide additional support to both clinical theories.

Infant research

Infant and caregiver form a dyadic system which either facilitates or inhibits the developing self and the ability of the infant to self-regulate and be aware. When an infant's earliest relationships are problematic and dangerous, the infant may be forced to dissociate. Since the core of the developing self is pre-verbal, a sense of agency and capacity for awareness are also ingrained pre-verbally. Sanders identifies a sequence of tasks which must be accomplished between a mother and infant which can lead to increasing

> recognition of inner awareness, purpose, and intention – shaping conscious organization. The bridge to the therapeutic level is constructed

as therapist and patient build increasingly inclusive and coherent moments of recognition between themselves . . . which act as corrective experiences, bringing the patient's own senses of "true self" and of "agency-to-initiate" to new levels of validity and competence.

(Sanders 2002: 1)

In a healthy child–mother interaction this process is enhanced. In an unhealthy infant–caregiver system, there can be massive inhibitions and potential pathology as infants become increasingly unable to be aware of their states and therefore to use their own experience as guides for action. Children whose caregivers cannot provide the necessary attunement will attune to the parent, hide their own needs, and abort their own sense of agency to "serve" the needs of the parent.

> [They] . . . feel compelled to remain either unaware of inner experience as a central referent for feelings and thoughts or dissociated from them, as they constitute a continuing threat to [their] own security. Throughout life pathological accommodation will continue to be distinguished from normal accommodation by the fact that the former will continue to require the abandonment of connection with innermost perception as central in the organization of experience, making it therefore compulsory.
>
> (Brandchaft 2010: 153)

Both reflexive compliance and robotic submission can then contribute to a sense of existential despair and meaninglessness. Depression, grief and rage (usually out of awareness) result. With no sense of agency, one is not living one's own life.

In these situations, the parents' limitations are experienced by the child as a confirmation of his own intrinsic defectiveness, badness, and unlovability. The new therapeutic relationship can help such patients shift this self-experience to see it less as a factual, shameful ingrained quality of their being, and more as a *consequence* of parental rejections or absence of attunement.

If the therapist provides consistent attunement, inevitably unmet dependency needs will emerge in the therapy, accompanied by self-loathing and a conviction that expressing them will result in the loss or destruction of this new relationship. These patients' early life experiences have severed any trust in human relationships and separateness feels terrifyingly isolating, but safer than reaching out to another.

> It is ultimately the new relationship of attachment with the therapist that allows the patient to change. To paraphrase Bowlby (1988), such a relationship provides a secure base that enables the patient to take the

risk of feeling what he is not supposed to feel and knowing what he is not supposed to know . . .

(Wallin 2007: 3)

Stolorow, one of the founders of intersubjectivity theory, defines trauma as a two-fold event; the traumatic event per se and the subsequent failure of empathy of the emotional surround (Stolorow 1998: personal communication). When children are unable to either express their needs and reactions safely, nor leave the parent, the normal fight or flight response is curtailed. In these circumstances, experiencing agency feels hopeless. Helplessness is the result. Without an authentic self, there can be no nourishing contact with another. One never learns to be authentically oneself *and* with another *at the same time.*

Because the patient's capacity for self-support and contact is frozen in the essentially non-verbal parts of the developing self, the therapist needs to attend to that aspect first:

> [T]he ways in which the nonverbal dimension is organized affect such familiar dynamic issues as safety, efficacy, self-esteem, mutual recognition, intimacy, separation and reunion, boundaries, self-definition, and aloneness in the presence of the partner
>
> (Beebe and Lachmann 2002: 34)

Both Gestalt therapy and intersubjectivity theory are field theory based and view the therapist and patient as mutually influencing each other. The therapist's state of mind and calm self-reflective capacities have a direct effect in the field on the patient's brain organization. This non-verbal process between adult patient and therapist has similarities with what Sanders describes as the:

> role of infant "agency" to self-regulate in the resolution of the dynamic tension between neonate and caregiver by the joining of directionality between them, that is, the caregiver's specificity in timing of intervention in relation to the availability of the neonate's agency in the awake state to initiate feeding. (Sanders: 24) . . . the early experiencing of the infant shapes and modifies the morphology of the baby's brain . . . [leading] to new understanding, both of long-term effects of certain negative features in an infant's early experiencing, such as trauma and recurrent pathogenic encounters, and, on the positive side, amplifying the development of the brain's potential. (Sanders: 26) . . . Each task of adjustment . . . for a given system – [will] depend on the infant's emerging awareness of its own inner state and intention as well as the mother's widening perception of her infant's changing inner states, intentions, meanings, and so on. We use the term recognition process

as the conveyor of this widening specificity in the gestalt perception of each.

(Sanders 2002: 31)

Since the capacity for affect regulation is a function of mutual regulation, failures within the relationship force infants to manage their arousal states on their own. This adaptive adjustment is not to be confused with genuine self-support. If all goes well, the

> infant begins to experience an awareness of its own state . . . [showing] the brain's capacity to construct gestalts of expectancy amid the recurrence both of affectively positive "moments of meeting" and of the affectively negative experience of further constraint to spontaneity of initiative.
>
> (Sanders 2002: 36–37)

My patient, child of a depressed mother (presented more fully later), is preoccupied with both regulating arousal by narrowly constricting her world, and with monitoring my inner states. Any nascent self-experience which might potentially conflict with me causes her to become either disorganized or dissociated.

> [C]aretakers possess enormous power to inhibit, undermine, or destroy the development in the child of his innate capacity for self-reflection, which might afford him the opportunity for correction, choice, and independent judgment when these alone could offer an escape route from his imprisonment. The child becomes incapacitated because he cannot integrate experiences that contradict the constructs of the parents.
>
> The result is what I have come to believe is the most pervasive and disabling disorder of our times. The tormenting doubt, never settled, about who and what one is, the absence of sustaining internal referents for one's sense of one's own self, and the lack of confidence, courage, and freedom to choose a course of one's own are all rooted in this existential conflict.
>
> (Brandchaft et al. 2010: 92)

With patients whose sense of agency has been subverted and who are crippled by shame and a sense of wrongness about their own experience, the therapist's on-going willingness to initiate repair of perceived disruptions, to non-defensively acknowledge their own part in those disruptions, and to maintain a stance of sustained empathy, is particularly important. "It is a misunderstanding . . . to equate mutuality with interactive regulation and autonomy with self-regulation. Both autonomy and mutuality require processes of self- and interactive regulation" (Beebe and Lachmann 2002: 225–226). Our capacity to grow, to explore our world, will always be enhanced by having a trusted empathic other behind us.

Gestalt therapy and intersubjectivity theory

Fritz Perls was influenced by eastern meditative techniques, by Kurt Lewin's field theory, by Husserl's Phenomenology, and by Lowen's work with the body. Gestalt therapy has always emphasized the validity of subjective experience and the "awareness continuum" was seen as a predominant therapeutic technique. Situating mindful awareness in a new context requires integrating these important Gestalt therapy contributions with more recent developmental theories of infant–caregiver relational patterns, neurobiology, and intersubjectivity theory.

Intersubjectivity theory is a contemporary psychoanalytic theory which also values subjective experience and operates from a field theory approach. Robert Stolorow and George Atwood developed intersubjectivity theory in the 1970s. Like Gestalt theory earlier, they addressed the larger relational field and

> offer a "lens" through which to illuminate the personal subjective world of an individual in the context of a *specific* relationship with a *specific* "other" . . . meaning is constantly co-created by both members of the dyad. The dialogic process is an "open system" in which the mutual give and take of both participants affects how an interpretation is understood.
>
> (Sapriel 1998: 40)

Intersubjectivity theory also asserts that pathology, resistance, even dreams, are a property of the contextual field, and not just products within the patient arising in isolation. Stolorow and Brandchaft propose that "what is called 'borderline' is not a pathological condition located solely in the patient but phenomena arising in an *intersubjective field*" (Stolorow et al. 1994: 36). Both Gestalt and intersubjectivity theory view the therapist as needing to understand the patient's experience as a "field influenced one." Gestalt therapy has always emphasized field theory, but historically, the technology of awareness was more figural, field theory more ground. A more contemporary view of Gestalt sees them as being related in a constant figure/ground fashion. In traumatized individuals, that stream of awareness is massively inhibited. Perception itself is too dangerous. Breathing stops, looking is forbidden, the body tenses to inhibit feelings and actions. Vitality is severely depleted. With such patients, because of the perceived danger in allowing themselves to become aware, mindfulness and body awareness work must be contained in the safety of the therapeutic relationship, in which patient and therapist are continually inextricably mutually influencing each other.

Conflict and anxiety are avoided by disowning one's perceptions, and safety and security maintained, but at the cost of real dialogue and nourishing contact.

> Experimenting with body-awareness ... awakens resistance and anxiety. But it is profoundly important ... much reintegration will be necessary before you clearly sense *what* you yourself are doing, *how* you are doing it, and *why* you are doing it.
>
> (Perls et al. 1951: 86–87)

Awareness work and mindfulness practice also develop a sense of agency. "The notion that 'thoughts' on their own initiative and without any help from you 'enter your mind,' must give place to the insight that *you* are thinking the thoughts" (Perls et al. 1951: 85). Both the psychotherapeutic relationship and mindfulness practice can help patients with trauma and dissociation develop an attitude of curiosity, not judgment, in tracking their own process.

My patient despairingly believes that if she let herself feel, she'd be impacted and feeling everything *all the time*, which of course is accurate. Her shame at being affected, and the prohibition against revealing her experience, create constant tension, and consequently, a layered reactivity that confirm to her that she is "overreacting." Mindulness practice can help because

> [b]y not identifying with, not holding on to, and being embarrassed by whatever arises, the meditator moves inexorably from a narrow focus on the content of her experience to an ever-widening focus on the process itself. Thoughts and feelings, stripped of their associated pride or shame, gradually lose their charge and come to be seen as "just" thoughts or "just" feelings.
>
> (Epstein 1995: 124)

If normal reactions are experienced as defective, then one strives to "be good," keeping one's experiences out of awareness. Ultimately, however, this doesn't work, since

> it does not eliminate "undesirable" emotions from the person, for it cannot repeal the way nature designed organisms to function. [It] ... complicate[s] further the already intricate organism/environment field by setting up a great number of situations which, unless avoided, are immensely emotion-arousing.
>
> (p. 97)

Perls goes on to say:

> emotion is a continuous process, since every instant of one's life carries in some degree a feeling-tone of pleasantness or unpleasantness . . . it is a crucial regulator of action, for it not only furnishes the basis of awareness of what is important but it also energizes appropriate action.
> (Perls et al. 1951: 94–95)

Infant research and neurobiology research show how the ability to use one's awareness as a guide to action is inextricably intertwined with the relational contextual field. If one's caregivers are experienced as dangerous, the infant cannot safely turn to them, and therefore emotions cannot be contained and integrated, and are then experienced as disruptions, rather than as valid signals to the self. To minimize "disruptions" as much as possible, isolation becomes the creative adjustment. Freezing action freezes the emotion. "The word emotion is composed of the prefix 'e' and the stem 'motion.' Emotion means to move out. All our feelings are body perceptions" (Lowen 1965: 9).

Practicing consistent mindfulness benefits self regulation, contains arousal, and increases empathy for oneself. "By separating out the reactive self from the core experience, the practice of bare attention eventually returns [us] to a state of unconditioned openness that bears an important resemblance to the feeling engendered by an optimally attentive parent" (Epstein 1995: 117). Encouraging such patients to risk agency, possible conflict, and ultimately, genuine contact, is a necessary part of growth as a self. The risk of humiliation and rejection increases when we use our emotions as guides to action, but so does the likelihood of experiencing authentic contact, a lessening of isolation, vitality and joy.

Brain/mind/research

Our language illustrates how emotions are expressed physically. English has phrases like: "hang your head in shame," "strike out in anger," "feel paralyzed with fear," "reach out when happy." Fear inhibits these natural biological emotion/action gestures. Early deprivation limits learning and growth capacities as well as the ability to take in anything positive from the environment. When a person feels imprisoned by shame and a conviction of intrinsic unlovability, it seems inconceivable to be authentically oneself in the world and be accepted. Therefore, it becomes impossible to believe in the authentic sincerity of someone else's care and love. The defenses originally created to manage unbearable disappointment and devastation have now become prison walls that keep out the good as well as the dangerous. This can result in a continuing sense of feeling "starved in the midst of plenty."

> Neuroscience research has rediscovered the notion that the function of the brain is most of all the organization of effective action . . . effective treatment may need to involve (1) learning that it is *safe* to have feelings and sensations through mindfulness and . . . (2) learning to modulate arousal, and (3) learning . . . to re-engage in taking effective action.
>
> (Van der Kolk 2006: 160)

When affect arousal can be managed in the safety of the therapeutic relationship, awareness can occur, and self-reflection becomes possible so that overwhelming feelings can be experienced as *states of mind*. "The stance of the self toward experience predicts attachment security better than the facts of personal history themselves" (Wallin 2007: 1). Mindfulness is becoming a recognized effective tool for the therapist; an encouraging finding to help these patients overcome a disastrously traumatic history.

Psychotherapists generally have tended to focus more on verbal exploration of meaning. With patients who dissociate, shifting the focus to include working directly on the patients' relationship to their bodies so that connection and integration can occur, is essential. The psychoanalytic community and psychobiologists are mining the recent interest in neurobiology and are re-discovering what Gestalt therapy has always known; the importance of the body. This process of re-connection requires careful, non-judgmental, mindful attention; to feelings, thoughts and body sensations as they arise in the present moment. Siegel suggests that:

> mindfulness involves a form of internal attunement that may harness the social circuits of mirroring and empathy to create a state of neural integration and flexible self-regulation . . . This is the reflexive state of awareness that is at the heart of mindfulness . . . This . . . internal attunement alleviates suffering and creates a stabilizing sense of being connected to both moment-to-moment experience and to our authentic sense of self . . . the qualitative feel of such an open state is the foundation of love.
>
> (Siegel 2007: 131–132)

Giving and receiving love require a state of openness. Openness and creative play require a sense of safety. For most of us, turning inward increases self awareness in a positive way. Unfortunately, with traumatized individuals, awareness activates further trauma and over-arousal, inducing panic, anxiety, and disorganization. The therapist can carefully monitor the rise of fear, anxiety and disorganization, and calmly encourage mindfulness, a little at a time.

> Self-regulation requires human contact and attunement. Pervasive failures of attunement can result in a valid fear of intimacy. Instead of

the promise of closeness, comfort, and respect, turning to others activates emotional memories of hurt and abandonment, and can endanger self-regulation, which then may have to depend on isolation and self-soothing. Even the longing to turn to another, which can be activated in therapy (if all goes well), can be a signal for potential pain. It . . . may precipitate a re-living of the trauma . . . it is critical to . . . explor[e] ways of regulating physiological arousal, in which using breath and body movement can be extremely useful.

(Van der Kolk 2006: 178)

Initially, my patient resisted doing anything for herself, and was unwilling to practice mindfulness. In exploring her reluctance and resentment, we discovered that, for her, the very act of my suggesting tools that she might use when alone activated a deeply ingrained organizing principle; namely: "once again, I have to do everything by myself." She uttered this with a mixture of despair and anger, convinced that I must be trying to get rid of her. She did not experience doing things for herself as self-care, but as an *isolating forced self regulation*. It re-activated her childhood feelings with her depressed mother, who could not attend to her and with whom she experienced herself as a burden. She was convinced the same was true for me. Often with infants of depressed mothers, the only way to experience closeness is to remain depressed or needy. There is a pervasive dilemma; namely: self-support means loss of the "other" (in this case me).

In Gestalt therapy, contact has the polarities of isolation and of confluence . . . The risk of moving toward contactful engagement is that the person will become engulfed by union with the other. In addition . . . is the fear that after the compelling, rending intensity is over, the individual's loneliness and isolation will be even greater than before. A person who has settled for the "security" of isolation fears dialogue as a disruption of this state.

(Hycner and Jacobs 1995: 57)

It is axiomatic that connection with one's own internal experience is necessary for genuine contact. "The awareness process . . . by implication is a precondition of dialogue" (Hycner and Jacobs 1995: 61). That is precisely what has made awareness so dangerous for these patients.

Case presentation

Some of the history of this patient was previously presented by me in *The Bridge – Dialogues across Cultures* (Sapriel and Palumbo 2005). The present account addresses different themes which emerged at a later stage in her life and in her therapy.

Carol is an intelligent professional single woman in her 50s. An important relationship in her life did not lead to marriage and left her feeling there would never be anyone else for her. Devastated after several failed therapies, she was referred to me for long standing depression. It was clear from the start that Carol needed long term intensive therapeutic support. Indeed, we have been meeting for over 10 years, three times a week. Carol comes from a fundamentalist Christian family where religious teachings held central place and reinforced family values and dynamics. "She describes her mother as 'selfless' (desirable), but depressed and burdened; her father as a successful professional who never talked about his or others' feelings. She cannot recall any early memories of being . . . touched . . . Early childhood needs and feelings were shamed, verbally or non-verbally. Feeling states other than cheerful ones were judged as 'good' or 'bad' in God's eyes, not understood or valued in their own right. Her primary survival strategy in this atmosphere was to become utterly self-sufficient, selfless, and numb/restrained in all her feelings, with invulnerability as a self-ideal" (Sapriel and Palumbo 2005: 256).

Self experience and attunement

Carol lived in chronic despair and hopelessness, crippled by shame, unable to look at me. Our early work revolved around her terror of placing any hope in another therapist. If I spoke too fast, she would become disorganized and dissociate even more. Frightened and over-aroused, she would lose the ability to feel herself and her own thoughts. I learned to modulate my responses to her, and inquired frequently as to how connected she felt to herself and to me. We gradually co-created our own unique system through dialogue. I would sit near her and she would hold my hand. Touch provided her with a non verbal contact she could experience, as well as giving me an additional avenue to sense her dissociation. "She revealed with some humiliation that she needed my affect attunement . . . to help with her self-regulation . . . yet her conviction that I could only experience her needs as an unwelcome intrusion motivated her to strive to eliminate them, even from herself" (Sapriel and Palumbo 2005: 258). It was safer for her to "not perceive," "not notice," her inner states. Remaining attuned to "the other" also gave her a sense of value and purpose. But it also left her feeling obscurely lonely and as she said: "not able to feel you."

Shame and isolation

Carol reported an abiding sense of isolation, worse at home, but also present with me. Any trust in human relating seemed inconceivable, or, at best, stupid.

All her efforts were aimed at not being affected by others. Any disappointment she might feel instantly meant that she had failed to prevent the interaction from happening; (her fault). Pervasive isolation and constant vigilance were the only ways to prevent life from surprising her into being affected.

We worked for years to decrease shame and to build trust. She can sense the slightest emotional shift in me, and be easily disrupted. My consistency and calmness were critically important in helping to calm her. My ability to acknowledge and repair times of misattunement were also important. Those early years were crucial ones in which we established a safe and secure relationship from which she could learn to grow. Only then could we begin to work on mindfulness and integration of her feelings with her body. She starts most sessions feeling "numb." Her face is covered. She first checks out where I am. Gradually, she reported periods of calmness when in the session with me, usually when holding my hand. This also allowed her to directly experience my presence and I could discern and name subtle withdrawals of her self, sometimes even before she herself was aware that anything had happened. I would then inquire if she'd felt or thought something forbidden, or sensed a shift in me which had affected her. Any annoyance with me, or differing with me, or even a longing towards me, would cause her to dissociate. She had no sense of agency, complying reflexively with what she perceived as my needs. When I asked her to voice her fears, she would answer: "why would you welcome my longings to be close to you?" "Why would you want to hear my anger?"

Mindfulness and body awareness

She used to start each session lying down, her face covered. Recently, she is sitting up, though she still finds looking at me difficult. I start by asking her to pay attention to her breath and see what emerges. She almost always starts to cry from the release of tension. "I've been holding myself together when away from you." At the start of every week together, after a three-day break, she re-experiences a fear that her feelings and needs would not be welcome to me so she starts the session once again dissociated. As she experiences my presence, she feels calmer. Feelings and thoughts emerge, and the conflicts also emerge which are inherent in any nascent sense of agency. There is a constant figure/ground relationship between self awareness and her fear of expressing and acting on her awareness. Subtle internal shifts in my state instantly trigger in her a return to a numb state. I then refocus her on her breath and her body. "Where is the tension?" "What does she want; from herself or from me?" She worries that having a need towards me means that I'll find her "too much." I encourage her to notice her feelings without judgment and suggest that our relationship now feels secure enough that she can become aware of her longings for comfort and risk expressing them to me.

Carol feels predominantly two states: "paralyzed" or "driven." We are naming a "top dog," an internal voice speaking with great authority: "You must, you should, if you don't then you'll never." She identifies with that part and believes herself "incapable of doing what she should be doing." This voice is responsible for her feeling pushed around without regard for her feelings. She objectifies herself as she was once objectified by her parents. There are massive obstacles to her becoming aware of the "under dog," as she reflexively dismisses and invalidates any perceptions emanating from that position. I ask her if she is afraid that if she didn't force herself, she would never do anything at all. She agrees. "I wouldn't feel like doing anything." "I'd live in a cave." She believes her self-experiences represent factual truths, and is only gradually seeing that they are a response to the relentless "top dog." A dialogue is slowly becoming possible between these two parts, so that she can begin to experience them as states of mind.

Unable to turn to the adults in her life for caring and containment, she had to prematurely turn to herself, creating a closed system in which living up to a relentless ideal to "always be productive and a good girl" helped her function and warded off the devastating pain of her hurt and rejection. Had she not creatively adjusted by dissociating from all her longings, she would have disintegrated. She lived in constant terror that a catastrophe would happen and controlled everything to ward off her reactions. By trying to control her environment, she is attempting to control being affected as well as trying to prevent the disintegration that had already occurred in her infancy. The catastrophe that she fears is awaiting her in her future is one that has already occurred in her past.

Carol now conducts a dialogue between this ever vigilant "armed guard" (who feels male), and the inert child-part being yanked like a rag doll into action. He says: "I can't stand you, you never do anything, you're so incompetent and afraid and useless . . . and you keep me from having the things I want in life." I suggest she switch to the other side. She collapsed, crying "why do you treat me this way?" "I can't do anything," "I feel inert, like a lump," "Tell me what to do." She is unaware of fear or conflict between these parts, only helplessness. I encourage her to become aware of the underlying conflict.

Often in the early stages of our sessions, I will experience her as "away," and unavailable in any genuine way, while simultaneously talking to me. In the past, she reports this as feeling "like I can't find you." She feels frustrated by this inability to satisfy her longing to "be with me." We have come to see that this longing to be close requires her to not have her own experience. So of course paradoxically, she feels further and further away from herself and from me. When I have suggested she side with her resistance, what emerged was a strong prohibition about letting me see her and a sense that "I must not let you matter to me, because if I do then you'll go away too, like my mother, and my boyfriend, and my first therapist." She also could become aware of an unbearable exquisite vulnerability if she allows me to "matter." The more she could identify with the resistance and express her grief, and anger, the more "real" she felt and the more genuine the contact between us.

While to her, any authentic sense of herself as an "I" speaking, can instantly feel dangerous, separate and isolating, through this internal dialogue she is gradually feeling less alone. Locating her agency is a process: (1) feel her conflict, (2) side with her resistance, (3) locate her determination, (4) decide to support agency, not self-annihilation, and (5) reframe her helplessness as "I won't" instead of "I can't." As she feels understood by me, she reports a spontaneous impulse to hold her hand out to me, but it is instantly inhibited by a prohibition (retroflection); she dissociates and the impulse is lost.

Currently, I consistently focus on her present body sensations and any impulses towards movement and on her feelings towards me in the present. Is she disappointed, discouraged, sad, annoyed, angry, longing? Her hopelessness rises quickly: "what is the point of having feelings?" "Why tell you?" "It's not going to change anything." If I fail to demonstrate any change in my behavior or am not activated by guilt towards her in response to any expression of her needs or feelings towards me, she feels reconfirmed in her insignificance. How then will she know that she matters? She is inherently insignificant if I am not impacted. The notion that feelings belong to her, and therefore "matter" to her, is alien, since she learned early on that "she did not matter." She feels insubstantial and unimportant. She is learning from our relationship to experience a different meaning as we reconfigure the field between us. She is building a new template, one where her feelings and reactivities are welcomed by me. If she can trust that she matters to me, it allows space for her to question why and how she does not allow her feelings to matter to her. However, ownership of her feelings is still not commonplace. It seems that experiencing her agency is still inherently dangerous and means isolation, not opportunity for contact.

Experiments

Carol fears any experience of loss, whether of a person, a belonging, or a cherished belief. She is also terrified of death, which constitutes the ultimate confirmation of her lack of control in the world. The notion of physical death has become the concretized metaphor for any awareness of personal limitation in her life. My suggesting she experiment with "surrender to what is" does not feel like a relief, but rather like resignation to the will of the other, or collapse into disintegration. I suggest she experiment with the idea of "letting go." I ask her what that feels like. "I'll never do anything," was her first reaction, which then evolved into a forlorn, inconsolable cry of "what will become of me?" "Who will take care of me?" "Who will comfort me?" It was very poignant for me to hear the "little girl's" cry of terror facing the unbearable. When I asked her to be aware of the "terrified child part" within, she didn't know what I meant. "I am terrified," she told me. "It doesn't feel like a part." Mindfulness is the path to converting these states into an awareness that they are "states of mind."

I suggest to her another experiment: that she connect to her breath until she feels some connection to her authentic self. I encourage her to then sustain that connection and try to support an authentic dialogue with me. Initially, the reflex to dissociate and "pretend to be a normal person" takes over. Her voice is high and her breath constricted. She breathes slowly and feels more connected. I suggest we stand together, side by side. I will hold her hand so she knows she is not alone. She asks me to close my eyes. I do. I ask her to slowly repeat the words: "I am; I am me." She dissolves into grief. "I don't know if I can." She then repeats the words a few times and becomes aware of an impulse to lean away from me. I inquire if that represents her true desire or a fear of something in me. "It's not what I really want," she says, "but I feel I should protect you from me." "You've had enough of me." She dissolves into sadness. I tell her that I want to continue to stand next to her and hold her hand. She cries harder. After calming down, she says "We've done enough for one day," and returns to the couch. We reflect on what happened; how she always longs for more contact, feels she "never gets enough," yet when someone is there who wants to give her more, she pulls away and stops it. She saw how hard it is for her to take in love and comfort. She feels sad, while acknowledging that "what we did today is very important."

Conclusion: growth and progress

Through mindfulness work and our relationship, Carol is developing a self-reflective witness part so that she can "have" her feelings instead of being entirely consumed by them. As indicated earlier, this ability is essential for overcoming an early traumatic history. To date, Carol's depression and despair are much less. Her capacity for self-reflection is growing. She sees the importance of self-care, while simultaneously still fearful that I will use that as an excuse to distance myself from her. There is grief for a past she cannot undo, and awareness that she does not have to live imprisoned by it. She has started a weekly yoga class. She enrolled in a six week Mindfulness Meditation Research class at UCLA, in a program started by Dan Siegel. Carol is integrating mindfulness into her life, both in our sessions and while alone and driving her car. She is meditating on the inevitability of impermanence and death. She has taken a tai chi class. Although we still meet three times a week, she has asked me to increase my own authentic responses to her so that we can practice conflict and dialogue together, as she now feels much stronger and does not require me to exclusively attune to her. Carol is risking more dialogue with me in the present moment. She has recently begun to share positive experiences, while still fearful that I will stop being available to her if she is not only in dire need. "I can see growth; I actually enjoyed decorating the house with Christmas ornaments." "I am buying furniture I like for my home." "I'm making decisions." "I accomplished something myself!" Carol is reaching out to more friends, has a dog she loves, and in general is feeling substantially less helpless and more equipped to effect changes in her life. "I'm feeling hopeful; it scares me to tell you and I want to savor it with you."

References

Beebe, B. and Lachmann, F. (2002) *Infant Research and Adult Treatment; Co-Constructing Interactions*. Hillsdale, NJ: The Analytic Press.

Brandchaft, B., Doctors, S. and Sorter, D. (2010) *Toward an Emancipatory Psychoanalysis: Brandchaft's Intersubjective Vision*. New York: Routledge.

Epstein, M. (1995) *Thoughts Without a Thinker: Psychotherapy from a Buddhist Perspective*. New York: Basic Books.

Hycner, R. and Jacobs, L. (1995) *The Healing Relationship in Gestalt Therapy*. Highland, NY: The Gestalt Journal Press.

Lowen, A. (1965) Breathing, movement and feeling: a discussion of the basic concepts underlying the work with the body in therapy. Lecture presented at the Hotel Biltmore, New York City, Fall.

Perls, F., Hefferline, R. and Goodman, P. (1951) *Gestalt Therapy*. New York: Dell Publishing.

Sanders, L. W. (2002) Thinking differently: principles of process in living systems and the specificity of being known. *Psychoanalytic Dialogues*, 12, 1: 11–42.

Sapriel, L. (1998) Can Gestalt therapy, self-psychology & intersubjectivity theory be integrated? *British Gestalt Journal*, 7, 1: 33–44.

Sapriel, L. and Palumbo, D. (2004) Psyche and culture. In T. Bar-Yoseph Levine (ed.) *The Bridge*. New Orleans, LA: Gestalt Institute Press.

Siegel, D. J. (2007) *The Mindful Brain: Reflection and Attunement in the Cultivation of Well-Being*. New York: W. W. Norton & Co.

Stolorow, R., Atwood, G. and Brandchaft, B. (1994). *The Intersubjective Perspective*. Northvale, NJ: Jason Aronson, Inc.

Van der Kolk, B. (2006) Clinical implications of neuroscience research in PTSD. Paper presented at The Embodied Mind Conference at UCLA Extension, March.

Wallin, D. J. (2007) *Attachment in Psychotherapy*. New York: The Guilford Press.

Acknowledgments

I am grateful to the following people for their invaluable contributions to my clinical thinking, writing and professional development: Bernard Brandchaft, Robert Stolorow, Judith Broder, and Bob Martin; and to Talia Bar-Yoseph Levine and Joseph G. Metscher for their on-going encouragement.

Chapter 11

The four relationships of Gestalt therapy couples work

Gary Yontef

Introduction

The gestalt literature is replete with discussion of abstract principles. There are also articles that use the gestalt therapy attitude, gestalt therapy techniques, or one principle of gestalt therapy theory. What is also needed are articles connecting the major principles of gestalt therapy with clinical applications. This chapter does this with couples work. There are articles and books on couples, some within the gestalt therapy sphere, but what is needed is a discussion of how to apply the paradoxical theory of change, phenomenological exploration, dialogic relationship, and active experiment together in a clinical application. Moreover, there is a need to discuss how these principles are applied in working with couples as opposed to the individual therapy focus to which the principles are usually applied. This chapter starts to address this as yet unmet need.

This chapter will focus on how gestalt therapy principles guide work with couples. I will discuss how the principles of dialogic contact, awareness (especially the phenomenological method), and the paradoxical theory of change organize gestalt therapy work with couples and how these principles apply differently in work with couples compared to individual therapy. My approach is a contemporary relational perspective and includes a discussion of appreciation of differences, destructive couples' cycles, and the importance of recognition of character patterns. I end with clinical examples.

Although I use heterosexual marriage language for ease of discussion, the principles are equally applicable to gay and lesbian marriages, married and unmarried couples, and "couples" of different arrangements, e.g., a three-person "marriage."

Working with couples is a natural extension of gestalt therapy principles. It has been a most significant and satisfying part of my work for 45 years. Gestalt therapy principles provide excellent support for assimilating many observations and interventions suggested by writers such as Gottman, Wile, Schnarch, Johnson, and Perel. Making the adaptations necessary to do effective couples work illuminates the nature, variety and range of gestalt therapy. The range of possible gestalt therapy approaches to couples can be seen by the very different approach to couples of gestalt therapists Michael Vincent Miller (1995) and Robert Lee (2007).

Contact times four

contact . . . is the simplest and first reality.
(Perls et al. 1994/1951: 3)

Gestalt therapy focuses on the immediacy of contact between therapist and patient. Organizing principles for a gestalt therapist are "meeting" the patient, clarifying immediate experience, making sense together of the patient's life, and then experimenting (Yontef and Bar Joseph 2008). The paradoxical theory of change states that one changes by knowing and accepting oneself and not by trying to be who one is not (Beisser 1970). In accordance with this belief, the therapist does not aim for directed change but rather enables growth to emerge from dialogic contact, focused awareness, and phenomenological experimenting (Yontef 1998).

Dialogue in gestalt therapy is usually discussed in the context of individual therapy. But the dialogic principles of inclusion, authentic presence, and commitment to dialogue apply in all applications of gestalt therapy, including couples work.

In couples work there are simultaneously at least four relationships: There is the relationship of the therapist with each member of the couple, the relationship of the couple to each other, and the relationship of the therapist to the couple as a whole. The four relationships are always going on simultaneously. Good therapy work with couples requires picking an effective but shifting focus while establishing and nurturing all four relationships.

In individual therapy the therapist–patient relationship can receive prolonged attention, individual processes can be allowed to run their course, and this process can be a model or learning opportunity that the patient can apply in his or her life outside the therapy room. But whereas in individual therapy the important relationships in the patient's life might be the subject of work in the session, in couples work a large part of the patient's environment is actually present in the room. In couples work the marital relationship is present in the session and the application of the learning to the patient's life starts right in the session.

The dialogic principles are the same in couples as in the individual. The therapist meets the patients to make sense together rather than a programmatic attempt aiming to make them different. Growth emerges from aware contact, dialogue, and experimentation rather than programmatically aimed at. The presence in the hour of the complexity, nuances, and difficulties in the couples system, the demand for a fix from the couple, and the dangerous volatility that sometimes manifests, create a pressure for programmatic change that requires a sophisticated understanding of the basic principles for the therapist to adequately meet the demands of the situation and be supported by gestalt therapy philosophy.

The gestalt therapy attitude of creative contact and experimenting allows for a variety of styles. One style is to work exclusively with the contact between the partners in the room during the hour, exclusively focusing on the process of how the couple interacts. Even in this style, the therapist still must establish and maintain a relationship with each individual as well as with the couple as a whole. If the therapist insists on limiting focus to the interaction in a prescribed treatment sequence, it is a form of aiming at the therapist's preconceived view of a proper focus. This form of aiming may well miss the connection with one or both of the individuals in the relationship. This aiming by the therapist does not fully attend to all four relationships that must be a part of top level couples work.

My experience is that if this style is strictly adhered to, individual therapy for one or both of the couple may be required prior or concurrent with the couples work not only for the conjoint therapy to be effective, but also for it not to make the situation worse.

The strict interactive focus can be effective when the patients have the support to observe/reflect, to receive the therapist's observations on their process, to examine and be open with themselves and their partner about their vulnerable reactions, and are open to experimenting. But often the individual members of the couple do not have the skill or the personality organization to do this. Sometimes the partners are so bitter and hurt that they cannot fruitfully engage in the interactive approach. In fact, sometimes this interaction becomes destructive and makes the marital situation worse.

I prefer to mix work on the contact between the couple in the room here-and-now with work about their relationship out of the here-and-now and one-to-one work on issues arising from the interaction. This approach has more flexibility, can be more supportive, and the work can go deeper than a strictly interactive focus. Working with one in the conjoint session creates the opportunity to bring more understanding to what one person brings to the session, understanding what is triggered in the interaction, what one truly wants in the interaction, deconstruct how the person copes with these processes.

The mixed approach requires that the therapist understand the phenomenal experience of both partners, how the interactive system operates, and to spontaneously and flexibly shift focus and contact. Working with one partner brings both the opportunity and the necessity of also working with the other partner and with their interactive process.

This is an advanced perspective that is layered and complex. For example, work with one partner in conjoint session is influenced by the presence of the other. Some patients react with "good behavior," or opposite that, rage or fear preventing the kind of exploration that might be possible in an individual session. But sometimes the individual feels safer with the partner present and the exploration in the conjoint session is more effective than in an individual session.

Whichever of these individual and interactive processes arise, the therapist has to organize around all four of the relationships. As the therapist works with one, there is an impact on the significant other who is in the room. Working persistently, patiently, kindly with one party to get clear, and connected, practicing inclusion, giving voice to what is experienced, imagining the other person's experienced reality, has an impact on the other member of the couple.

What is that impact? There are a wide variety of reactions. Sometimes the other is pleased because the spouse is examining his or her part in problematic exchanges and therefore feels less blamed and more hopeful. Sometimes the other is touched and has a loving response. Sometimes the other will jump to the defense of the spouse that they themselves were attacking. But sometimes the other is pleased because the therapist is now seen as placing the blame on the other – and glad that the spouse is being "picked on." Of course, these all give a perspective on the system, and how the system operates outside the therapeutic hour, and is a basis for further exploration.

As one spouse works to own his or her previously unaware displacements and transference, a healthy move away from the old stuck system, the partner might not be able to listen without feeling blamed, needing to fix it, or even using the exploration of the other as an opening to attack. Sometimes the observing spouse will feel angry that the interactive time is being taken by the other, wanting the other to have their own individual therapy.

Contemporary advanced understanding requires the therapist to be aware and work with the complexity of the four relationships as they develop and change through the course of the therapy.

Phenomenological attitude and the paradoxical theory of change

Dialogic engagement is necessary for effective gestalt therapy, but not sufficient. A task orientation and methodology for working on the task are also necessary. The major task in gestalt therapy is working for awareness, including awareness of the awareness process. In gestalt therapy, contact is the relational vehicle for that exploration.

That exploration is organized by a phenomenological method. The aim is to help the individuals discriminate what they actually experience from what they habitually assume, guess, interpret, and were told to believe; to discriminate actual experience from mere verbalization.

How do we know what people actually experience? We know what people actually experience from the "work" of phenomenological exploration, i.e., focusing and phenomenological experimenting. It is not that the therapist knows and tells the patient what he or she "really experiences." The work is organized around description in which the practitioner puts aside the certainty that beliefs, biases, thoughts, interpretations, and so forth reflect objective reality. This creates an opening for new awareness. In other words, the patients explore with therapist support and skill to establish what their actual experience is. The test of this is the patient's own experience and not the interpretation of any other person, including the therapist.

Couples therapy is psychotherapy and what is revealed in the awareness work within the conjoint work often also sheds light on how the person functions in other contexts. The process of refining what one feels, observes, thinks, needs, senses, intuits applies in any context. As actual experience is clarified, communicated, and tested, behavior can be increasingly based on an aware sense of agency, a deeper sense of self and the world, with the person learning how to be more aware.

Appreciation of differences

Appreciation of differences is a central value in gestalt therapy and essential in healthy functioning. Differences between people are respected in gestalt therapy as a source of novelty and growth. In contemporary gestalt therapy with its clarification of relational epistemology and refined relational practice, respecting, valuing, appreciating differences is fundamental. Appreciation is central to dialogue. It is also a part of the open attitude of gestalt therapy phenomenology in which differences are accepted as valid phenomena. This is especially useful in cross-cultural contact (Bar-Yoseph Levine 2005).

This value is central in working with couples. If differences are not accepted, valued, the alternative is either unhealthy confluence or the demand for such. If the sameness is achieved, then the possibilities of excitement and growth are sacrificed. This would mean choosing the comfort and safety of confluence over the risk of intimacy, experimentation, novelty, excitement, and change.

Some of the vitality in marriages is the tension of complementary temperaments of the partners. But it is frequently also at the heart of marital discord. For example, what happens when a man of even and dependable temperament is together with a woman of passion? A happy outcome is a mix of his regularity and her variability. In the less optimal arrangement she uses her passion to put him down for his temperament and he puts her down for being hysterical and irrational. In one gay couple, one partner was an engineer and the other an artist, each functioning consistent with the stereotype. A key to progress was each moving from a defensive attack on the other to appreciation of what they have to offer each other.

Optimally, the contact and awareness work results in an appreciation of differences, a respect for the validity of different perspectives, wishes, values. The therapist demonstrates appreciation of differences by equally valuing and confirming the phenomenal validity of both partners, i.e., not taking sides. In couples work the recognition of differences and awareness of the process of how the couple deals with differences is central.

In individual therapy the individuals with the difference are the therapist and patient. The therapist has the dual role of participant and facilitator. But in conjoint session, the differences between the spouses exhibits in the room and the therapist is facilitator. Intolerance of differences has to be explored and hopefully what emerges from the unpacking of the old gestalt is a new one in which differences are valued. If the particular differences between the spouses do not form a more acceptable system, the couple is likely to either be in a dissatisfying long-term marriage or divorce.

In older style gestalt therapy work, with its confrontive and cathartic emphasis, the paucity of dialogic inclusion, and a lack of emphasis on the therapist having his or her own therapy, there was more danger of the therapist subtly, or not so subtly, taking sides in couples work. A lack of sufficient attention to the four relationships often doomed the couples therapy in that style.

Aiming, e.g., to insist on a set model, either from a manualized approach or from a bias of the therapist, usually means neglecting some aspect of the four relationships and thus limiting the effectiveness of the couples work.

Destructive cycles

One of the relational patterns that must be effectively dealt with early in therapy is escalating negativity. The chain of events has to be interrupted so that the rapid escalation and its basis can be brought into awareness and possibilities of more fruitful contact experimented with. Often there are also issues of physical safety that necessitate early interruption of the escalating negative cycle.

Passionate, open, and direct fighting can resolve and result in establishing and keeping intimacy and positive passion alive in a long-term relationship. But the destructive escalating type of fighting, in which the deepest emotions are interrupted and in which each partner does not allow him or herself to be positively influenced by the other, does not have this positive result and over time often gives rise to a marital situation beyond repair. The alternative of suppressing the fighting often results in alienation, seething resentment, and passive-aggressive tendencies. The destructive escalating and the fight suppressing styles both predict either a long-term unhappy relationship or divorce.

Gestalt therapy methodology of awareness includes bringing into awareness interruptions of important thoughts, feeling, sensations, needs, and observations. I think of this as "interrupting the interruption" so that the patient can be aware of this process and thus be able to exercise choice. This therapeutic interruption brings the awareness process itself into awareness.

All through the destructive marital cycles there is self-interruption. There is often an interruption of awareness of feeling hurt or scared, interruption of knowing the intent to hurt the other, interruption of awareness of power, motivation, interruption of shame affect, and so forth. There are also interactive interruptions such as interrupting the other person when they are talking, paying no attention to the other, paying attention only to argue with the other, controlling by retroflecting, and so on.

Example[1]

George and Bob repeatedly escalated from hello to rage; from what could have been a momentary lack of communication or awkward disconnection, their faces became flushed with rage and they stopped talking to each other. Resentment was in the air. How did it happen?

George: Came home from work, tired, stressed, not very responsive or talkative. This is not a rare occurrence. George does not appreciate the impact his mood and behavior has on Bob.

Bob: Takes this personally, but his self-image is that such things do not bother him, he is "thick-skinned." He interrupts awareness of his deeper experience of rejection and not getting the love and respect that he needs. His responses are fueled by the out-of-awareness conflict between his desires and George's state of mind.

Bob: What's wrong with you tonight? (Attacking, angry tone.)

George: Nothing. (Sullen, unresponsive tone.)

Bob: You are in one of your moods again. (Sarcastic, tone is even angrier.)

George: And you are being a jerk again. You always do that. Can't I get a few minutes of peace? (The name-calling is provocative to Bob.)

Bob: I just wanted a little contact. You are impossible.

As I helped George clarify what was causing his unresponsive state, Bob was a bit more receptive. I worked with Bob to get a deeper understanding of how he was affected, and this led to George being clearer about how important George's love was for Bob and Bob telling George how much he loved him, ... which was very healing for George. The words and demeanors of both

> were influenced by the deeper level of sharing that supported more awareness and vulnerability by George and Bob individually but also supported a pattern of being receptively influenced by the feelings of the other.

Character pathology

As in any psychotherapy, working with couples in gestalt therapy must take into account the organization of the personalities of the participants, especially those with borderline, narcissistic, or schizoid personality organization (Yontef 1993, 2001). The spouse of someone with a borderline personality organization may need help in understanding the often mystifying splitting process. "I don't get it. Last week she loved me and I was the greatest. Today I am the devil. How can I believe she loves me when she then says that I am the devil?" Both partners need help in holding both parts of the split (Yontef 1993).

Examples

These examples illustrate how the therapist must relate to both individuals and to the interaction.

> Betty and Carl. Betty frequently raged at her husband Carl both in session and out. My attempts to have Betty and Carl talk with each other and guide their interaction toward good relational practice were not productive. The interaction between them was too acrimonious; they both felt too injured, shamed, despairing, and overwhelmed. I recommended individual therapy for both of them. They did not follow that recommendation.
>
> In individual therapy I might make contact with Betty at first largely via empathic reflections, giving voice to feelings, thoughts, and associations generating the rage. These might be fright, hurt, shame, guilt, etc. With time what hopefully would emerge would be a clearer sense of the core configuration, deeper awareness and motivation, support by the patient for real dialogue, support for experimenting with other ways of being, and so forth. This would take patience, and development over time, focusing on "objective" reality, e.g., if the spouse is really as unreasonable as the raging patient believes, could be postponed if indicated.
>
> But, while Betty is in conjoint therapy with Carl not individual therapy, she needed me as she would in individual, i.e., to establish contact marked by

empathic reflection, to help her feel understood and accepted and to become aware of her core feelings. In the room with Carl, the person she is so angry at, she often does not feel safe enough to pause to allow the work we could have done if it were just the two of us in the room.

As I worked in the conjoint sessions with Betty, I was concerned with how Carl was affected. Did Carl feel neglected when the focus was not on him, that I was siding with Betty, or might he have been relieved and glad to be out of the spotlight – or firing line? Or, perhaps Carl might have taken it as Betty being "the problem." He might be compassionate or on the other hand might use her vulnerability against her. I needed to be alert to these possible reactions.

Carl used any opening to establish his superiority, being right; he was often condescending and shaming. In the face of this, Betty did not feel safe enough to let down her aggressive defenses. In working with Carl in the conjoint session we were able to bring awareness to what turned out to be a shame process that he defended against by shaming others. Over some months of work, Carl showed more insight, became more reflective, and talked to Betty without the condescension and shaming.

In turn Betty was able to identify hurtful or shameful triggers in the interaction and bring this to Carl's attention in real time in a way that he could hear. Betty often feels rejected and unloved by Carl. This has meaning in the context of her history of parental abandonment, abuse, and the resultant sense of being worthless and unlovable. Her rage covers a sense of impotence.

Carl was unskilled in recognizing and expressing emotions. While Betty wanted more, Carl felt threatened and tended to withdraw. This is a classic female-demand, male-withdraw pattern. Before our work, the angrier she got, the more he shut down, judged and criticized her; the more he judged and withdrew, the more ashamed and angry that she got. I interrupted this circular causality to share my observation and suggested experiments both in session and between sessions. We were able to successfully interrupt the circular causality and then the work on other aspects of their marital situation went much better.

The message here is that the therapist who works with one partner in the conjoint session has to observe, inquire, and work with the observing spouse while keeping in mind the couples' relational process. In this work the therapist must be able to move between focus on explicating the underlying meaning of an individual's behavior, the impact of the other on that person, and a focus with a wider lens in which the therapist observes and suggests observation and discussion of, and experiments, with the system as a whole.

Teri and Sam. Sam tends to withdraw, e.g., when he comes home from work. In the best of times he tends not to be very reflective or expressive of emotions or needs. Teri is more emotionally oriented and expressive. After being home with the children, and household chores, all day, she is hungry for adult contact. Understanding both of these individual subjectivities is rather easy. But how do they operate as a system?

Like Betty and Carl, their interaction manifests circular causality. Teri wants contact at the very time that Sam wants time alone. The more she demands, the more he withdraws. The more he withdraws, the more upset and demanding she gets. And so they escalate.

If both were well self-supported, and generally loving in their relationship, the specific problem of coping with the immediate entry of the working spouse into the household, a time in which commonly the house spouse is tired and the children difficult, could be handled pragmatically. But in the situation with Sam and Teri, as with many couples, this circular causality is not only in this specific situation, but recurrent and common in how they relate to each other.

For Teri, Sam's isolating defenses not only leave her feeling deprived, but also it triggers an old shameful sense of being unlovable. She defends against this by her criticism and attacks on Sam. Sam feels not appreciated, under attack, and unable to give Teri the emotional connection that she desires. For him it triggers a resentment of being trapped and never appreciated for what he does. There is a deep sense of inadequacy, shame, about his inability to feel and be passionate and he also has a belief that if he were a "real man" he would not tolerate such treatment.

The therapist has to establish, maintain and deepen a connection with both Teri and Sam, while also relating to the system in which each feels victimized and each is also a part of the negative circular causality in which they are trapped. The principle is to engage and not to aim; to observe and make sense of how they interact; and to experiment based on what emerges from the contact and emerging awareness.

Unlike Betty and Carl, Teri and Sam were able to work by contact with each other. We observed the process together. We experimented. For example I suggested that as an experiment they acknowledge what they heard the other saying before they responded, and then saying how they were emotionally affected. Of course, this took some psycho-educational work. As they understood the basic idea of understanding each other and responding with how they feel, both Teri and Sam were open to be influenced by the experience of the other. In many couples they are not, and that unwillingness or inability to be influenced by the other, to take the point of view of the other into account, becomes the focus for exploration. With Teri and Sam I suggested another experiment in which they could practice being in touch with their immediate experience, make here-and-now contact based on that awareness, and receive the same from the other. I suggested they move close enough to touch knees and talk to each other only expressing what they experience here-and-now and not asking questions. This was defined to include observations (not interpretations) and personal sensations, affect, desires, and imagery.

Harriet and George. George is a bright, intellectually oriented man that needs to be right, is rigid, pejorative, and abrasive in his mode of being right. This alternately makes Harriet angry, hopeless, depressed, and ashamed of not being able to deal better with George. I observe this in session. Exploration led him to become aware of an underlying shame process that his pejorative behavior kept out of his awareness. He also became aware that this behavior got him the opposite of what he wanted and needed. As this became increasingly clearer and his self-support increased, he realized that he also exhibited this pejorative attitude at work and this had alienated others and led people to be reluctant to promote him.

The awareness work has to include awareness at the level of interaction of the two, how the system as a whole works. Needed change that emerges primarily from the reflective/empathic work with each individual often gets sidetracked or overwhelmed, sabotaged by the interactions. George started to respond to the work in the conjoint session on his shame and shame defense, started to be open to getting his own therapy, was softening somewhat. As he did, Harriet's long pent up anger erupted. Rather than recognizing, supporting, being pleased at the changes George was making, it provided an opportunity for her to lay into George and let out her long pent up anger. With that aggression coming at him, George reverted to his less vulnerable, more familiar, more aggressive mode. Soon they were doing the same old thing and getting the same old results. As I worked with Harriet at the level of her more vulnerable feelings underlying her anger, George was able to restore the gains he had made in the therapy and she was able to talk to him rather than at him.

Discussion

As in individual and group gestalt therapy, new behavior can be suggested as experiments. This gestalt therapy use of phenomenological experimentation enables active interventions and organized new behavior without the therapist becoming an agent to programmatic, predetermined, or manualized change. If the therapist is really committed to phenomenological exploration, can explain and teach the phenomenological attitude, then the work on awareness in a dialogic and phenomenological mode can proceed. This requires treating whatever is reported or observed from the experiment as data that informs without judgment or demand to change. Difficulties can then be seen as phenomena worthy of exploration, data pointing the way to further exploration, rather than a resistance to the program, therapist, or change.

Gestalt therapy enables the blending of reflective talk, focusing, and experimentation. Often the therapist has to guide and teach, e.g., about the awareness process so that the patient can recognize the process of emerging awareness or active avoidance of awareness when these processes occur. Thoughts or feelings that otherwise get lost often come into awareness via phenomenological experiment. Sometimes fear, shame, guilt, anger come into awareness rather than the defense against these feelings. Sometimes softer, vulnerable more affectionate, loving feelings emerge.

With couples that talk without real contact, it is sometimes helpful to pose an experiment, e.g. the one I had suggested to Teri and Sam: Bring the chairs face-to-face until your knees touch, talk to each other just saying what you experience at the moment. No questions of each other, just here-and-now reports. If they agree to the experiment, and then can't do it, this is valuable information. If they start, then we can observe what happens, observe the working of their process.

From this particular experiment I have had couples make soft and loving contact, cry, say "Hey, I didn't know you felt that way," and so forth. Sometimes what is learned, what I learn, is that my timing is off, this couple does not have some of the requisite foundational skills, or sense of safety, and that my emphasis needs to be slower, with smaller steps, and more support building.

What is important here is that we can work creatively through dialogue, focusing, and experimentation in the context of full attention to all four relationships.

Note

1 All clinical examples are composites of actual clinical work with several couples.

References

Bar-Yoseph Levine, T. (ed.) (2005) *The Bridge – Dialogues Across Cultures*. New Orleans: Gestalt Institute Press.

Beisser, A. (1970) The paradoxical theory of change. In J. Fagan and I. Shepherd

(eds) *Gestalt Therapy Now* (pp. 77–80). New York: Harper. Online. Available: www.gestalttherapy.org
Lee, R. (2007) *The Secret Language of Intimacy: Releasing the Hidden Power in Couple Relationships*. Mahwah, NJ: Analytic Press.
Miller, M. V. (1995) *Intimate Terrorism: The Deterioration of Erotic Life*. New York: W. W. Norton & Company.
Perls, F., Hefferline, R. and Goodman, P. (1994/1951) *Gestalt Therapy: Excitement and Growth in the Human Personality*. Highland, NY: The Gestalt Journal Press. Originally (1951) New York: Julian Press.
Yontef, G. (1993) *Awareness, Dialogue and Process: Essays in Gestalt Therapy*. Highland, NY: Gestalt Journal Press.
—— (1998) Dialogic Gestalt therapy. In L. Greenberg, G. Lietaer and J. Watson (eds) *Handbook of Experiential Psychotherapy*. New York: Guilford Publications.
—— (2001) Psychotherapy of schizoid process. *Transactional Analysis Journal*, 31, 1: 7–23.
Yontef, G. and Bar Yoseph, T. (2008) Dialogic relationship. Chapter 9. In P. Brownell (ed.) *Handbook for Theory, Research, and Practice in Gestalt Therapy* (pp. 184–197). UK: Cambridge Scholars Publishing.

Chapter 12

Gestalt family therapy: a field perspective

Brian O'Neill

Family therapy has developed as a specific form of therapy which works with the family as a whole, as well as individual members. It is a therapy, or grouping of therapies, based primarily on systems theory and the application of cybernetics.

There are significant similarities between the worldviews of family therapy and gestalt therapy and it is initially surprising that more has not been written about gestalt family therapy. What seems to have restricted the application of gestalt therapy in working with families is the skewed development of gestalt therapy itself. While it began as a field perspective and broadly equated to a systemic perspective, gestalt therapy tended originally to translate to an individualistic clinical practice and paradoxically resulted in authors describing how to bridge the individualistic paradigm of gestalt therapy to systems theory (Armstrong 1988; Lynch and Lynch 2005; Zinker 1994).

Applying the gestalt approach to family therapy carries a challenge when linking to systems theory of not losing the uniqueness of the gestalt approach or contravening its core principles of practice. This is particularly difficult when family therapy has a well established and strong theory base which can tend to overshadow the uniqueness of gestalt therapy. Indeed some of the writing in gestalt family therapy appears as an adjunct to the family therapy approach, or an amalgam (Lynch and Lynch 2005; Zinker 1994), rather than a unique application of the principles of gestalt therapy to working with families. Others such as Kempler (1974) developed their own unique theory of gestalt family therapy based primarily on their practice, without the current emphasis on aspects such as dialogue and the field perspective.

This processes of amalgamation of the gestalt therapy theory with systems theory has arisen, it can be argued, because a theory of practice of gestalt therapy has been absent (Parlett 1993), particularly in relation to the field perspective. What has been described as contemporary gestalt the last decade or so has been an articulation of the field and dialogical perspectives and to refine or better describe field theory in linking theory to practice

(Latner 1983; O'Neill and Gaffney 2008; Parlett 1993; Staemmler 2006; Yontef 1993).

These current developments in gestalt therapy pave the way to apply and articulate a theory of practice of gestalt family therapy, building on the current writing on the field perspective, as well as the ascendancy of the dialogical influence. This is further supported by the increasing numbers of gestalt therapists choosing to extend beyond an individualist work practice and work with couples, families, groups and organizations. It is of particular note that Philippson (2002) pioneered a perspective of gestalt family therapy based not on the similarities with systems theory and as an amalgam, but based on his conceptualization of field theory. The importance of this is that, as well as noting the similarities between these two approaches, Philippson has described the differences between systems theory and field theory.

Understanding what works in family therapy – the importance of our worldview

The importance of the development of the field perspective in gestalt therapy is relevant in the support it provides to the teaching, supervision and practice of gestalt family therapy.

There is much that has been written about family therapy from other modalities, particularly systems theory, and much that has been researched. Simons (2006) states that the field of family therapy finds itself still unable to answer the critical question of what it is that makes family therapy work. He notes:

> The two dominant approaches to answering this question, the common-factors perspective and the model specific factors perspective, remain divided at this juncture by a fundamental difference of emphasis between the two.
>
> (Simons 2006: 331)

He proposes a way of integrating these two perspectives is through the hypothesis that the therapists achieve maximum effectiveness by committing themselves to a family therapy model of proven efficacy whose underlying worldview closely matches their own personal worldview.

This co-created process of worldview and principles matching the lived practice of the therapist is in keeping with research on outcome studies, particularly in areas such as domestic violence. Current research in domestic and family violence indicates that the relationship between the therapist and client system is paramount and is affected by the lens of the therapist (Alexander and Morris 2008; Levesque et al. 2008; Murphy and Maiuro 2008; Musser et al. 2008). In this context a clearer application of these developments in the gestalt field perspective to family therapy is timely and opportune.

The field perspective in gestalt family therapy

The field theory found in the seminal text (Perls et al. 1951) was presented not as a field *theory* but an ontological statement about reality – that the field is real. This is in accord with similar writing in physics, where the field was originally viewed as a model or representation, and was then declared to be real with the advent of Maxwell's four equations of the electromagnetic field (Bohm and Hiley 1993; Einstein and Infield 1938; O'Neill 2008).

An alternative field perspective in gestalt therapy has been based on the work of Lewin (1936) which offers the field as a theoretical epistemology, a method for understanding reality but not the reality itself – like a map – or, as Lewin termed it, similar to a handicraft.

In our current writing (O'Neill and Gaffney 2008) we have stressed that each of these perspectives are valid and are useful to inform practice. We gathered together the main commonalities and presented them as a field perspective, outlining the principles and practices which accord with both approaches and present a more unified and practical approach to field theory.

The following section outlines interlocking theoretical precepts which delineate the principles of the field perspective and their application to family therapy. It begins by outlining the principles of an integrative perspective, followed then by family therapy practices which flow from these principles.

Principles of gestalt family therapy from a field perspective

The following section outlines interlocking theoretical principles which inform and guide the work of gestalt therapists in working with families and that delineate the attitudes and practices utilized in the field perspective as defined by O'Neill and Gaffney (2008). What follows is a brief review of these principles and how they relate to gestalt family therapy.

Principle – the self as process

Gestalt therapy described the person as a fluid part of an organism/environment field. This does not take away the sense of separateness experienced by each person but contextualizes the experience of self within a wider field. As stated by Perls et al. (1951) in the seminal text: "The self is a system of contacts in the organism/environment field" (p. 228).

More importantly for gestalt family therapy, this theoretical perspective articulates wider "selves" or organisms similar to a biologist who may study a bee hive and not just the bee. Hence when two or more people become systematized in their contact with each other, they are a *self* from a gestalt perspective. When a couple births a child, the self of the family is also born and with that a wider, more complex system of contacts in the field.

Principle – the whole determines the parts

This principle finds commonality with principles in systems theory in family therapy. The subtle difference (which also carries through to practice) is that systems theory models attend to the dynamics *between* the people in the system, as compared to the field perspective which *works with the family as a whole*, as an entity in itself. The stereotyping of models in this way is purely a convenience to gain a sense of the difference between perspectives, with the acceptance that therapists may work and act with families from a variety of perspectives.

Systems theory is well aware of the impact of the system on the individuals in the family. The additional aspect of the gestalt perspective is to view the family as a "self" with *agency* as a "self." This is not dissimilar to where the current wave of family therapy is today, however from this perspective the gestalt approach offers ways of being with and a part of the wider "self" of the family plus therapist.

Principle – the parts determine the whole

As a mirror of the previous principle, this principle enunciates the importance of the elements of the whole, the impact of each family member on the overall family and the awareness, dialogue and movement between each for the therapist. The focus is therefore on *the relationship between* the whole and the elements or what systems theory calls sub systems (parents, adults, partners, children and individuals).

There are times when for example the therapist will attend to the importance of the singularity and uniqueness of the person, while at other times noting the relationship of the individual to the family or sub systems. This movement between the individual, sub systems and family is a choice of the therapist and there are times when the needs of the individual outweigh the needs of the family or sub system and other times when the family or sub system needs outweigh those of the individual.

Principle – the wisdom of the organism

The gestalt approach in seeing the family as an organism, a self, carries the premise that such an organism has an inbuilt wisdom, just like any other self or organism. Gestalt therapy sees the figure/ground formation (when allowed to operate unobstructed) as a process which attends to the immediate needs of the organism.

Families usually come to therapy with this figure/ground flow diminished in some way – fixed gestalten and redundant creative adjustments – and hence the work of the therapist is to assist the family to access their homeostatic and growth processes. This principle is also articulated by Zinker (1994) and Lynch and Lynch (2005) as in keeping with a blended gestalt and systemic approach. While they note there are differences in style with how this principle is applied, there is also space for creative intervention and direction by the therapist, as the therapist is also now part of the family system.

Principle – paradoxical agency

Paradoxical agency from the stance of the therapist is a key element or attitude of the gestalt approach to family therapy. After teaching gestalt therapy for close to three decades it is apparent that perhaps the biggest challenge in learning this approach is the movement of the student/therapist away from attempting to control and influence the therapy process to a therapeutic space of being present, aware and responsive in the field.

This is a paradoxical process of searching for balance between choice and acceptance and is described in the original text of PHG as the "middle mode" – the space between active and passive functioning, where the person is accepting, attending and growing into the solution, and the substitution of readiness (or faith) for the security of apparent control (Perls, Hefferline, and Goodman 1951).

Principle – needs organize the field

Perls et al. (1951) described two prime needs of the organism to be those of growth and homeostasis. Lewin presented an interesting addendum to this process in that the phenomenology of the organism (individual, or family) also plays a part in how the field is perceived. Hence a clump of trees in a field is seen as needing to be removed by a farmer, used as shelter by a soldier and a place for romance by a couple.

The gestalt therapist may note that while each individual in the process has their own individual needs (love, attention, etc.) these may not be the need of the family as a whole (i.e. mother attending to baby, adult children leaving home, etc.). Being able to have a bi-focal lens and note the patterns of individual and family process allows the therapist to work not only with the individuals and the relationships between them, but the family as a whole. From this awareness the family and its members can now choose and accommodate processes of the family organism of which they are a part, as well as the individuals in their own life space.

Principle – harmony within chaos: nothing unconnected ever happens

The field perspective requires the therapist to attend to what is figural or stands out and the process by which the family and its members pattern or make sense of what becomes figural for them. Frequently what is brought to therapy is the struggle of any organism to attend to conflicting figures, such as love and hate, or attachment and need for separateness.

Being attuned to and aware of these patterns of contact supports us as therapists to make sense of what appear paradoxical and self defeating behaviors, and understand families are doing what they do from some sense of need which is attempting to creatively adjust to the environment. Parlett (2005) states that as gestalt therapists we know that much of what seems inconsequential is in fact organized; that is, it is meaningful in some context of which we may be partially or completely unaware.

These patterns are harmonics within the apparent chaos of the family dynamics and underlie the initial problem in the family. These are the patterns of contact which develop, particularly when the environment is not meeting the needs and the organism must adjust creatively. From this principle the stance of a gestalt therapist is one of a phenomenological attunement to the organizing patterns of the life of the family, the individuals and other selves (i.e. couple, parent and child sub systems).

Gestalt family therapy

The next section outlines the way in which a gestalt therapist, working from a contemporary field perspective, would be guided to use these principles in the practice of family therapy.

The genesis of the family

The field perspective of gestalt therapy offers the therapist a lens to view the life of a family and the challenges each life stage brings. Today there are many variants of the traditional family, including single parent families, same sex parent families, step families, blended families and separated parent families, so much so that a household of two originally partnered people with their own children is close to becoming a fringe group. However for the sake of parsimony I will describe the traditional process of family development of a couple who decide to have a child.

From a field perspective the "self" of the family first becomes figural when, traditionally, a child becomes part of the parent system – in other words when the couple decides to have a baby. For simplicity the traditional (and Western) notion of the family will be used as this is simple. The identity of the mother and father start changing as they anticipate becoming "parents." Similarly the identity of the couple begins to change as the couple now becomes a "family."

Even after the child is born the couple are, for a long time, still the more figural "self" in the household – the "couple" have a child. Yet the impact of this on the identity of the "couple" starts to become apparent and the advent of another individual into the household brings into existence a field whereby other selves may become more figural. This includes the "mother-child" self, and the "father-child" self as well as the "mother-father-child" self, or family.

This development of a couple into a family also creates heightened attachment and belonging (there are more selves to be part of) and paradoxically more potential for loss of attachment and a sense of isolation (there are more sub groups I may not belong to).

The work of the therapist

Families, in whatever form they take, either decide on or are referred to a family therapist because one or more of the people in the family are experiencing some form of disorder. This is also evidently connected to processes within the family as a whole which cause the individual to seek help.

Much of what a family brings to therapy is initially hidden or implicit. The work of the therapist is to attend to and be aware of the experience of these implicit realities of the field of the family, particularly in how they manifest for the therapist in their own felt experience and imagery, as well as the external figure ground formation of client and therapist. Hence in working phenomenologically the therapist needs to attend to her own experience of self in the family/therapist field and not only noticing what the family and the individuals do.

Like a compass which picks up and discloses "invisible" magnetic fields, the compass needles of proprioceptive experience, imagery and external figure ground formation can be the guides to the therapist in this more intimate setting of family therapy work. The work of the therapist is to be aware of, attend to and experiment with these rich figures which present.

There are four ways of being as a therapist which are practiced by all gestalt therapists and which indicate that they are operating from a field perspective (O'Neill and Gaffney 2008). These are titled – field sensitive practice; field insightful practice; field affective practice; and the practice of being field present.

The following section will now explore these as they relate to family therapy from a field perspective.

Field sensitive practice – being aware of the field of the family and therapist

A field sensitive approach in practice is one which the therapist attends to whatever becomes figural even though it may not at first seem organized or meaningful. This means trusting in the emerging figure, knowing that eventually patterns will emerge and will start to make sense. This is learning not to "force" a pattern or meaning, nor to attempt to work it out analytically or cognitively, but to allow meaning to emerge from the field and within a dialogue with the family. In the life space of the family we discover meaning in the way in which they individually and collectively organize their world and their hidden or implicit needs and drives become understandable and explanatory.

For example if a child is having trouble with school, how does each member of the family and the family as a whole make sense of this? One parent may sound understanding, another parent critical and a sibling may make jibes. There may be no clear meaning for the family as a whole. If we hear from the child that they are being bullied (for example) this may alter the meaning for the individuals and family as a whole – both parents may become supportive and outraged at the school and the sibling likewise may want to stand up for their younger sibling. The family as a whole may demonstrate a solidarity and protection with the underlying meaning that "we might attack each other but no one may attack our family" etc.

So as the phenomenology of one is understood (the child), the phenomenology of the family as whole can change and the patterns of meaning which separate the family and draw it together start to emerge – a picture of how the family views the world and events that happen, particularly here and now. Hence with phenomenological exploration the therapist may support the individuals to shift from their own separate life spaces to a more connected and collective one, enabling each member to become more sensitive to the life space of the other. These individual shifts also bring about a shift for the family as a whole, creating a greater sense of solidarity and sensitivity to each other's life space.

Field insightful – making sense of the family and of how they make sense of the world and each other

The application of being field insightful is evident when gestalt therapists enquire about a wide field of influence and possibility of connection, keeping a fluid openness to the possible interconnection of people, events and situations. There is also the practice of giving relevance to each event as not random but ordered and to seek to make explicit this order by enquiry and experiment. In this way the gestalt therapist is constantly an action researcher, finding out the meaning and connections being made by the family through inquiry in an experimental cyclical fashion, very much in the same way a systemic family therapist does.

Like physics, this attitude in gestalt therapy is one which is relativistic and where while a separate reality may exist, the person will always have a relative view of this within the field. Thus gestalt therapists will accept that while they may feel their view is the right one, there is space for the other view as part of a wider reality to the possibility that they are simply wrong. This does not mean giving up one's view but realizing there is more or different views being held by others. As Parlett (2005) states, there is a willingness to address and investigate the organized, interconnected, interdependent, interactive nature of complex human phenomena.

The various maps of gestalt therapy previously mentioned are applicable at this point, and each person is able to express and experience the process and theme that is developing. Usually the theme is one in which polarities are in operation and shaping the field in the same way two magnets shape a field of iron filings. For example silence in a family, when explored, may happen when people are both angry and frightened. There are the polarities of fight or flight in operation. If members are unable to express either of these we may witness a family with one or more members being depressed. As they are able to express either fear or anger safely, the link to depression becomes more evident. They can then consciously choose to withdraw or voice anger instead of being together in a silent depressed state.

The work of the gestalt therapist is to assist the family to understand and experiment with these polarities so that they do not become "fixed gestalten" which hold the family in a stuck place. Being able to understand the existence of underlying polarities, such as fight or flight, allows the family to experiment with what might happen as first one and then the other polarity is acknowledged and expressed.

Field affective

The practice of this stance is found in the enquiry of gestalt therapists about the present moment. This supports experimentation and enquiry around exploring what happens as the context changes – in what way does the self change. The therapist may encourage experimenting with themes such as exploring what might happen if one told another they were hurt as well as angry – what is this like? This is guided by techniques of exaggeration/ reversal and repetition/reformulation of apparent polarities.

An example of this may be in how each family member tolerates the polarities of love and hate. A family that maintains a strong sense of love for each other but does not tolerate anger requires individual and collective creative adjustments to "deal with" anger. These of course can take many forms and as the family have the opportunity to "be angry" without needing to creatively adjust or take it out of the family, they find ultimately that the closeness of the family paradoxically grows. In other cases, where anger is present regularly, its polarity may be that expression of hurt is disallowed. When hurt is allowed the field will once again change.

This willingness to experiment is a key element in gestalt therapy and offers a significant ability to both the therapist and the family to not stay stuck with repetitive cycles of behavior and instead explore different and more freeing ways of being with each other as a family. The son and father who constantly end with the father angry and the son sullen may evolve as a family when the father risks telling the son he is also hurt and the son risks saying he also loves his father.

Field present

Ultimately a field perspective which is enfolded in the practice of dialogical psychotherapy becomes a practice which is present, inclusive and committed to dialogue.

From the field perspective the therapist and family explore the experiences of having the therapist present in the intimate space of the family. As the family experience another person is present with them and that as well as the "family" there is the "family and therapist" then the work becomes apparent in its attention to dialogue. This offers an experience by the family of another person who responds to them as a family in a way that is unique and in relationship. A simple question from the therapist such as "how do you imagine I see you and even feel about you as a family" is one of significant dialogical impact and usually requires the family to be in a place where they are able to integrate and trust such feedback from the therapist.

This is a realm of work where the therapist is both a part of the family/therapist field and is also experienced by the family as an "other" – in dialogical terms as a "Thou." This then affords the therapist the possibility of a dialogical approach both with individuals within the family and the family as a whole. For example if the therapist tells the child who is being bullied that they think they are truly brave to bring this into the family, then this will affect the child, the parents, the other siblings and the family as a whole. A simple yet profound intervention from a gestalt perspective – being present with the family, including ourselves in the life of the family, being committed to be in dialogue with them and showing that how we are as therapists is something that is lived and not a technique or style of intervention alone, similar to the congruent empathy of Rogers (1961) and as detailed by the work of Martin Buber (1958).

Conclusion

The ways of being a gestalt family therapist mentioned above, of being field sensitive, insightful, affective and present, offer subtle yet key practices which define the field perspective, and add a dimension to the gestalt approach with families, as yet to be more fully explored and described.

At a philosophical and theoretical level, gestalt therapy and traditional family therapies can learn, parallel and synthesis in the rich interchange which becomes possible as the frozen or fixed gestalt melts. In systems theory terminology this can be described as the change that happens as the dominant discourse of a system or family is altered as the hidden discourse emerges. The richness and similarities between systems theory and gestalt therapy around these processes offer more possibilities for cross fertilization and enrichment.

At clinical practice level the gestalt therapist has much that can be offered in annunciating the dialogical and experimental aspects of family therapy, while the phenomenological roots of gestalt therapy are in accord with family therapy concepts of discourse and hypothesis. At a field perspective level, gestalt therapists offer the potential exploration of the subtle movements in the paradoxical elements of therapist control and surrender, and the paradoxical control discovered through surrender. Particularly in the work which is developing with couples and families where violence, control and social control are very figural, Gestalt therapy offers a paradigm which allows for heightened engagement through attunement to client needs and the explication and lived reality of the authentic self, which is a subtle living of a field perspective practice and a way of life.

References

Alexander, P. and Morris, E. (2008) Stages of change in batterers and their response to treatment. *Violence and Victims*, 23, 4: 476–494.

Armstrong, D. (1988) Gestalt therapy: a systemic approach to individual change. *Australia and New Zealand Journal of Family Therapy*, 9, 4.

Bohm, D. and Hiley, B. J. (1993) *The Undivided Universe*. London: Routledge.

Buber, M. (1958) *I–Thou*. New York: Scribner Books.

Einstein, A. and Infield, L. (1938) *The Evolution of Physics*. New York: Simon and Schuster.

Kempler, W. (1974) *Principles of Gestalt Family Therapy*. California: Kempler Institute.

Latner, J. (1983) This is the speed of light: field and systems theory in Gestalt therapy. *The Gestalt Journal*, 6, 2 (Fall): 71–90.

Levesque, D., Driskell, M., Prochaska, J. and Prochaska, J. (2008) Acceptability of a stage-matched expert system intervention for domestic violence offenders. *Violence and Victims*, 23, 4.

Lewin, K. (1936) *Principles of Topological Psychology*. New York: McGraw-Hill.

Lynch, J. and Lynch, B. (2005) Family and couples therapy from a Gestalt perspective. In A. Woldt and S. Toman (eds) *Gestalt Therapy: History, Theory and Practice*. Thousand Oaks, CA: Sage Publications.

Murphy, M. and Maiuro, R. (2008) Understanding and facilitating the change process in perpetrators and victims of intimate partner violence: summary and commentary. *Violence and Victims*, 23, 4: 525–538.

Musser, P., Semiatin, J., Taft, C. and Murphy, C. (2008) Motivational interviewing as a pregroup intervention for partner-violent men. *Violence and Victims*, 23, 5.

O'Neill, B. (2008) Post relativistic quantum field theory and gestalt therapy. *Gestalt Review*, 12, 1: 7–23.

O'Neill, B. and Gaffney, S. (2008) The application of a field perspective methodology. In P. Brownell (ed.) *Handbook for Theory, Research and Practice in Gestalt Therapy*. Cambridge: Cambridge Scholars Publishing.

Parlett, M. (1993) Towards a more Lewian gestalt therapy. *British Gestalt Journal*, 2, 2: 115–121.

—— (2005) Contemporary Gestalt therapy: field theory. In A. Woldt and S. Tomen (eds) *Gestalt Therapy: History, Theory and Practice*. Thousand Oaks, CA: Sage Publications.

Perls, F., Hefferline, R. and Goodman, P. (1951) *Gestalt Therapy: Excitement and Growth in the Human Personality*. London: Souvenir Press edition (1984).

Philippson, P. (2002) *Self in Relation*. New York: Gestalt Journal Press.

Rogers, C. (1961) *On Becoming a Person*. New York: Houghton Mifflin.

Simons, G. (2006) The heart of the matter: a proposal for placing the self of the therapist at the center of family therapy research and training. *Family Process*, 45: 331–344.

Staemmler, Frank M. (2006) A Babylonian confusion? – The term "field." *British Gestalt Journal*, 15, 1.

Yontef, G. (1993) *Awareness, Dialogue and Process: Essays of Gestalt Therapy*. New York: The Gestalt Journal Press.

Zinker, J. (1994) *In Search of Good Form: Gestalt Therapy with Couples and Families*. San Francisco: Jossey Bass.

Chapter 13

A neo-Lewinian perspective on gestalt group facilitation*

Seán Gaffney

Introduction

Kurt Lewin (1890–1947) managed, in his relatively short life, to leave behind him a legacy of influential work in many areas. Field theory, group dynamics, action research, social change – all were initiated by his inquiring mind, his research focus, practical applications and strong support for the on-going and further work of his students and associates (Marrow 1969).

The focus of this chapter is based on Lewin's field theory, an influential though historically often unacknowledged ingredient in the theory and development of gestalt therapy. Indeed, it was not until almost 50 years after the first explication of gestalt therapy (Perls, Hefferline, and Goodman 1951/1994) that Lewin's influence began to be more fully recognized (Wheeler 1991; Parlett 1991, 1993, 1997; McConville 2003; O'Neill and Gaffney 2008).

The purpose of this chapter is to explicate how a contemporary revision of the work of Kurt Lewin, integrated with such basic gestalt therapy constructs as "contact" and "self", can yield meaningful theoretical and practical advances where Gestalt with groups is concerned. In particular, a distinction is made between "life space" and "field", and the revised life space construct becomes central to the chapter. In addition, the construct "contact boundary dynamics" is introduced as a bridge between the psychopathologizing of aspects of contact in traditional gestalt therapy theory, and the more normal psychology of Lewin's person/environment.

Theoretical perspectives

An issue which arises in teaching and applying Lewin is that, while he used the terms "field" and "life space" synonymously (Staemmler 2006: 69), it is

---

* Previously published in *Gestalt at Work: Integrating Life, Theory and Practice.* Collected papers of Séan Gaffney, Volume 1. Used with permission.

possible and useful to distinguish between them. One approach here is through the distinctions between the ontological, the phenomenological and the epistemological perspectives (O'Neill and Gaffney 2008). Such an approach yields the conclusion that Lewin is primarily phenomenological and epistemological – while not discounting the ontological.

Another issue is that Lewinian field theory has been used both as a meta-theory *and* a theory in its own right (Gold 1990). In this respect, the life space of a given person is phenomenological, and a worthy subject of research based on the premises of the meta-theory. At the same time, there arises the question of how the person and environmental others of a particular life space organize the always porous and dynamically changing interaction between them, as well as between them and their "surroundings" (Staemmler 2006: 69). The "surroundings" is what Gold calls "the social facts beyond the boundary" (Gold 1990: 78), the boundary here being that which delimits the phenomenal life space relative to that which is "outside" of it. This is relevant to the earlier question of the ontological nature of the field, since the use of terms like "surroundings" or "the social facts" assumes their existence, while they are, at the same time, not – or not yet – part of the person's experience, or life space.

Georges Wollants quotes an interesting and relevant perspective on this issue:

> "Having existence for the person" is a phrase from Lewin, who, in pragmatic fashion, understands by existence anything having demonstrable effects on the person. Consequently, elements of which the client is unaware are also included to the extent that, through observation the therapist can determine that they have effects (cf. Cartwright 1952: xi–xiii).
>
> (Wollants 2008: 189)

A similar perspective is provided by Margharita Spagnuolo Lobb:

> I believe that the field in gestalt therapy has to do with this idea: it includes things (or events) we are not aware of, but which are there, and they might become aware, changing the whole perception we have of the field. The more we grow in our awareness, the more we are aware of where we belong to. The field includes the many possibilities of the phenomenological event.
>
> (Spagnuolo Lobb 2003: 53)

Mention of boundaries also raises the principal issue that traditionally-focused gestalt practitioners have with Lewin: that he is suspected of supporting the notion of fixed and closed boundaries from an intra-psychic perspective, rather than the fluid and co-created contact boundary of gestalt therapy (Bloom, personal communication, 2009). Both Staemmler's and Wollants' summaries of Lewin's position point in another direction, and one with which I fully agree:

> In Lewin the phenomenal person and the phenomenal environment form a shared field, within which their respective forces influence each other.
> (Staemmler 2006: 76)

> The focus of interest is not on the state of the inner courtyard of an isolated self, but the process of contact in which the person–environment interaction takes shape.
> (Wollants 2008: 14)

To sum up, and declare my position here: a field is dynamically co-created in and of a fleeting present moment, forever becoming, it is process in process. A field, at any moment, can be hypothesized as ground to the emerging figure of the life space. Here, metaphorically, the life space is a cross section of the dynamic process of the field, given phenomenological structure as that which is figural as environment for a person at any given moment, and with which she may engage in a mutual interaction.

These theoretical perspectives can serve as an initial ground to the extrapolations on Lewin that are at the core of this chapter, and its proposal: that a neo-Lewinian field perspective on groups and group facilitation can advance the theoretical development and practice of gestalt therapy-based group facilitation, whether the setting be group therapy, personal and professional development groups, or group-work in organizations and society as a whole. In removing the focus on therapy, this is also in line with the proposal that Gestalt is a "philosophy of being" (Bar Yoseph Levine, this volume).

Life space and field

Lewin is the author of the formula $B = f(P, E)$: behaviour is a function of the person and environment. He gives examples of how the same, apparently ontological, environment will be perceived phenomenologically in distinctly unique ways by a variety of persons, depending upon their roles, circumstances and needs. A hilly clump of rocks and thick bushes in the middle of a piece of fertile land may be seen by a farmer as an obstruction to be removed in the interests of increased acreage and easier harvesting; a soldier might see it as a place of ambush or hiding; two rambling lovers might see it as an opportunity for some private moments. This is the life space, where $B = f(P, E)$. As such, each person's life space carries its own distinct set of phenomenologically informed characteristics as a sub-set of whatever totality may exist ontologically – including the person – this totality being anyway the person/environment field at any moment.

Should any of the persons in the example change roles and circumstances, then their experience of the hilly clump will change. If the soldier becomes a farmer, then that in which he once hid and found safety or cover will now be either an obstruction to be removed, or a reminder to be cherished, as the context or situation is changed. To paraphrase Lewin's thinking, the need self-organizes the field; our needs, desires, ambitions organize our experience – that is, our life space, our understanding of who we are in relation to what or whom we experience as our environment. What we see as our environment, how we see it thus and how we then respond is related to our needs. Naturally, when the environment is not a clump of rocks and bushes, but rather other people (the social field), then needs meet needs, actions evoke responses which in turn evoke responses and all the unpredictability of being in and of the world comes into dynamic play as forces of the field being co-created, or vectors, as Lewin called them, borrowing from physics: forces with an origin, a direction and a magnitude.

For the sake of as much clarity as may be possible with such complexities, what follows is a highly simplified and minimalist description of a neo-Lewinian Field Theory. An introductory comment here: the person *has* a life space (person/environment). By this I mean that she has a sense of an environment which is influencing her behavioural choices, both now and in the foreseeable or expected future. Her chosen behaviours will be in relation to her environment as she experiences it. At the same time, the person is of the totality, the wholeness, of that specific person/environment field of which she is an intrinsically influenced and influencing part. This distinction, which is core to this chapter, will hopefully become clearer and its relevance more obvious as we proceed.

The person will have a sense of being able to observe and describe her experience of the environment – her life space. Since we cannot observe the fullness of that of which we are ourselves a part, the person is unable to describe the wholeness of the person/environment field of which she is an integral and influential part. She can however describe her experience of being influenced – and as soon as she distinguishes what or who is influencing her, and whom she may influence, she is taking a life space perspective.

The life space is the world as perceived by a person relating to it, usually depicted by Lewin as a Jordan curve, that is, a phenomenologically boundaried time and space, where surrounding forces or events only become phenomenal aspects of the life space when and if they become salient to the person. This is the complex meeting of the ontological and the phenomenological referred to above.

Whilst the environmental other/others constitute the life space of the person, the wholeness of the person and her environment is the person/environment field, where each element is dynamically contributing to the self-organizing in the moment and, thus, also over time. In this way, a person experiences quite a different sense of agency in respect to her life space than in respect to the field of which she is a contributing force.

This point becomes clearer when the environment of the life space of A is another person, B, and viewed from that other's perspective also, and simultaneously. Here, the life space of A is B in relation to A. Simultaneously, the life space of B is A in relation to B. Merged and inextricably linked, they constitute the field of AB, to which may be added other environmental factors which each brings with them in the "totality of coexisting facts which are conceived of as mutually interdependent" (Lewin 1951), and of which each of them may have been in some awareness prior to their interaction. Concretely, each brings with them their past experience as they express it in the present and their future aspirations as they choose intentional behaviours in the moment – and these behaviours are dynamically field-emergent, always in the context of the totality of the AB field. Whilst field-emergent, their behaviours may be experienced by each party as acts of agency in relation to the environmental other of their life-space.

Assuming that A is a group member, as are B, C, D and so on, the presence of the facilitator (F) now adds both a life space for A (A/F) as well as a life space for F (F/A). The same applies to B, C, and D and so on, representing each and all of the other members of the participant group. The group facilitator is meeting each as a client and the group-world of that client as she experiences it. Together, the combined life spaces dynamically constitute the facilitator/member's field, where each is both influencing and being influenced by all the other forces of that field.

This is a good place to add an essential aspect of the perspective being presented here: the slash (/) in the construct organism/environment, usually taken to denote the *contact boundary* in gestalt therapy theory, is functionally identical to the line in the Jordan curve which is used to distinguish the person from the perceived environment in Lewin's original work. So the Jordan curve highlights the person/environment dynamics of organism/environment, though more explicitly from a psychological perspective. We are indebted here to Frank M. Staemmler for his exciting distinctions between biological and psychological models in his ground-breaking article on field theory/theories in Gestalt (Staemmler 2006).

In a therapy group, the therapeutic process resides as much if not more in the *contact boundary dynamics* of membership along with other members, than in the interventions of a therapist with individuals. Relating to others in their life space is the work of group members. This includes relating to the group therapist, and vice versa.

Group, group facilitator, life space and field

From the perspective briefly outlined above, the life space of each member, as well as that of the group therapist, is the subjective, emergent figure to the dynamic ground of the totality of each person/environment field. At one and the same time, there is a multiplicity of emergent life spaces of the field, thus being co-created moment to moment as the forces (vectors) self-organize. To capture something of the complex mutuality of these processes, the term "emergent creation" has been proposed (O'Neill and Gaffney 2008).

Of particular interest here is the gestalt group facilitator in her formally designated function of therapist and/or group facilitator. This function distinguishes her from group members, individually and collectively.

The facilitator is clearly of the facilitator/group members' field at the same time as her field-emergent life space perspective is one of the multiplicity of life spaces, which are, simultaneously, both of and dynamically co-creating the field from moment to moment. The wholeness of the field at any moment influences each life space; changes or fixities in each life space influence the field in its becoming. Metaphorically, this is a dance of process and structure, not as opposing opposites, but rather as analogous to a yin/yang symbol of interdependent relatedness.

Implications for gestalt group facilitation

The seminal work on Gestalt with groups of Elaine Kepner (Kepner 1980), was further developed by a colleague, Mary Ann Huckabay (Huckabay 1992). Group analyst Yvonne Agazarian (Agazarian and Peters 1981; Agazarian 1997; Agazarian and Gantt 2000) combined systems thinking with Lewinian field theory in her development of group theory and practice. A summary of their thinking, along with my own, can posit that the environmental other – separately and together – of the group facilitator's life space, can be described as follows, in ascending order of complexity:

> The group-work context (however understood)
> Group-as-a-whole
> Sub-groups
> Interpersonal
> Intrapersonal

Here, the intrapersonal may be considered as the stuff of individual therapy, the person's sense of self, and experience of self-in-the-world. Already here, the interpersonal – that is, the person's relations to and exchanges with others – is involved, and can be seen as a life space perspective. Sub-groups are both formal, i.e. recognized as such and relatively stable over the life of a group, and informal, i.e. arising in and of the moment, often around a shared perspective on any given theme, and open to dynamic change. The group-as-a-whole is the collection of group members who formally identify as members, however their commitment to or engagement with others is expressed. The context may be, for example, a training institute group or publicly advertised open therapy group, etc. In each case, the context will be a force of the facilitator/group members' field as well as an aspect of the facilitator's life space perspective. For a faculty member of a training institute, this aspect may be more figural than for a guest trainer, for whom "my reputation", or "more work" may be more significant. The context also includes the socio-cultural aspects involved, the political situation, world events – anything that may potentially become figural to anyone in the room. Or where the absence of such influence may itself become figural: this latter is what is sometimes colloquially called "the elephant in the room".

Figure/ground dynamics are important here. Hypothetically, each and all of the potential environmental others mentioned earlier may become figural to the facilitator. Much will depend on her openness to accepting each and all as her environmental other, and she as theirs. For example, an identifiable sub-group of members A, B and C emerges, representing, say, the vector "more theory". This is clearly of interest to each individually, to them as ABC, and is also representative of a force of the group-as-a-whole. The challenge here for the traditional individually-focused gestalt therapist is to imagine a sub-group of persons having sufficient collective agency, in or out of awareness, to be met as an entity in itself, and for that entity to be a dynamically constituent part of the whole.

This challenge becomes more complex – and, I argue, more exciting and rich with possibilities – if and when the gestalt group facilitator is willing to explore the possibilities of the group-as-a-whole as the environmental other of her life space, with which she may find herself in dynamic interaction. At times, this may carry a sense of mutual agency, where, for example, group members have agreed on a consensus around some issue, which they, collectively, wish to address to the facilitator through a spokesperson. This would be an example of two life spaces – the facilitator's and the group's – meeting and thus co-creating a field of forces likely to lead to negotiated organic change. At other times, the facilitator and members (individually and collectively) may experience that something inexplicable and even irrational is occurring, out of their control and utterly unpredictable in outcome. This is the joy of uncertainty, risk and spontaneity, the creative moment in group work.

From theory to practice

Here is an attempt to exemplify the above from the perspective proposed here, fully aware that a multitude of other meanings may be ascribed with equal validity. A group session is scheduled for 9 a.m. At the appointed time, the facilitator is in place and most, though not all, of the group members. Those members present continue the social chit-chat in which they were engaged, maybe even including the facilitator in their exchanges. Time goes by. Here are some possible scenarios:

1   A group member glances at the clock and says "We might as well wait for them – I hate starting and then restarting." The others agree, and the chatting continues.
2   A group member glances at the clock and says "I think we should start."
3   A group member says "I think we should start" and another says "No. We can wait for the others."

In 1), this can be seen as the group-as-a-whole coming late. In 2), a sub-group of "present" is forming and thus creating a sub-group of "absent". In 3) two sub-groups (at least) are forming around the absence of a third sub-group. This might well develop into a series of interpersonal exchanges, either between individuals with differing views or even between a number of individuals representing the sub-groups. In this latter case, a third sub-group may well emerge, of those losing interest and/or expecting the facilitator to decide.

In each case, the facilitator has at her disposal the full range of gestalt therapy methodology in engaging with collective entities (sub-groups or group-as-a-whole) as her environmental other, and she as the other to it.

I have elsewhere (Gaffney 2006a, 2008, 2009) introduced and developed the construct "contact boundary dynamics" which I use instead of such more established gestalt therapy constructs as "resistances", "disturbances" and "interruptions" to contact, as well as "contact styles", "contact functions" and "contact modalities", each of which seem to suggest and even encourage an intrapersonal focus. As a construct, *contact boundary dynamics* is meant to convey the mutuality of self/other interactions. It is also equally applicable to the organism/environment core construct of traditional gestalt therapy (Perls, Hefferline, and Goodman 1951/1994), as well as the person/environment model of Lewin. *Contact boundary dynamics* is the contact boundary, the event that is the field-emergent self of gestalt therapy theory and practice. Whilst the group facilitation approach proposed here does not necessitate accepting and applying this construct, the construct is certainly consistent with the thinking involved.

The core issue is the same: what is the facilitator's experience of contact with whatever environmental other is figural as that of her life space? How can she use her awareness to support her interventions? How does she support possible variations on life space perspectives? This last question introduces a particular complexity of the approach proposed here, involving considerations of both figure/ground and the relationship between wholes and parts. Figures emerge as the person's experience and that which is not figural thus becomes ground. We know from Rubin's vase/two faces drawing from 1915 (Kennedy 1974) that we cannot see the figure and its ground simultaneously. We can, however, shift from one to the other, thus making figural that which previously was ground.

The "possible variations on life space perspectives" mentioned above in relation to the facilitator's intervention choices involve a variation on the Lewinian theme that the need organizes the field – the perspective also organizes the field. A group facilitator with an individual therapy focus is likely to experience the intrapersonal issues of each group member as figural. For another, interpersonal exchanges between members will excite interest. The facilitator with a perspective which allows the group-as-a-whole, i.e. the members as a collective entity to be the environmental other of her life space, and thus a constituent part along with herself of the facilitator/group field, will experience all events as field-emergent at a collective level, even when expressed by an individual. The behaviours of individual members, their interpersonal exchanges, the dynamics of sub-group formation and interactions between them, can all be viewed as expressions of parts in the becoming of the whole. In the context of this proposal, each person as a group member and each sub-group is a part of the group-as-a-whole. The formation of the group-as-a-whole as a collective entity is the group evolution process over time. Any collection of individuals coming together in any way as a "group", with a designated facilitator, is always identifiable as an entity in an inter-subjective relationship with its environmental other, the facilitator. The gestalt of the group (Gaffney 2006a, 2006b) at any given moment is a metaphorical cross-section of this evolutionary process.

Group evolution here is analogous to the change process as a client in individual therapy may sense increasing field-emergent self-support in the therapist/client relationship. As such, the group facilitator working from the perspective presented here will be willing to regard the group-as-a-whole (group members collectively) as her life space environment. This entails accepting that she is the environmental other of the group's life space. With this perspective, intrapersonal, interpersonal and sub-group dynamics are all equally available as energized figures for the facilitator, with the group-as-a-whole as ground. At any time, she can re-configure the group as her environmental other, informed by her experience of contact with a part of that whole.

The field-emergent self of the facilitator is of the facilitator/group field, where contacting includes that with individuals, sub-groups as entities, and, of course, the group-as-a-whole, and the contact boundary dynamics involved. Because of the mutuality of these dynamics, we can posit a field emergent self of any sub-group as well as that of the group-as-a-whole. Or at least, a sufficiently distinct psychological entity to be analogous to "self", fully consistent with "the socially field-emergent phenomenal self of gestalt therapy" (Bloom 2009).

In conclusion

This chapter is an attempt to summarize my thinking with regard to gestalt therapy applied to more socially complex clients than individuals in one-to-one therapy, focused on – though not limited to – groups: most work in organizations and societies takes place with groups as influential parts of the relevant whole.

Further, it proposes that working with wholes, comprising small (sub-groups) or larger collectives of persons (group-members-as-a-whole), is equally within the competence and methodological skills of the Gestalt practitioner, as is working more exclusively only with individual group members, or members in interpersonal interactions. This latter may be described metaphorically as not seeing the woods of the whole for the trees of the individuals, and is still a noticeable trend for many Gestalt practitioners (Feder and Frew 2008). My proposal is for those Gestalt group practitioners willing to see the ecological system, the forest, the woods, the entwined saplings as well as the trees, each and all of the field of their interconnected glory.

A more explicit purpose here has been to propose that a nuanced contemporary revision of the contribution of Kurt Lewin is not only possible but useful, and can yield meaningful theoretical and practical advances where Gestalt with groups is concerned.

References

Agazarian, Y. M. (1997) *Systems-Centred Therapy for Groups.* New York: Guilford Press.

Agazarian, Y. M. and Peters, R. (1981) *The Visible and Invisible Group.* London: Tavistock/Routledge.

Agazarian, Y. M. and Gantt, S. P. (2000) *Autobiography of a Theory.* London: Jessica Kingsley Publishers.

Bloom, D. (2009). Commentary I: the cycle of experience re-cycled: then, now . . . next? Let's go round again: cycle of experience or sequence of contact? Dan Bloom has another go with Seán Gaffney. *Gestalt Review*, 13, 1: 24–36.

Feder, B. and Frew, J. (2008) *Beyond the Hot Seat Revisited.* Metairie, LA: Gestalt Institute Press.

Gaffney, S. (2006a) Gestalt with groups – a cross-cultural perspective. *Gestalt Review*, 10, 3: 205–218.

—— (2006b) Gestalt with groups – a developmental perspective. *Gestalt Journal of Australia & New Zealand*, 2, 2: 6–28.

—— (2008) Gestalt group supervision in a divided society. *British Gestalt Journal*, 17, 2: 27–39.
—— (2009) Using the gestalt approach in developing social change practitioners in the north of Ireland. In J. Melnick and E. Nevis (eds) *Mending the World*. Cape Cod, ME: Gestalt International Study Center Press.
Gold, M. (1990) Two "field theories." In S. Wheelan, E. Pepitone and V. Abt (eds) *Advances in Field Theory*. London: Sage.
Huckabay, M. A. (1992) An overview of the theory and practice of gestalt group process. In E. Nevis (ed.) *Gestalt Therapy – Perspectives and Applications*. Cleveland, OH: Gestalt Institute of Cleveland Press.
Kennedy, J. M. (1974) *A Psychology of Picture Perception*. New York: Sage.
Kepner, E. (1980) Gestalt group process. In B. Feder and R. Ronall (eds) *Beyond the Hot Seat*. New York: Gestalt Journal Press.
Lewin, K. (1951) *Field Theory in Social Science: Selected Papers* (D. Cartwright, ed.). New York: Harper Brothers.
Marrow, A. J. (1969) *The Practical Theorist – The Life and Work of Kurt Lewin*. New York: Basic Books.
McConville, M. (2003) Lewinian field theory, adolescent development, and psychotherapy. *Gestalt Review*, 7, 3: 213–238.
O'Neill, B. and Gaffney, S. (2008) A field perspective in gestalt therapy. In P. Brownell (ed.) *Gestalt Therapy: Theory, Methodology and Research*. Cambridge, UK: Cambridge Press.
Parlett, M. (1991) Reflections on field theory. *British Gestalt Journal*, 1, 2: 69–81.
—— (1993) Towards a more Lewinian gestalt therapy. *British Gestalt Journal*, 2, 2: 115–120.
—— (1997) The unified field in practice. *Gestalt Review*, 1, 1: 16–33.
—— (2005) Contemporary gestalt therapy: field theory. In A. Woldt and S. Toman (eds) *Gestalt Therapy: History, Theory and Practice*. Thousand Oaks, CA: Sage Publications.
Perls, F., Hefferline, R. and Goodman, P. (1951/1994) *Gestalt Therapy – Excitement and Growth in the Human Personality*. Highland, NY: Gestalt Journal Press.
Spagnuolo Lobb, M. (2003) Therapeutic meeting as improvisational co-creation. In M. Spagnuolo Lobb and N. Amendt-Lyon (eds) *Creative License – The Art of Gestalt Therapy*. Vienna: Springer-Verlag.
Staemmler, F. M. (2006) A Babylonian confusion – the term "field". *British Gestalt Journal*, 15, 2: 64–83.
Wheeler, G. (1991) *Gestalt Reconsidered*. Cleveland, OH: Gestalt Institute of Cleveland Press.
Wollants, G. (2008) *Gestalt Therapy – Therapy of the Situation*. Turnhout, Belgium: Faculteit voor Mens en Samenleving.

Epilogue

Chapter 14

Awareness instead of rules: Gestalt ethics

Ernst Knijff[1]

> Freedom means doing the right thing.
>
> (Metzfer 1962)

Introduction

In the area of people working with people, we often notice articles and discussions about the limits of roles and working areas:

> When is a priest no longer a priest but rather a psychotherapist?
> When can someone call himself a supervisor or coach and when not?
> As a coach, can you go into the more personal, private issues of a client or should you stick to the work issues?
> How open can you be as a therapist? Can you speak about your own intimate, personal issues?
> How strict should an ethical code be?

These kinds of question are quite familiar during staff meetings and conferences in The Netherlands and, as far as I can see, also in other countries inside and outside Europe.

These are issues and questions with some quite significant ethical implications. It has to do with being clear about the different approaches in a multidisciplinary cooperation but, most of all, it has to do with the integrity of the professionals involved.

Unfortunately, many of these discussions end up in a formalistic and restrictive way of defining limitations and restricted roles.

One would expect that this over-investment in defining and re-defining would lead to a need for dealing with these ethical questions and issues. The illusion persists that problems can be solved by improving the definitions and filling up the gaps with rules.

Roles and functions

It seems so easy to prevent confusion inside situations of guidance by just defining the different roles inside the relation. Let us look at an example:

> In a psychiatric hospital, one of the therapists had started a sexual relation with a patient. As a first reaction to all the consternation and feelings of insecurity, the management had clarified and tightened up the rules again and for a while, this gave some peace . . . until the next incident occurred and the management reacted in the same way.

This kind of reactive behaviour is not only very logical, but also very adequate as a first step in the process. It did give some relief by reminding about and tightening up the rules concerning the therapist–patient relationship.

However, it was a misunderstanding to think that this crisis was caused by a lack of rules and therefore that more or stricter rules would be the best solution to this crisis.

In my view, the problem is not caused by a lack of rules, but by a lack of awareness of the field[2] and of the specific functions in this field.

Reactively focusing on the rules will not solve this problem, but rather lead to a pattern, that might even create or increase inadequacy. This has to do with the psychological law that we are created by what we react to or, in other words, that we are strongly defined by what we try to restrict or deny. So, what is needed here is not more focus on rules and defining the roles, but rather creating more awareness of the field and the functions in the field, hence follows the Gestalt philosophy of practice.

To understand this better, we first have to look into the difference between role and function.

    1. Role
We can define a role as:
    a. a formally defined behaviour, which is legitimized by an authority
    b. clearly recognizable and visible for others as such
    c. the behaviour which clearly fits into the system of authorization.

On stage and in court, the "actors" dress up to make their role clear. Police officers and soldiers wear uniforms to make clear to the public that in their role and behaviour, they are only very slightly influenced by their personal views, preferences and feelings. Their behaviour is defined and legitimized by the authority, to whom they accede and to whom they subject themselves. By their uniforms, they clearly represent the authority and the power that is given to them by the authority.

Normally, the person with a specific role will be punished if he does not behave according to his role. The fact that this person cannot step out of his role and for example become visible or recognizable as a unique person, sometimes leads to inner conflicts or to corrections by the authorities. A clear example was the situation in Belgium where the king refused to sign a new law on abortion. He resigned for just one day to have someone else sign the law and then got back on his throne again.

Other examples are: the soldier who refuses to participate in killing civilians or, from a totally other dimension, the father who has sex with one of his children.

I can imagine that some people will ask now: does this example of the father belong here? To give an answer to that, we first have to look at the word "function".

2. Function
We can define a function as:
"a whole of inter-depended and 'synchronized' behaviour, which includes all participants in a certain field".

A father, mother and child are functions in the field that we define as "family". If in this field the relation of the father and mother becomes the figure, we leave out the function of the child and we no longer speak of father and mother, but of man and wife. Having sex has a place in this relation or field of man and wife. If a father has sex with his child, we can speak of inadequate behaviour in this field "family" and because of that, all functions in the family get confused. Because the father is abusing his function.

So, being a father is not having a role, but having a function in a specific field, called family.

Let's look at another example of a functional view: Supervision includes at least two persons and therefore two functions: the supervisor and the supervisee. These two participants have to agree on two items:

a. What does it mean to have supervision?
b. Are both of them willing to fulfil their functions in this field?

This demands clarification of the field of supervision, which does not mean that we have to come to a clear, strict definition of supervision. We need a description which helps both supervisor and supervisee to increase their awareness of this field. A nice illustration here is the approach of the Dutch Flemish Association for Gestalt Therapy and theory (NVAGT) which states: "*Supervision is meant to awaken, develop and refine the awareness of the supervisee on what is happening in his/her professional relation.*"

This way of describing the field of supervision does not put things into strict structures, but creates space for adequate action by defining the intention and the direction of the specific relation. In that way, it acknowledges the organismic character of the field.

Within the mutually accepted description of the supervision relation, both supervisor and supervisee agree on the specific function they have in this relationship and also on the characteristic of this relationship, which is the asymmetry. After all, if the asymmetry disappears from this relationship, the part "super" (from superior) disappears and the relationship – if the same intention and direction remain valid – becomes an intervision relationship. The aspect "inter" stands for "between equals". We don't have to put this asymmetry into rules and roles, because the agreement on this asymmetry enables the participants in the field to function in such a way that the intention and direction are fulfilled. The asymmetry is a condition to enable the intentions and goals of the supervision. In that way it clarifies the relation.

By this way of looking at the phenomenon of supervision, questions such as: can a supervisor be intimate with the supervisee, or can a supervisor go into the private issues of the supervisee, or can a supervisor judge the work of his supervisee, or provide theory etc. are no longer relevant.

Actually, a supervisor can do anything, as long as he is aware of the intention and goals of the supervision and his function in the field and as long as he thinks that this intervention contributes to these goals. As long as the supervisor has this awareness, the supervisee will feel comfortable and challenged enough to explore his own awareness of the case he put forward.

This approach clearly encourages and increases awareness, which is the main goal of supervision. Putting the relation and behaviour of supervisor and supervisee under strict rules rather limits this awareness and is, for that reason, clearly contradictory to this main goal. What has been fixed stops per definition what has to be flexible: namely – awareness.

It might seem as if we should never have specified roles and clear rules in situations of guidance. This is not the case.

In some situations, it is very legitimate to have strict role-definitions and even control on how people should handle the rules, e.g. when we are dealing with severe borderline-relations or dealing with people whose capacity for field awareness is very low or even absent. In these cases, we hinder rather than increase awareness by not offering the defined roles and rules. However we will offer these roles and rules as an experiment to awaken awareness.

Function and freedom

The following question might come up now: are we not just playing with words and moving from defining roles towards defining functions and fields of guidance? In other words: instead of discussing the definitions and limitations of roles, we are now discussing the definitions and limitations of, for example, therapy, supervision or coaching. "When can we speak of educational therapy and when does it become supervision or vice versa? Or, when can we speak of counselling instead of coaching?" Where is the difference? And indeed, there might be a chance that a therapist out of insecurity about his function will search for clear definitions of therapy. In that case, it will not help at all, because it will not increase awareness.

Therefore it is important to see to it that neither therapy nor the specific functions in this field should be put into strict rules. They need to be dialogued. Having a dialogue on therapy we are involved in is the most appropriate way to keep everyone's awareness awake: awareness about one's own and awareness about the other's specific function in this relationship. And if by chance, the therapist notices that he is focused on the topic of rules during a meeting with a client, he will look at it as one of the possible phenomena in the field, which means that he is aware of the fact that this topic is part of the therapist/client field and can be explored like any other topic in this field.

Actually, one can say that putting things into rules during a meeting with a client comes from a lack of awareness, unless the guide offers his rules as an experiment to increase the client's awareness on the topic.

To fulfil his function as a therapist, he can take on whatever quality, hobbies, or characteristic he has. He can do that as long as he is aware that his interventions are experiments serving the intention and direction of the therapy. This is his freedom, because being a therapist is not a strict role, but a fluent function.

Freedom means here the ability to choose; to choose to be involved with the situation and the people involved. This is what we call responsibility. Freedom is the ability to respond in a certain situation.

In this way, freedom does not mean "to be freed of . . .", but "to be free to . . ."

We are always free to think and wish whatever we want, but when it comes to the realization of our thoughts and wishes, we are always defined by the conditions of the situation, e.g. my own biography, my own body, the circumstances etc.

If one would say that a fish is restricted in his functioning by the water around him, one would simply deny the fact that it is a fish.

Therefore, freedom can never mean to be free of the field or situation in which one is involved, but free to be able to respond in this field or situation.

And because therapy takes place in a very specific, defined situation, freedom in a guidance situation is defined as a being free to respond in this specific situation. I should like to state that this is a condition and not a limitation.

Whereas a function is part of its circumstances, a role is characterized by the fact that it has to be free of changing circumstances. The person with a specific role has to be independent from internal and external influences as much as possible. Respons-ability here means to do the right thing according the given law.

However, every legislator realizes that a role person is not something like an automaton or a machine, in which you put some laws and rules to have him do the right thing. Sometimes it is even expected that the role person will make his own considerations. A clear example is the Israeli Army. Israeli soldiers can not appeal to the automatism "Befehl ist Befehl". This robot-like attitude has cost the life of many fellow-countrymen during the Second World War. However, even in the Israeli parliament – after the many refusals by pilots to bomb the Palestinian areas – there are people who like to get rid of the possibility to doubt given orders.

Confusion of fields

Confusion of the client

Normally, we are quite capable of changing fields and functions without having to stop and think, e.g. it rarely happens that the function of consumer is confused or mixed with the function of friend or husband or child. Actually, we can say that if someone is not capable of making adequate distinction between different fields and not capable of fulfilling his appropriate function belonging to a specific field, this might indicate a need for support or therapy.

However, in our function as a therapist, we are often confronted with clients whose awareness on these aspects is confused: a manager who is not leading, a father who is treating his daughter as a partner, a customer who thinks he is a king, a psychotic person who thinks he is the psychiatrist, etc.

Such cases demand a therapist to be extra clear on his field of guidance and his function in this field, because we can not ask or expect this clarity from the client. His confusion on fields and functions is exactly the reason why he came for help.

Therefore, a therapist has to ask himself if he is able to work with such a confused client and fulfil his function within this field.

The contract, which both therapist and client will agree on, must include that the function of client becomes clearer during the process of therapy. However, sometimes the difference between the expectations of the client and the ideas and possibilities of the therapist within this specific field are so great that it is impossible to make a therapeutic contract.

> *An example*
>
> A couple has come for support in their process of divorce.
> Therapist: "When I listen well to both of you and hear what you are looking for, I think you are better off with an attorney than with a therapist."
> She: (after a long silence) "Actually, we do not want to face that yet."
> He: "*You* don't want to face it." (. . .)
> Therapist: "Is this the problem, you want to work on: that one of you already wants to settle the divorce, while the other is not yet willing to face it?"
> The clients decided to have couple therapy and the therapist made up therapeutic contract with them.

Confusion of the therapist

Of course, it is also possible that the guide gets confused about his function and the goal of the contract with his client. This fear could lead to a need for "defining roles and rules", which will only create more confusion. The only thing a therapist can do to handle this confusion is to explore it, which, of course, is only possible if he is aware of this confusion.

An example

A clear example of this kind of confusion is a therapist who falls in love with his client. Being in love, the therapist risks getting confused about the field and the functions in the field. What can help him is to be aware of everything that is happening within the situation with him and his client. And most important, he should realize that his being in love is part of the therapeutic field and in that way has a therapeutic function in this field.

The ethical code, which is very common in handbooks on psychotherapy, says that a therapist should immediately break off the therapeutic relationship with this client and send him or her to another colleague. However this is totally opposite to the gestalt approach, which sees this falling in love as a phenomenon in the field which should be explored as such, while maintaining the boundary defined by the therapeutic relationship.

Breaking off the therapy stops the awareness of the therapist and the client of this phenomenon and therefore can never be a good intervention from a gestalt point of view.

To put it even stronger: to break off a therapeutic relation, the moment a phenomenon of this relation becomes a clear and strong figure means that we interfere with the awareness of the field, and that is unethical!

There is a great chance that, by doing this, the therapist is exactly doing what the client already knows from other relations. In fact, this might have been the reason for the client to come for therapy in the first place. Thus the therapist has become part to the client's pattern and, by breaking off the relation, increases this pattern instead of increasing awareness of the pattern. By increasing the awareness of the client, the therapist might be helping the client become freer or more flexible in this pattern.

From the same point of view, the therapist does not have to go and work on himself by looking into his needs and then to take care of this need for love somewhere else. If he starts dealing with this question, he is becoming a client himself instead of fulfilling his function as a therapist in this relationship.

What he has to do is ask himself the question what the meaning is of his being in love within this relation: "What is happening here between me and my client that I am falling in love? How can I increase my awareness of this situation?" This exploration is part of the therapeutic work. However, it is possible that the therapist is so confused that he is not able to be aware of these questions and not able to deal with them. In that case supervision is needed.

Another example concerns the rule that a coach should not go into the private problems of her coachee. She should restrict herself to purely work-related issues instead of issues that belong in a therapeutic relationship.

However, if a coachee tells her that he prefers to speak about his problems with his wife instead of his problems with his manager, the coach has to realize that this wish has a function within the coaching relation. It is not a question that undermines the coaching, but it is a part of the field of coaching. And even if this wish would undermine the coaching, that fact is still part of the field and should be explored as a phenomenon in the field of coaching.

The coach can explore with her coachee the parallels between the coachee's wife and his manager, but she can also explore what she perceives as an "undermining behaviour" of the coachee.

Basically, the main point is that a therapist should perceive all phenomena in situations of support as phenomena of the field, even if the client brings in phenomena from another field. By bringing them into this field they become part of this actual field. So, discussing what should or should not be possible or allowed is just missing the point, namely the essence of getting aware of what is happening.

In the example above, where the therapist is falling in love with his client, the question is not: "Can he do that?" because he already has, but: "What in this situation does the therapist recognize from other situations of his client and is this phenomenon possibly the same as in these other situations?"

In other words: the therapist is using the principle of the parallel process. This means that he is aware that in the therapist–client relationship phenomena may occur which also occurred in other situations of the client.

An example

During supervision, a social worker in the field of probation brings in a case: he had to support a former manager of an institute for mentally handicapped children during his period of community service. This period of community service is part of the punishment this man got for sexual abuse of one of the children. The social worker was terribly angry with his client, because the client told him that the punishment was not fair: the child had asked for this sexual contact. How could he, as this man's social worker, make the service meaningful if his client is convinced that he does not deserve the punishment?

According to the contract in the care for people with a mental handicap, the manager has the function of manager *and* caretaker and the child the function of client. A typical characteristic of a client – especially in this field – can be that he is not able to know his function. In such situations, it is part of the function of the caretaker to recognize this lack of knowledge and to understand the behaviour of the client within this context.

In this case it means that this manager/caretaker should have interpreted the expression of sexual desires by this child as part of the support situation and not as a personal request to him to satisfy her sexual needs, even if this request was personally formulated this way.

This is not an example of the fact that intimacy should not be allowed in situations of support. It is an example of having a lack of awareness on the side of the manager/caretaker. The manager/caretaker did not handle the need for intimacy from the very important aspect of asymmetry. With awareness of this asymmetry, of his own function and the function of the child he must have been able to give a different answer to the need for intimacy than satisfying it in a sexual way. A healthy sexual relation is based on symmetry, not asymmetry. Therefore, I like to state again that this case is not a proof that intimacy is inappropriate in a situation of support; it only proves the inadequacy or lack of awareness of the manager/caretaker in dealing with the topic of intimacy.

It has already been mentioned that a specific contract (the clearness of the field) may not be fulfilled or realized, because the necessary functions can not be fulfilled. During supervision this would be the topic to look at. Supervision should not be restricted to analyzing the client, but should focus on the therapeutic relation.

The therapeutic relation of this social worker with his client (the manager/caretaker) was quite complicated: the social worker also had a physically handicapped child and was in a process of placing this child in an institute.[3] However, it was clear during the supervision that the social worker had enough awareness on the influence of his relation with his daughter on his functioning as a social worker in this field.

The figure was the anger he had because of the violence of his client towards the child and his own violent tendency toward his client. Furthermore, the social worker did not really believe in supporting this ex-manager because he did not show any feelings of guilt. This made it almost impossible to give meaning to his service.

And therefore, the question arose if we can speak of a situation in which the contract of support cannot be fulfilled. The ex-manager refused to accept his function of being the client and the social worker was not able to fulfil his function of guide because – due to his private situation – he was not able to focus on the support.

On the other hand, it is a fact that exactly these phenomena are indisputable parts of the field which is defined as the field of probation: the refusal of confessing a crime, the violence involved: the violence of the manager (sexual abuse is violence) and the violent feelings of the social worker as well as the polarity power and impotence. The fact that the client has to accept support is in fact a main topic and paradox in this field.

Therefore, a quick conclusion that support in this situation is impossible would be a clear sign of identification[4] with the violence–impotence pattern and a sign of a lack of awareness. Because this identification comes from a reactive impulse, resistance, it is possible that ending the relation of support will only increase the pattern: a social worker who is stuck in his anger and who will probably act inadequately on the one hand, and a violent client who stays that way and will probably become a recidivist on the other hand.

Beside many other possibilities, a possible way to dis-identify is to do exactly the opposite from what one would do out of this reactive behaviour. In this case, the supervisor suggested that the social worker explore the possibility of expressing his anger and sadness about the abuse of the child towards his client. In other words, not withdrawing from the relation of support but continuing it.

Possibly, the fact that the social worker did not trust himself to fulfil his function as a guide in relation to his client could interfere with this strategy. In fact, it would be very likely that for the social worker his function of being a father might not be able to distinguish from his function as a social worker in the field of support and thus to keep the right asymmetry.

Therefore, they chose a construction, where a colleague of the social worker would facilitate a (possibly confronting) meeting of this social worker with his client. If the outcome of this meeting was that the social worker was no longer capable of supporting this client, the colleague would take over.

The confrontation in itself would be an important experiment within the context of the obligated support of probation. If, however, the outcome of the meeting would be that the asymmetry between the social worker and his client could be renewed, the social worker would have regained his mandate and therefore should continue the support.

This experiment was in fact an answer to a conflict which had become figure within the relationship of support and not an action to avoid this problem. The effect of this approach was that the social worker got very emotional during the meeting with his client. This touched his client so strongly that he was willing to take on guidance and support at last.

Notes

1 Translated from Dutch by Frans Meulmeester.
2 Field is defined as *"the whole of interactions, a person and his environment exchange and all the aspects which become actual in this interaction"*.
3 The context of the supervision does not necessarily ask for exploring the relation of the social worker with his child. Of course, this relation will have its influence, but it is another field. It could be explored in a therapy situation, e.g. the process of chronic sorrow and the process of mourning because of the admission into this institution.
4 The word "identifying" refers to acting out of illusions and without sufficient awareness. With dis-identifying, we mean acting where illusions can have their place, because of the awareness the person has. There is no confluence with the illusion. The prefix "dis" fits better here than the prefix "de", because the latter suggests one can handle without any illusions. We always have illusions, that is not the problem. Having or not having awareness of them, that is the question.

Reference

Metzger, W. (1962) *Die schöpferische freiheit.* [Creative freedom.] Frankfurt a.M.: Waldemar Kramer.

Chapter 15

Culture change: conversations concerning political/religious differences*

Philip Lichtenberg

Gestalt therapy's dialogic approach to therapy and to organizations can be effectively extended to the wider social world. We can use it in everyday conversations so as to change the culture, since cultures are created and re-created in the interplay of persons at all times. Promoting dialogue in such conversations will change the underlying gestalten which characterize any society.

Gestalt therapy embodies commitment to democratic and egalitarian functioning of persons in the therapy room, in organizations, and in the everyday life of our culture. If we are confined by our professional roles to the background, or even there a minority voice, we nonetheless represent an orientation vitally needed for the various societies of our time. The pulse of democratic, egalitarian functioning is weak, indeed, and nowhere is it heard more faintly than in conversations among family, friends, neighbors, and co-workers in everyday life. My purpose in this chapter is to suggest what these everyday conversations might look like and how we may begin to address strengthening of democracy and egalitarianism, as gestalt therapists.

One year before the publications of Perls, Hefferline, and Goodman's *Gestalt Therapy* in 1951, another sophisticated and profound work was published directed to promoting a democratic world. This massive psychoanalytic work of Adorno, Frenkel-Brunswik, Levinson, and Sanford, *The Authoritarian Personality* (1950), aimed to understand what made ordinary people potential fascists, what aspects of personality functioning provided for acceptance of anti-democratic living and relating. (I was very much influenced by that work and I did my master's thesis on Religious Conventionalism and the Authoritarian Personality under the direction of Daniel J. Levinson, one of the authors of that book.)

While this research was attacked because it focused on right-wing and not left-wing authoritarianism, it provided a powerful set of ideas that are

---

* Previously published in *Studies in Gestalt Therapy: Dialogical Bridges*, 2008, (3) 1, pp. 45–63. Used with permission.

relevant to modern gestalt therapy, and in this day of authoritarian political and religious leaders the reappearance of these ideas may be useful. With the absence of a strong socialist presence in modern life, the days of unreflective anti-communism (or "knee-jerk anti-communism") may be past. Democratic and egalitarian activities, basic to therapy, may be less vulnerable to charges that they are communist and therefore unacceptable. Milton Rokeach (1960) attempted to overcome the left-wing bias with his work on dogmatism. He did not make much difference, primarily because he focused on ideology and shunted personality theory aside. Bob Altemeyer (1996) continued the work on right-wing authoritarianism over the years.

The big notions in *The Authoritarian Personality* (Adorno et al. 1950) concerned faulty projecting, problematic introjecting, intolerance of ambiguity and ambivalence, and great fears of dependency, all of which made for ethnocentrism, racism, homophobia, and sexism, not only in the institutions of society but in everyday discourse. In my offshoot of that massive work, for instance, different religious orientations reflected varying degrees of such faulty modes of experiencing. Religious sects could be placed on a continuum from a humanistic to a fundamentalist/conventional differentiation. It is not difficult to find these variations today with authoritarian religion, whether Christian, Jewish or Muslim.

The need for a theory that can lead to action in our everyday lives

While *The Authoritarian Personality* (Adorno et al. 1950) was very perceptive and powerfully diagnostic, it did not lead us to take actions toward shifting the balance from a more authoritarian to a more democratic culture. Overcome by the anti-communism of the Cold War, deflated by its overlooking of left-wing authoritarianism, and promoted primarily in the academic sphere, its thrust was diminished and it very nearly vanished. Here, again, diagnosis without suggestions for action can lead us to helplessness and despair. It remains for us as therapists, persons devoted to practicality and actions based on theory, to revive the democratic orientation bequeathed to us by Dewey and Goodman and the other founders of therapy as well as these psychoanalytically-oriented research scholars.

Under the umbrella of anti-communism two strands of thought were confounded. On the one hand, anti-communists opposed the authoritarianism of the so-called socialist states led by the Soviet Union and Red China, and perhaps some therapists enlisted in this. On the other hand the leaders of American society conducted profound anti-democratic activities throughout the world. I will focus on the USA where I have been active though I know that many other Western and other societies were involved in the anti-communist efforts. For example, in Iran, in 1953, the United

States and Great Britain were involved in ousting a democratically chosen leader and in re-installing a Shah (Mohammed Reza Pahlavi); in Chile, in 1973 the USA was implicated in overthrowing Salvador Allende, the democratically-elected President of Chile; and in Guatemala and Nicaragua we destroyed democratic regimes in the name of anti-communism. The Vietnam war was fought in this endeavor as well, even while it appeared that the Vietnamese would have democratically chosen Ho Chi Minh as their leader. Today, Cuba today still suffers from this orientation, and I could name many governments and movements that have suffered the same fate. How could this happen? How could generally humane cultures be caught up in such destructive processes? Further, are the leaders of each of these societies so insulated that they do not reflect tendencies abroad in the land?

I suggest otherwise. Leaders express the "common sense" of society's people, as Gramsci (1948/1971), Italy's democratic left-winger put it, and as Thorstein Veblen (1899), the great American social thinker, argued years before that. Leaders are understood and put in positions of power because they reflect what Sanbonmatsu (2004: 145) called the "underlying Gestalten or perceptual structures" that are normative in any society. That is, the "common sense" in any society is what persons in everyday life include and exclude in their awareness. It is the familiar, obvious way of thinking and feeling. Hitler could not have accomplished what he did had he not personified tendencies in German culture exaggerated by profound economic distress, and had he not been supported by the German judiciary and the political leaders of his time who themselves reflected the underlying perceptual structures of that society.

The everyday application of gestalt therapy: principles in the practice of difficult conversations

By looking at our conversations with each other through the lens of gestalt therapy, we can discover our common sense and we then can experiment with different ways of altering social discourse. With a different way of experiencing daily life, citizens will put into positions of authority persons with fewer authoritarian characteristics. One "point of application" of therapy, as Kurt Lewin (1947) would frame it, is daily conversation around politics and religion, a lost art in modern America.

As a start, I bring a basket of examples from my everyday life to show what I mean, hoping that everyone will take this approach and develop it beyond me.

I was at a dinner after George W. Bush and Dick Cheney took the United States and its allies to war in Iraq. Shortly after our arrival my friend remarked that he had been at a Catholic wedding the previous day. In the midst of the wedding service the priest had asked that attendees pray for the President. My friend looked at his compatriots and rolled his eyes, which they did in return. Upon hearing this, I playfully said, "Why not blurt out, 'No'?" That, of course, went down like a lead balloon. Rightly so. But then I suggested that my friend might have gone over to the priest after the service and voiced his disapprobation of President Bush. My friend retorted that this was a wedding and he did not want to disturb the atmosphere of the moment. I voiced my concern about our propriety and our retroflecting our truth on such occasions such that we keep a right-wing and fundamentalist culture going.

You may have noticed that my friend and I were both imagining that the priest was in support of George Bush. The election was not distant and many Catholics supported Bush because he opposed abortion. That assumption came from our projecting. Some time later, I used this example in a group on conversations with persons who differ politically to show how when we retroflect our differences, we become implicated in the ongoing assumptions. A Presbyterian minister in the group reminded me that it is commonplace to bless a leader, not necessarily in support of that leader's policies, but merely to wish that the leader would be wise and productive in service to the country.

Thus, if my friend had pursued the priest and was openly curious about what the priest had in mind in this blessing, he might have engaged in a politically and socially useful exchange. Had the priest actually meant to encourage the group to favor the President and his war, my friend might have disagreed with him and shared his own moral perspective. Had the priest merely followed a custom and, upon questioning, would have voiced his own opposition to the war in Iraq, my friend would have had a venue for his own political stance without disrupting a pleasant wedding party. In either case, he would not have had the unfinished business that led him to his remark to me at his dinner party. And my own projecting would have been foreclosed. This is an example of a missed opportunity.

As I talk about this topic at gatherings in my retirement community, I come across numerous stories of unfulfilling encounters between my friends and their family members who differ with them politically. Three of my friends describe right-wing relatives, a sister, a sister-in-law, a niece with whom they have unfinished business. Each situation poses its own challenge pertaining to how to proceed in the relationship. When I hear their tales I become excited and exclaim that these are the conversations we need to pursue, to experiment with, and learn what works and what does not.

A man tells me he is a moderate Republican and his sister-in-law is a right-wing Republican with whom he regularly disputes. One or the other of them brings up their difference on any of several topics – abortion, war, gay marriage and they have a repetitive intellectual dance and do not meet. It slips out in our talking together that my friend believes his sister-in-law is "stupid," but when I point out his angry judgment, he becomes confused and breaks off. He is carefully not aggressive in his life. He and his sister-in-law titillate each other in their talks and have a continual agreement to disagree without moving from their own starting positions. When onlookers to our discourse tell me they see what I am doing, and it gives them impetus to try experimenting in their own domains, I feel successful. My friend told me later that he liked our engagement.

I facilitated another group in my community concerning "difficult conversations with family and friends." A man asserts that he is to have a difficult conversation with another man in the group. Both men have had an encounter in a previous committee meeting that was unfinished. The making of a bequest to the community was being talked about and the man who was being addressed by the protagonist in my group had spoken vigorously against a proposal concerning the allocation of the gift. This second man is a trial lawyer, a big man, with a strong voice, and he had influentially stopped the process in its tracks. The two men, whom I will call Alex and Zed, agreed to have the conversation with my facilitation.

Alex said he had felt bullied by Zed when I asked what it had been like for him in the committee meeting. In retrospect, I did not pick this up as actively as I might. To feel bullied is to say that the other is a bully, but it is not to say what happens inside in the presence of a bully – a common attribution of an internal process to a social relation. A good intervention would have been to ask further what it felt like internally to be bullied. Zed replied, however, that he knew he would be seen as a bully and he presented a rationale for his actions. As a lawyer he knew what others did not know, that the legal situation was being misrepresented and he was basically asserting the law. When I urged him to tell us what it was like for him inside when he saw what was happening, he acknowledged, after some resistance, that he saw a juggernaut happening, a car rushing to hit him, and that he felt alone, and he felt responsible for upholding the law. As Zed revealed his inner life, and I emphasized his feeling alone, Alex moved toward him emotionally, and they quickly came to a mutual understanding of how to proceed at the next community meeting. In my terms, they had a "meeting" in our presence, a view confirmed by a woman in the group who remarked that both men were more open and relaxed after they reached their understanding.

The promotion of dialogue through the inclusion of each man's inner experience of vulnerability led to a beautiful coming together. It also allowed me to speak about openness to vulnerability in our culture. We hear much from politicians about strength and strong measures of law and order and of tough love, and much from religious leaders about our weakness in the world, but neither politicians nor ministers do this in a growth-producing manner. To be super-strong without being aware of our weakness in life is to be in denial of death. So the exclusion of vulnerability from daily discourse is harmful. Reflecting this exclusion, political leaders act as if they are invulnerable.

Yet being open about our vulnerability is ambiguous. On the one hand, persons can be manipulative by claiming their weakness while handing over power and responsibility to others. When they assert their weakness without also showing their continuing capacity to be influential, they disempower themselves. On the other hand, persons can be realistic about their vulnerability and still not surrender their influence in the world. A person can be both weak and strong in relating to another. Therapists practice this all the time in doing therapy when confused or anxious and yet remain in connection with clients.

Several of the examples I have presented come from groups in which I was a leader or facilitator. As actors in everyday life, changing the culture need not depend on organized groups. Even as we function in egalitarian mode as therapists or consultants, we can quicken conversation at social gatherings from our gestalt therapy base. We do not have to come only from a privileged position. Therapists give themselves more freedom to use dialogue with clients than they permit for themselves in normal everyday discourse.

Conversations and themes in theory derived from gestalt therapy

Our thinking as gestalt therapists is part of the practice of having difficult conversations. This presents several themes from gestalt therapy. Everyday conversations are locales for experiments in dialogue. Gestalt therapy is essentially experimental, and grounded in dialogue. Immediately possibilities in how to promote dialogue come to mind. For instance, one can particularize self and other in exchanges that take place commonly. Persons often speak to each other as if the other could be substituted easily. They say things as if that other could be almost anybody. We can suggest such a person talking to us to might add a personal statement such as "Say that to me as someone unique in your life." Or, "Are you shaping what you say according to what you know about me or might want from me specially?" Alternatively, through our self-invention, self-discovery and self-disclosure, we might delineate ourselves more fully in the eyes of the other. We often remain obscure. We can say to our friend, "Here is how I am reacting to you right now." Or we can ask, "How are you responding to me given what I've just said to you?" Colleagues who have understood my ideas about development of a distinct "I" and a distinct "You" in contacting use these ideas (Lichtenberg 2000). I there refer to "four corners in contacting" which each participant must engage if full dialogue is to happen. A first corner is "This is what I want and who I am." A second corner is "I want you to tell me what you want and who you are." A third corner is "Tell me how you are reacting to what I have said or done," and a fourth, obviously, is "Here is how I am reacting to what you have said or done."

When involved in such a focused way of relating we need to be respectful of resistances to such transparency and disclosure. One can never be sure how others will use one's revelations and we live in a paranoid and litigious world. Yet there is considerable space for more self-disclosure and more interest in others' personal experience. Attending to self-disclosure brings me to a second theme from gestalt therapy.

We know well the paradoxical theory of change – one must become who one is before true and useful change is possible. The other side of this is that we cannot coercively change the other in some productive way. Of course, we can kill other persons, or oppress them, or exploit or dominate them, and thereby change them in a destructive fashion. We have learned, however, from our democratic, egalitarian stance, that the best we can do is to meet the other, coming from our own truth, and we can then hope that the other will want to become different if our truth has value, and be ready ourselves to become different if we find otherwise. To meet the other is to be open in two senses – open about ourselves, as in self-disclosing, and open to being influenced by the other. By modifying ourselves in the relationship, we open the door to the other changing self.

The notion of meeting the other is a third theme from gestalt therapy, that of healthy confluence. Feeling close to another has its own problems. Spontaneous merging at the climax of contact means giving up one's separateness and also one's control over the relationship. There is a kind of surrendering in the contacting–withdrawing process in that we give up our egotism as we lose ourselves in this new, temporary unit that is larger than its component participants. As I have earlier suggested, healthy confluence is the loss of boundary with awareness of self as separate from the other. Herein is our gestalt therapy variant to Freud's Eros–Thanatos ongoing dialectical relationship: they are antagonistic yet also mutually supportive of each other. As the fetus grows both by the expansion (Eros), and by pruning of neurons, with cell-death or apoptosis facilitating that pruning (Thanatos), so all growth later in life depends upon individuation in dialectical relation with inclusiveness. It is scary to give way to such merging, and we find ways to avoid closeness just as we find ways to obscure our individuality. The experience of faulty confluence, of being dominated and submerged in the other, or too readily obscuring self while enhancing the other, may make us fearful of healthy confluence.

When we lose our sense of separateness outside of awareness, without each of us being openly particularized, we become anxious at the moments of meeting when a new, larger unit is likely to appear. The loss of self is perceived as costly to the previously hurt individual. Observing and studying resistance to closeness is an undeveloped field, and everyday conversations may be the place to start. I ask you to reflect on loving our clients in the process of therapy as also raising anxiety about closeness. Such worry about closeness may also contribute to lack of egalitarian political conversations.

A fourth theme from gestalt therapy available to casual discourse is the value of staying with ambiguity, uncertainty and confusion until clarity in the dialogue is reached. Ambiguity may be manifested in contrasts or contradictions between verbal and non-verbal communications, or the uncertainties may be contained in the verbal content alone. Isadore From responded to verbal/non-verbal communication with, "You are saying something sad and you are smiling. Are you aware of this?" Or, rather than asking about the person's awareness, one might note: "I am confused by what you are telling me." Sometimes in therapy work I have experienced someone as self-critical, yet saying this to me with a triumphant look on her face. We know this phenomenon from the discussion of self-conquest in Perls, Hefferline, and Goodman (1951), yet I have never heard any comment on it outside the therapy room. Why not reflect on this more generally, in order to be more comradely? All language is incomplete and ambiguous; much in verbal communication is open to uncertainty. If we pay attention in everyday conversations to ambiguous comments and encourage clarity or directness, we will have many new opportunities and may have more fun.

If staying with ambiguity until mutual understanding is attained or approached is one consideration in conversations, so too is the idea of finishing what is unfinished, however that may be defined. I persevered on the unfinished at the party concerning remembrance of the Catholic priest and his prayer for the President, yet did not find completion. I brought the subject up later in another context and then saw both more possibilities and how my projecting may have limited my vision. And I still can finish this when I next socialize with my friend. We often tell clients they can re-open unfinished business if they have withdrawn too soon. We can do the same outside of therapy. We have countless opportunities that we neglect because we have adapted to the cultural norms and do not consider that risking excitement, confusion or failure in living outside of these norms is in some degree a responsibility we can choose to assume.

The place of strong feelings in daily discourse

People project onto others in unhealthy ways when their arousal level is more than they can support and I may seem contradictory when I propose that we would do well to bring intense emotions into our daily discourse. Yet I urge promoting more vitality in our usual relationships. Of course, almost all modern societies foster unwholesome projecting. We can remind ourselves of "infidels," "terrorists," or other characterizations of negatively conceived out groups. Yet, high arousal need not promote projecting. What is important are the conditions in which arousal takes place. The distinction is between arousal determined by sensory over-stimulation, which is arousal associated with projecting, and arousal created by the joining of a person's urges and inner subjective interests with the sensory reception of what is presenting itself in the person's surround – emotional fullness.

We know sensationalism from advertising where sight and sound are used to attract our attention. We are less familiar with "emotional fullness" – arousal in which we complexly experience simultaneously what is coming up inside us and what is impacting us from our surround. An example from that domain may be helpful.

In a group, a woman told me that she had been very angry with me for two months. She spoke directly to me, described my action, yet she was not explosive in her comments. She was deeply hurt by my remark I had made in passing.

I remembered what I had said, paused to allow myself to get beyond being defensive, and owned my underlying anxious feeling when I made that flippant remark. I expressed my sincere regret. We looked closely at each other and felt a beautiful togetherness.

One observer in the group said to us that there seemed to be no emotion in the encounter. Both my critic and I were astonished by her viewpoint and told her that it was a rich conversation, full of feeling and very rewarding. Emotional fullness is not necessarily visibly excitable, as a sensationalist society would have us mistakenly believe, and which our observer seemed to assume. The conversation had contained emotional fullness for my woman friend and for me.

Everyday discourse and the possibility of cultural change

The understanding of awareness in gestalt therapy can be helpful in addressing this issue of authoritarianism raised by Adorno et al. (1950) more than 60 years ago after the experience of Nazi Germany. Racism, importantly derived from projecting, obscures interocepts and brings the person to focus primarily on percepts. We know about homophobia in the former Soviet Union and Cuba as well as the racism in what was once a socialist-oriented Israel as well as South Africa and the United States. So, too, images of the enemy have this very characteristic, whether these images arise in a capitalist or a socialist context. They are significantly projections.

As I hope to have shown here, gestalt therapy may offer us a way through this problem. Awareness is the combining in equal measure of "interocepts," that is, of one's interior, and percepts, that is, of one's surroundings. Further, awareness as directed inwardly and outwardly to one's surroundings offers an opening to an egalitarian discourse, the cornerstone of community. With its special methods of addressing awareness within ordinary human functioning in everyday relationships, gestalt therapy offers us the tools for every single one of us to apply ourselves to these humane, democratic, egalitarian tasks.

The culture embodied in everyday life is the ground of what ails us, and everyday life can very well be the arena in which we need to address our wisdom that comes from the consulting rooms and organizations within which we live and work. I beseech gestalt therapists to engage in culture change by adapting gestalt therapy and the gestalt philosophy of being to the details of everyday discourse. The enterprise can be surprisingly exciting, challenging, and productive.

References

Adorno, T. W., Frenkel-Brunswik, E., Levinson, D. J. and Sanford, R. N. (1950) *The Authoritarian Personality*. New York: Harper & Brothers.

Altemeyer, B. (1996) *The Authoritarian Specter*. Cambridge, MA: Harvard University Press.

Gramsci, A. (1948/1971) *Selections from the Prison Notebooks* (Q. Hoare, ed.). New York: International Publishers.

Lewin, K. (1947) Frontiers in group dynamics. In D. Cartwright (ed.) (1951) *Field Theory in Social Science*. New York: Harper & Brothers.

Lichtenberg, P. (2000) Creating a distinct "I" and a distinct "You" in contacting. *The Gestalt Journal*, XXIII, 2: 41–50.

Perls, F. S., Hefferline, R. and Goodman, P. (1951) *Gestalt Therapy: Excitement and Growth in the Human Personality*. Highland, NY: Gestalt Journal Press, 1994.

Rokeach, M. (1960) *The Open and Closed Mind*. New York: Basic Books.

Sanbonmatsu, J. (2004) *The Postmodern Prince: Critical Theory, Left Strategy, and the Making of a New Political Subject* (p. 145). New York: Monthly Review Press.

Veblen, T. (1899) *The Theory of the Leisure Class*. New York: Penguin Books, 1979.

Index

Locators for headings which also have subheadings refer to general aspects of the topic.

absolutism, moral 20, 21, 23, 24, 25
actual situation 33, 34–5
actualization 54, 55, 84
aesthetics in psychotherapy 10
affect regulation 110, 114. *see also* emotion; feelings; self-regulation
affect-state dependent recall 86
agency: couples 127; groups 155; infant 108, 109, 110; life space/field 153; and mindfulness 112, 117, 118, 119, 121; paradoxical 141
ambiguity 27, 29, 176, 180, 182
anger: couples 126; culture changes 178–9, 183; field affective practice 145–6; projection 64–5, 67–8; therapeutic relationship 172
anti-communism 175–7
appreciation of difference 34, 127–8
arousal, and projection 182–3
articulation 43
arts/humanities 49–50
asymmetry, relationship 171, 172–3
attachment to therapist 108. *see also* love
attention 76, 90
attunement 65; infant-caregiver 107, 108; and mindfulness 114, 121; neuroscience perspective 89; psychotherapy 42, 108, 117; and self-experience 116
authentic self 108, 109
The Authoritarian Personality: (Adorno et al.) 175–6, 183
authoritarianism 175–6

awareness 57, 71–2, 80–1; biological/phenomenological fields 79–80; case study 171; and consciousness 71–4, 79–80; couples work 127, 129; culture changes 183; of difference 3; and ethics 166, 167; historical perspectives 72–4; and interpretation 91; and mindfulness 111, 114–19; neuroscience perspective 90; organism/environment and self/world fields 77–9;. reworking/reconfiguring 75–7. *see also* consciousness; experience; *and see below*
awareness instead of rules 163; confusion of client 168–9; confusion of therapist 169–73; function and freedom 167–8; roles/functions 164–6

befriending the field 5, 9
behavior 33, 151
behaviorism 73
being. *see* philosophy of being
Bible 23–4, 95. *see also* religion; spirituality
biology/biological: fields 77–80, 153; holism 31–2. *see also* environment; organism
body awareness, and mindfulness 117–19. *see also* experience
boundaries 150–1; contact 63, 153, 156; disturbances 4; self-other 84, 181; therapeutic relationship 169–70
breath 117, 120

Index

The Bridge – Dialogues Across Cultures xviii, 115
bridge too far metaphor. *see* holism
Brownell, P. 94, 96-98
Buber, M. 7, 98, 146
bullying 179
Bush, George 177-8

calmness, therapist 117
caregiver-infant relationships 107-11, 113; neuroscience perspective 88-9
Cartesian worldviews 59-61, 62, 63
case studies: couples 129-33; flexibility 21-2; interactive field 43-5, 46-7; mindfulness 115-21; sexual abuse 171-3
category mistakes 31, 35
change: contact episodes/cycles 3-5; engineering profession 2; and personality 57; practitioner as healer 8-10; process model of growth 2-5. *see also* paradoxical theory of change
child development. *see* development; infant/s
Chile 177
clarity 182
Clemmens, M.C. 40, 42
client/therapist relationship. *see* therapeutic relationship
closeness: fears 176; and individuality 181
coherence theory of truth 62
common-factors perspective 138
communism/anti-communism 175-7
communitas 7
community life xix, xx, 18, 22-3
compliance, child 108
confusion, roles; client 168-9; therapist 169-73
connection 39; couples work 132; family therapy 142; and mindfulness 120; and personality 54-5. *see also* contact; interactive field
consciousness: and awareness 71-4, 79-80; conceptions 31-2; as knowing 74-5; reworking/reconfiguring 75-7. *see also* awareness
consistency/constancy: and fluidity 16-17; need for 17-18; therapist 117. *see also* continuity; flexibility

contact: and awareness 74; biological/phenomenological fields 79; boundaries 63, 153, 156; and change 3-5; consciousness-awareness continuum 76; couples work 124-6, 128, 129, 130, 132; culture changes 181; episodes/cycles 3-5; and growth 7; and mindfulness 115, 119, 120; neuroscience perspective 86; organism/environment and self/world fields 79; relational theory of self-in-context 84. *see also* connection; interactive field
containment, therapeutic relationship 111-12
contextualization of experience 20, 25
continuity 54. *see also* consistency/constancy
conversations. *see* dialogue/dialogic approaches
counterpoint 15-16, 19, 25. *see also* flexibility
couples work xx, 123-4; case studies 129-30, 130-3; character pathology 130-3; contact dynamics 124-6, 128; destructive cycles 128-30; difference appreciation 127-8; discussion 133-4; phenomenological attitude/paradoxical theory of change 126-7
Crocker, S. 35
Cuba 177
cultural perspectives xviii, xx, 48, 52-3, 115
culture changes 175-6; action towards democratic cultures 176-7; conversations/themes derived from gestalt therapy 180-2; and daily discourse 183-4; gestalt therapy applications 177-80; strong feelings, role in daily discourse 182-3

death: fear 120; mindfulness 121
defenses: couples work 131, 132; relational patterns 89, 110, 183; shame 133, 134
definitions: consciousness 74, 75, 79-80; field 149-50; functions 165; holism 29-30; knowledge xviii; projection 63; psychotherapy 167; roles 164, 166; transcendence/immanence 94; trauma 109

demand-withdraw patterns of relating 131–2
dependency fears 176
depression 110; case study 116; child development 108, 109, 115; family therapy 145; and mindfulness 121
deprivation 113. *see also* infant-caregiver relationships
destructive cycles, couples work 128–30
development, child: infant research 107–11; neuroscience perspective 88–9, 90. *see also* caregiver-infant relationships
dialogue/dialogic approaches 7; couples work 123, 124; culture changes 180–2; family therapy 137–8, 146; philosophy of being 1; and projection 65, 66; psychotherapy 40; in psychotherapy 67; role of strong feelings 182–3. *see also* interactive field
difference 3; appreciation of 34, 127–8; resolution 2. *see also* language
directness 182. *see also* openness
disgust, case study 46–7
dissonance 16
dualism 59–61, 62, 63
dynamics: couples 124–6, 128; family 142

eastern thought 94, 100
Ego, Hunger and Aggression (Perls) 27, 29
ego functioning 77
elephant in the room metaphor 155
embodiment: case study 43–5; consciousness 76; and observer perspective 40; psychotherapy skills 41–3; self/world fields 79; shame 45–7. *see also* experience; interactive field
emergent phenomena 87; group facilitation 154; mind 97; neuroscience perspective 90–1
emotion: embodiment 113; and memory 86; and mindfulness 112–13, 115; regulation 110, 114. *see also* feelings; self-regulation
empathy 24, 114
engineering profession 2, 128

environment: field 141–2, 151–2; and spirituality 96–7. *see also* biology; organism
epistemological perspectives 150
ethics. *see* awareness instead of rules; morality
exaggeration 145
existentialism 16
experience, sensory 3, 31–2, 40, 41; and attunement 116; and awareness/consciousness 77, 80; case study 44; couples work 126–7; contextualization 20, 25; and holism 34; and mindfulness 117–19; organism/environment and self/world fields 77–8; and projection 64–5, 65–6; in psychotherapy 67 to include both sides truth; shame 45. *see also* interactive field
experiments, gestalt 57; conversations/themes derived from gestalt therapy 180; couples 123; family therapy 146; mindfulness 120; phenomenological 133–4; thought 59–60
expert practitioners 6, 60

family therapy xx, 137–8, 142–3, 146–7; development, family 142–3; field affective practice 145–6; field insightful practice 144–5; field present practice 146; field sensitive practice 144; field theory principles 139–42; harmony within chaos 142; needs organize the field 141–2; paradoxical agency 141; perspectives/understanding what works 138–9; psychotherapy 143–4; self as process 139–40; systems theory 137, 140, 142–3; wisdom of organism 139–40
fascism 30
feelings, role in daily discourse 182–3. *see also* affect; emotion
field/s: affective practice 145–6; befriending 5, 9; biological 77–80; confusion of client 168–9; confusion of therapist 169–73; definitions 149–50; insightful practice 144–5; and life space 151–3, 154; needs organized 141–2, 151–2; organism/environment and self/world 77–9;

pneumenal 97–8; present practice 146; sensitive practice 144
field theory xix, 1, 27; client/therapist relationship 45; and embodiment 41; family therapy 137–8, 138–9, 139–42; group facilitation 154–5; and holism 32–3, 35; process model of growth 5; theoretical contradictions 64. *see also* interactive field
fight or flight 145
fixed gestalt 5, 6, 89, 91; couples work 126, 133; family therapy 145
flexibility: case study 21–2; constancy and fluidity 16–17; correspondence vs. coherence 62; couples work 125; point and counterpoint 15–16, 19, 25; Life Focus Communities 22–3; morality 19–22; personal identity 17–18; 'shoulds' 23–5; therapeutic relationship 170
freedom xvii, 16: and function 167–8; quotation 163; and responsibility xvii, 167. *see also* flexibility
function, awareness instead of rules 165–6, 167–8

gating, attention 90
gestalt: philosophy of being. *see* philosophy of being; therapy. *see* psychotherapy
Gestalt Therapy (Perls, Hefferline and Goodman) 4, 27, 62–4
God xix, 93, 96–7. *see also* religion; spirituality
Goldstein, K. 31–2, 84
Goodman, P. 2-4, 6-9, 16, 17, 27, 28, 33, 50, 59, 67, 141, 149, 156, 176, 182
grace 8
group facilitation 149, 158; life space and field 149–50, 151–3, 154; practical application 155–8; systems/ field theory 154–5; theoretical perspectives 149–51
growth: and mindfulness 120–1; process model 2–5; rehabilitation/healing 6–8
guilt, therapeutic relationship 172

habit of loyalty 56–7
harmony within chaos 142

healing/health: journey 6, 8; neuroscience perspective 86; philosophy of being 2–3; practitioner as healer 8–10; and rehabilitation 6–8; and relationship 90
holism xix, 35–6; actual situation 33, 34–5; and awareness 73; definition 29–30; Lewin/field theory 32–3; organismic 31–2; and personality 49–51; philosophical 30–1; role in therapy today 27–8
Holism and Evolution (Smuts) 29, 30
humanities 49–50
hyper-beings 51–2

I-It relationship 7
id functioning 77
identification 172
identity: constancy and fluidity 17–18; and personality 51–2, 56. *see also* self
immanence 94–6. *see also* religion; spirituality
in between 40
inclusion 42
individualism, neuroscience perspective 90
individuality: and closeness 181; and connection 54–5; and environment 32; and society 52–3
infant/s, mindfulness research 107–11. *see also* caregiver-infant relationships; development
Inquiry into the Whole (Smuts) 30
insight, family therapy 144–5
interactive field 39–41, 47–8; articulation 43; attunement 42; case studies 43–5, 46–7; embodiment 41–2; resonance 42–3; shame 45–7. *see also* dialogue/dialogic approaches
interpersonal group facilitation 154–5
interpretation, and awareness 91
intersubjectivity theory 109; and gestalt therapy 111–13
intimacy needs 171
intrapersonal group facilitation 154–5
introspection 73
Iraq war 177–8
irreversibility 4

isolation, and mindfulness 115, 116–17, 119
I-Thou relationship 7, 8

Jacobs, L. 7, 39, 40, 66, 81, 115
Jordan curves 152, 153
journey, therapeutic 6, 8

knowing, and awareness/consciousness 74–5, 79, 80
knowledge, definition xviii

language xviii; and personality 53–4, 56, 57. *see also* dialogue
layers of personality 4
leadership 6; political 177
Lewin, K. 32–3, 85. *see also* group facilitation
Lichtenberg, P. 27, 180
Life Focus Communities 18, 22–3
life space 149–50; and field 151–3, 154
listening 7, 24
love: -hate polarities 145–6; and mindfulness 114; therapeutic relationship 108, 169–71
loyalty, habit of 56–7

manipulation 51, 56
materialist approach, neuroscience perspective 86–8
medical model of illness 5–6, 9
meeting, other 181. *see also* self-other
mental handicap case study 171–3
metaphor 150, 154; bridge too far. *see* holism; elephant in the room 155
mind: and self 97
mindfulness xx, 107, 120–1; attunement and self-experience 116; body awareness 117–19; case study 115–21; couples work 129; experiments 120; infant research 107–11; intersubjectivity theory/ gestalt therapy 111–13; neuroscience perspective 113–15; shame/isolation 116–17
mirror neurons 85, 91
mirroring 90, 114
model specific factors perspective 138
morality xx; and flexibility 19–22; Life Focus Communities 22–3; and personality 56; pluralism 20, 23; and religion 20, 163; 'shoulds' 23–5. *see also* awareness instead of rules
mother-infant relationships 107–11, 113; neuroscience perspective 88–9
movement 3, 5
music and psychotherapy 15–16
mysticism, New Age 34

natural world, and spirituality 96–7. *see also* environment
Nazi Germany 31, 175, 183
needs: intimacy 171; organize the field 141–2, 151–2
negativity, couples work 128–30
neuroscience perspective xix, 83, 91; healing 86; materialist approach 86–8; mindfulness 113; psychotherapy 89–90; relational development 88–9; relational theory of self-in-context 83–6; therapist knowledge about client 90–1
New Age 34, 35
numinosity 95; *see also* religion; spirituality

objectivity: couples work 127; psychotherapy 60, 61–2, 63, 67, 91. *see also* truth
observer perspectives 40
ontological perspectives 150, 152
openness 182; couples work 125; and mindfulness 114; self-disclosure 181; to vulnerability 179–80
organism: and awareness/consciousness 77–9, 80; fields 77–80, 153; wisdom of 139–40. *see also* biology; environment
originality, return to 3
other, meeting 181. *see also* self-other

paradoxical agency, family therapy 141
paradoxical theory of change 18, 56, 89–90; couples 123, 124; culture changes 181; fields 172; and phenomenological attitude 126–7
parallel process 171
parenting. *see* caregiver-infant relationships
Perls, F. 4, 27, 29, 62–4, 84, 113
personal experience. *see* experience
personality 49–51, 52; and awareness/ consciousness 77, 78; connected individuality 54–5; and culture

52–3; flexibility 17–18; functioning 55–7, 78, 80; and identity 51–2, 56; and language 53–4, 56, 57; layers of 4; and self 49, 56

perspectives: Cartesian 59–61, 62, 63; cultural xviii, xx, 48, 52–3; epistemological 150; family therapy 138–9; life space 151–3; model specific factors 138; observer 40; ontological 150, 152; phenomenological 150, 152; in psychotherapy 64–5, 66, 67–8; spiritual 94, 96–7; theoretical, group facilitation 149–51

phenomenology 27, 64; and awareness/consciousness 79–80; couples work 123, 125; experiments 133–4; family therapy 144; and paradoxical theory of change 126–7; perspectives 150, 152; personality functioning 78; philosophy of being 1; theoretical contradictions 64

Philippson, P. 35, 77, 84, 89, 90, 94, 138

philosophy of being 1–5; contact and change 5–6; and holism 30–1, 33, 34–5; practitioner as healer 8–10; process model of growth 2–5; rehabilitation/healing 6–8

pluralism, moral 20, 23

pneumenal field 97–8

point and counterpoint 15–16, 19, 25. *see also* flexibility

polarities, field affective practice 145–6

political leadership 177

politics, gestalt therapy applications 177–80

Polster, E. 2, 3, 18, 98

pornography 21–2

power imbalances, in therapy 60

practitioner as healer 8–10

presence 39, 146

process: model of growth 2–5; oriented elements 94; self as 139–40

projection xix, 59; clinical problem of 65–6; clinical solutions 66–8; correspondence vs. coherence 61–2, 65; culture changes 176, 182–3; definitions 63; misuses 59–61; theoretical contradictions 61–4; theoretical solutions 64–5

psychology and spirituality 96, 97, 98

psychotherapy: aesthetics 10; applications to culture changes 177–80, 180–2; and awareness/consciousness 73; constancy and fluidity 17; family therapy 142–3; interactive field 39, 40; and intersubjectivity theory 111–13; medical model of illness 5–6; mindfulness 114; and morality 19, 21, 24; and music 15–16; objectivity 60, 61–2, 63, 67, 91; power imbalances 60; and projection 60, 61–2, 63, 65–8; role confusion 169–73; and spirituality 98–9. *see also* couples work; family therapy

recognition processes 109–10

reductionism 49–50; biological 34; neuroscience perspective 86–8

rehabilitation and healing 6–8

relational dialogue. *see* dialogue; interactive field; language

relational patterns: demand-withdrawal 131; infant research 113

relational theory of self-in-context 83–6

relationship: asymmetry 171, 172–3; case study 21–2; couples work 124–6; to environment 32; Gestalt philosophy of being 2, 3; and growth 7–8; and healing 90; I-Thou 7, 8; neuroscience perspective 88–9; personality functioning 78; process model of growth 3; and spirituality 7–8, 94. *see also* caregiver-infant relationships; therapeutic relationship

relativity, moral 20, 21

religion 116; and the authoritarian personality 175–6; and ethics 20, 163; gestalt therapy applications 177–80; 'shoulds' 23–4. *see also* spirituality

repetition 145. *see also* fixed gestalt

research, infant 107–11

resistance, stages 4

resonance: case study 44–5; psychotherapy skills 42–3

respect, for difference 34, 127–8

responsibility and freedom xvii, 167

return to originality 3

roles 164–6, 168

rules 163, 164, 166, 167. *see also* awareness instead of rules

sacred 98. *see also* religion; spirituality
safe emergency 16
Sartre, J.-P. 16
science: and arts/humanities 49–50, 73; medical model of illness 5–6, 9. *see also* biology; reductionism
sculpting, child 88–9. *see also* development
self xix; authentic 108, 109; and awareness/consciousness 77, 78–9; constancy and fluidity 17; disclosure 181; and mind 97; neuroscience perspective 90–1; and personality 49, 56; as process 139–40. relational theory of 83–6; /world fields 79, 80. *see also* experience; identity
self-other 55; boundaries 84, 181; relationship 7, 8
self-regulation 3, 4; contact and change 6; infant research 110; and mindfulness 114–15, 116; needs of organism 141; neuroscience perspective 89–90
Seligman, M. 24
sensitivity 144
sensitization 42
sensory experience. *see* experience
sexual abuse, case study 171–3
sexuality 52; projection 63
shamans 9
shame 45–7; couples work 130–1; defensive 133, 134; and mindfulness 112, 116–17
'shoulds' 23–5. *see also* morality
Smuts, J. 29, 30, 31, 33
society, and individual 52–3
speech. *see* dialogue; language
sphere of immediacy 32
spirituality 93–4, 99–100; application to practice 98–9; healing 9; and natural world 96–7; orienting perspective 94; pneumenal field 97–; and psychology 96, 97, 98; and relationship 7–8; transcendence/immanence 94–6. *see also* religion

Staemmler, F. M.- 61, 62, 67
stagnation 5, 6. *see also* fixed gestalt
Stern, D. 85
stuckness. *see* fixed gestalt
submission, child 108
supervision 165–6, 171–2
systems theory xx; family therapy 137, 140, 142–3; group facilitation 154–5, 157, 158

theist worldviews 96–7. *see also* religion; spirituality
theoretical issues: group facilitation 149–51; projection 61–5
therapeutic journey 6, 8
therapeutic relationship 45, 107, 108; affect regulation 114; attunement 117; boundaries 169–70; containment 111–12; couples work 124–6; family therapy 138; parallel process 171; supervision 171–2
therapist, role confusion 169–73
thesis/anithesis 15
totalitarianism 30
touch, couples work 133
transcendence 8, 94–6. *see also* religion; spirituality
transference, couples work 126
trauma 109, 114
truth: correspondence vs. coherence 61–2, 65; hierarchy 60; neuroscience perspective 91; and projection 65; in psychotherapy 60, 61–2, 63, 67, 91. *see also* objectivity

Uncommon Ground (Polster) 98
United States 176–7

Vietnam war 177
vulnerability, openness to 179–80

wisdom of organism 140–1
withdrawal: family therapy 145; patterns of relating 131–2
words. *see* dialogue; language

yin/yang 154
Yontef, G. 28, 32, 71, 75, 124, 130, 138